OCTOPUS

OCTOPUS

Sam Israel, the Secret Market, and
Wall Street's Wildest Con

GUY LAWSON

CROWN PUBLISHERS

NEW YORK

Library of Congress Cataloging-in-Publication Data

Lawson, Guy.
Octopus : Sam Israel, the secret market, and Wall Street's
wildest con / Guy Lawson.—1st ed.
p. cm.
1. Israel, Samuel, 1959-   2. Stockbrokers—United States—
Biography.   3. Hedge funds—United States.   4. Wall Street
(New York, N.Y.)   I. Title.
HG4928.5.L39 2012
332.64'524092—dc23
2012003095

ISBN 978-0-307-71607-1
eISBN 978-0-307-71609-5

Printed in the United States of America

Book design by Maria Elias
Jacket design by Christopher Brand
Jacket illustration by Brian Levy

10 9 8 7 6 5 4 3 2 1

First Edition

For Lucy and Anna

We are never deceived, we deceive ourselves.

—Johann Wolfgang von Goethe

Contents

Author's Note

In reporting this story over a period of three years, I spent hundreds of hours interviewing Sam Israel in prison and on the telephone. I also exchanged countless e-mails with Israel and Dan Marino, the former CFO of Bayou Funds. To authenticate Israel's account, interviews were conducted with the FBI in New York and the Serious Fraud Office in London. I reviewed thousands of pages of legal documents, analyzed hundreds of financial records, and conducted extensive Freedom of Information searches. Much of the evidence related to Israel's case had been placed under seal by federal prosecutors in an attempt to keep the record secret—but I was able to obtain it all through confidential sources. Over the years, I also interviewed dozens of Israel's associates, legitimate and criminal. Traveling to Europe multiple times, where the amazing finale to Israel's adventure took place, I uncovered ongoing international financial frauds that have yet to be investigated by the authorities—conspiracies that continue to this day.

When I began to talk to Israel, he promised to tell the truth, no matter how unflattering or brutal it was. "I will not lie to you," he said. Given his history, I treated this vow with profound skepticism. Indeed, I soon discovered many of the events he described did defy belief. But I also learned that in virtually every instance where the facts could be checked, other sources confirmed and/or corroborated his account, if not his interpretation. Inevitably, however, there are twists and turns in Israel's tale that have to be taken on his word alone. Readers should bear in mind that this is the story of a self-confessed con man. Confidence games are a strange blend of fact and created fact, the narrative constructed by a con artist luring his prey into a world of deception. So it was for Israel as he perpetrated his fraud at Bayou and then ventured into the deadly embrace of the Octopus.

Readers should also be aware that, owing to the legal complexities of publishing the names of people involved in crimes that remain unprosecuted, in several instances I've had to use pseudonyms (a complete list appears on page 343). Anyone interested in further information regarding the scams and scammers portrayed in these pages can visit guylawson.com or my page on Facebook.

Guy Lawson
New York, New York
July 2012

Introduction

On Monday, June 9, 2008, a disgraced Wall Street hedge fund trader named Samuel Israel III decided to end it all. Given the desperation of his circumstances, the only way out seemed to be suicide—or at least the appearance of it. For nearly a decade he'd been the mastermind of one of the largest and most complex frauds ever perpetrated on Wall Street. The discovery that his $450 million hedge fund was a Ponzi scheme had cost Israel his reputation, his fortune, his freedom. Sentenced to twenty years in prison, he was almost certain to die behind bars. Once he had been the promising scion of a wealthy and prominent family of traders; now, at age forty-nine, he was at the end of his rope. Years of heavy substance abuse, a dozen back operations, and open-heart surgery had left his body in ruins. Israel was addicted to painkilling opiates and dreaded the prospect of kicking drugs in prison. Broke and broken, he reasoned that if he was gone at least his children could collect on his life insurance policy. Ending it all would also allow him to retain a measure of dignity and autonomy. It would be a final act of atonement—and defiance.

On the cloudless June day that Israel was supposed to report to federal prison in Massachusetts to begin serving his sentence, he drove his red GMC Envoy toward Bear Mountain Bridge in upstate New York. The suspension bridge spanned the Hudson River in a state park an hour north of Manhattan. Making his way along the winding road, Israel was tormented by conflicting emotions. The thought of perishing in prison filled him with dread. So did the prospect of what he was about to do. As he rounded a curve, the half-mile-long bridge came into view. He tried to calm his racing thoughts. Jumping to your death was the time-honored fate for a failed financier like Israel. *Body rain* was the term on Wall Street.

Like the legendary Faust, Israel had sold his soul in return for earthly powers. Standing before a wall of computer screens in Bayou's beautiful converted boathouse overlooking Long Island Sound, he had played the role of a modern-day necromancer who could create money out of thin air. For years, Bayou had provided investors with an annual performance of 18 percent. But it had been just that: a performance. Like Faust, Israel had been granted exactly twenty-four years to live out his dream—from the Reagan tax cuts of 1981 to Bayou's implosion in 2005. Now it was time to give the devil his due.

As Israel neared the bridge, he tried to make sense of the swirl of events that had pulled him into an abyss. He wasn't just another Wall Street scammer. There was another story—one that hadn't been told. At the height of his fraud, as he desperately searched for a way to make hundreds of millions of dollars to save Bayou and himself, he'd discovered a secret bond market run by the Federal Reserve. The labyrinth of this shadow market dwarfed Israel's own grand deception. Grappling with the many-tentacled beast he came to call the Octopus, he'd often feared for his own life. As he traveled to the financial capitals of Europe—to London, to Zurich, to Frankfurt—his companions had been CIA hit men, moneyed aristocrats, and the puppeteers who controlled the world's financial system. On this journey, Israel had glimpsed the terrifying reality exposed during the global financial crisis of 2008: Investment banks were perpetrating systemic fraud, the international financial system was a scam, and the Federal Reserve was operating a vast Ponzi scheme. At least that was the reality he'd experienced.

Driving onto Bear Mountain Bridge, Israel wondered if he'd ever know the full truth—or if the Octopus would once again succeed in remaining invisible. One thing he knew for sure was that he wasn't going to allow himself to disappear into prison forever. As he neared his destination he concentrated on the specificity of what lay ahead: the road, the bridge, the end. Reaching the middle of the bridge, he pulled to the side. "Suicide Is Painless" was written in the dust on the hood of the Envoy; he'd left a note at his house. Sam got out of the vehicle and climbed over a cement divider onto the pedestrian walkway that carried the Appalachian Trail over the Hudson River. The bridge had no surveillance cameras; only the video from the toll-booth recorded him as he disappeared from view. Looking around to see if he was being watched, he stepped onto a narrow ledge. He stared down: 156 feet, high enough to reach terminal velocity. The suspension bridge seemed to sway in the haze. Sam told himself he wasn't afraid. He'd soon be forgotten, just another disgraced Wall Street scammer who got what he deserved. Body rain. He took a deep breath. He leapt . . .

CHAPTER ONE

Trust

A ll Sam Israel ever wanted to be was a Wall Street trader. For generations, the men of the Israel family had been prominent and hugely successful commodities traders. For nearly a century they and their cousins the Arons had been major players trading in coffee, sugar, cocoa, rubber, soy, precious metals—the substance of modern American life. Along the way, the family became fantastically wealthy. Long before the term was coined, the Israels were real-life Masters of the Universe.

But it was Wall Street that attracted Sam, not the commodities market. As a boy growing up in New Orleans he'd sat on the lap of his legendary grandfather, Samuel Israel Jr., watching the ticker tape from the New York Stock Exchange and imagining what life was like in that distant place. When the Israels moved to New York and his father took a senior position in the family business, which had grown into a multi-billion-dollar multinational conglomerate named ACLI, Sam dreamed about trading stock in the skyscrapers of Lower Manhattan.

In the summer of 1978, at the age of eighteen, Sam got the chance to try his luck. At the time, he was a newly minted graduate of Hackley, an elite prep school outside New York City. Although the Israels were very rich, Sam was expected to earn his own pocket money. Thus he was spending the summer working odd jobs and training to try out for the freshman football team at Tulane University, alma mater of his father and grandfather. In the Israel family it was assumed that Sam would go to work for ACLI when he finished college. He was smart, charming, athletic, extremely likable. But Sam had a propensity for lying. In his mind, they were harmless lies, teenage lies, about girls, sports, deeds of derring-do. It was his way to be liked, to be funny, to get attention, to make himself feel good.

Sam had been blessed with all the good fortune any young man could hope for. But he didn't want to follow in the footsteps of his illustrious ancestors. He didn't want to be the beneficiary of nepotism, with all of its attendant resentments and insecurities. Despite the Israel family's outward appearance of perfection, Sam's relationship with his father was deeply troubled. Sam wanted to be his own man, shaping his own destiny, proving his own worth.

"My father asked me if I wanted to come into the family business," Israel recalled. "But I said no. I didn't want to be like my father in any way. I was only a kid, but I could see what was going on. My father had gone into the business, and his father had treated him poorly. My grandfather was always on my father about one thing or another. Nothing could ever please my grandfather. My father was doomed to that life. He was never going to break away and be on his own. It would've been the same for me.

"If I became a Wall Street trader, I wouldn't be working for my father. I'd be trading stocks instead of commodities. It may seem like a small distinction, but it was huge to me. At my father's business I'd be the kid who had been born into the right family. On Wall Street I'd be on my own. I was always told that the New York Stock Exchange was the greatest place on earth. It was where the smartest people went. It was the hardest place to get ahead. Wall Street traders lived by their wits. It wouldn't matter that my last name was Israel. It wouldn't matter who my father and grandfather were. On Wall Street, anybody could make it—if they were tough enough and smart enough."

One fine June afternoon in his eighteenth year, Sam was working as a bartender at a garden party in his uncle's backyard. The crowd was middle-aged, well dressed, seemingly unremarkable—pretty wives and pale-faced men with paunches and high blood pressure, drinking too much, smoking too much. But Sam knew that beneath the milquetoast appearances, these men were Wall Street's ruling class.

Standing behind the bar, Sam was approached by a heavyset man in search of a cocktail. The man was just under six feet tall, weighed more than two hundred pounds, and had an unruly mane of brown hair and a ruddy complexion. He was wearing expensive clothes, but he was slightly disheveled and had the twinkle in his eye of a prankster. Sam instantly recognized him. Standing before Sam was the famous Freddy Graber—the man they called "the King" on Wall Street. Sam had heard his father and uncles talk about Graber's exploits. Still only in his early thirties, Graber was already famous for his unbelievable ability to trade stocks.

Instead of accepting a partnership offer at Lehman Brothers,

Graber had started something called a "hedge fund." In the seventies, hedge funds were exceptionally rare and mysterious, a secret realm run by the high priests of high finance. Only the wealthiest people even knew of the existence of hedge funds. Only the greatest traders gained entrée to the select society. Freddy Graber was in that number. His hedge fund acted as a broker for major investment banks, clipping a few pennies in commission for executing trades on the floor of the New York Stock Exchange for companies like Goldman Sachs and Morgan Stanley.

But Graber's true genius was the way he traded his own money. Unlike most Wall Street traders, Graber didn't bet with other people's money. This was a dare within a dare. Normally traders who "ran" money invested their own funds, along with money given to them by banks, insurance companies, pension funds, high–net worth individuals. Not Graber. He traded for himself exclusively. His stake in the early seventies had been $400,000. In less than a decade he'd turned it into $23 million. Cash. It was the kind of feat that had made the Israel men famous. In 1898 Sam's great-uncle Leon Israel had started with $10,000, and by 1920 he had $25 million—the equivalent of $500 million today.

Graber carried himself with confidence that bordered on arrogance. But at the same time he was unpretentious, quick to grin, instantly likable. He was also a serious drinker. Graber asked the young Israel for a vodka and cranberry juice on the rocks, with a chunk of lime. Israel handed over the drink and introduced himself—knowing his last name would be recognized. Graber was polite but didn't take much notice of the eager teenager.

When Graber returned for another drink a few minutes later, though, Sam was ready. "Vodka and cranberry on the rocks," Sam said, mixing the cocktail before Graber could order. "With a chunk of lime."

"You have a good memory, kid," Graber said. "You any good with numbers?"

"I'm very good with numbers," Israel said.

"You could make a living doing what I do," Graber said.

"I'd love to see what you do, Mr. Graber," Israel said.

"Come up and see me anytime," Graber said, handing over his card. "The door is always open."

From Graber's offhand manner, Israel knew it was an empty invitation. But Sam wasn't going to let this opportunity pass him by. The next Monday morning, he dressed in his best suit and caught the early train to Manhattan.

"When I walked up the subway stairs into the sunlight at the corner of Wall Street and Broadway for the first time it was like I was entering a new universe," Israel remembered. "The streets were teeming with action. Secretaries hustled by. Shoe shine guys, newsstand boys, hot dog vendors, everyone was on the make. To me it was the most incredible place on earth. It was like a giant casino. It was pure glamour. It was everything I'd dreamt about."

Frederic J. Graber and Company operated on the thirtieth floor of 1 New York Plaza, a fifty-story skyscraper that housed Goldman Sachs, Morgan Stanley, and a host of powerful law firms. Graber's trading room was in a suite of offices with a dozen or so other independent hedge funds. At the time there were only a few hundred funds running perhaps a few billion dollars, compared with the trillion-dollar industry that would emerge in the coming decades. Israel stood awkwardly at the threshold watching the early-morning commotion. Sitting behind a large marble desk in the trading pit, Graber didn't recognize Israel at first. Then Sam summoned the courage to remind the older man of his offer. Graber grinned at Israel's nerve. He could have sent

Israel away, but he was gregarious by nature, inclined to be generous, and Sam was obviously keen. Graber sent Sam down to the trading floor to see how things worked there. By sending him to the floor, Graber was making it plain that Sam was on his own. It could easily have been his first and last day. But Sam had other plans.

In the late seventies the floor of the New York Stock Exchange was a madhouse, a roiling sea of humanity being tossed by waves of greed and fear. The exchange was divided into a series of rooms, each with huge boards to record the hundreds of millions of dollars being traded at every moment, each filled with brokers and clerks screaming their orders and jostling for every eighth of a point. In this oversized fraternity house, the kind of place where men played Pin the Tail on the Donkey and sprayed shaving cream for practical jokes, the intensity was so high a trader could fall over from a heart attack and trading wouldn't stop. There would be a moment of concern, perhaps, as the trader lay gasping on the floor, but trading would go on as the paramedics arrived with a stretcher and took him away.

The teenage Israel walked through the pandemonium for the first time in a state of awe. The floor was chaotic, but the action was also choreographed. Brokers with numbers on their chests took orders from clerks, who worked banks of phones; runners known as "squads" sped the orders to specialists, who checked the trades and then posted them to the ticker tape on the big board. The noise and speed were bewildering. Buffeted by the mob, Sam slowly found his way to Graber's booth, number 0020. The tiny space was crammed with a hundred telephones, each connected to a different broker. There stood Graber's trading clerk, a short, dark-haired, stout man twenty years older than Israel—Phil Ratner.

"Phil was a tough old bird who knew everything about trading,"

Israel recalled. "By the time I made it to the floor it was nearly lunch-time. I watched, but no one was really talking to me or telling me any-thing. Not that they were rude, they were just busy. So Phil sent me to get pizza. I went and bought eight large pies, with extra cheese, extra toppings. When I got back to the floor, I was stopped at the door. The guy working security told me that food wasn't allowed on the floor. All the phones and wires in the systems would be damaged if people took food or drink onto the floor. But I wasn't to be denied. I started to argue. The governor of the floor came over and started screaming at me for bringing pizzas into the exchange, asking me who the fuck I thought I was. I pointed at Phil and I said, 'That man over there has the power to give me a job, and I'm not going to lose that chance. I'm bringing him these pizzas unless you knock me out.' I was a kid. I still had zits. I shoved past the governor of the exchange. That was how determined I was to please those men.

"Phil and the guys started pissing themselves laughing. The gov-ernor was bent over double. It was all a setup—a prank. They wanted to see if I had the mettle. I was being hazed. I laughed along with them—I pretended to laugh. But I was very serious. Nothing was going to stop me from becoming a trader. At the end of the day, I asked Phil if I could come back the next day. Just to watch, I said. I was scared he was going to say no. But he took pity on me, I guess. Or he thought I would be good for a laugh. Being able to laugh at yourself, that was one of the most important things on the Street. Phil said okay. From that day forward, I was in, and no one was going to get me out."

Sam spent the rest of the summer as a runner on the floor of the NYSE with Phil and his crew of clerks. Graber had an account at the members' smoke shop in the NYSE, so Sam was sent to fetch cigarettes and snacks. In idle moments, Sam was taught "liar's poker," a game of chance, based on gambling on the serial numbers of dollars, that prized the ability to deceive. The floor of the exchange was completely foreign to the well-heeled teenager, and he set about learning its ways with the attention to detail of an aspiring samurai. "Downstairs" was the name for the floor. "Upstairs" was where Freddy Graber and the other traders made their decisions about buying and selling.

"All of the brokers downstairs came from Brooklyn and Staten Island—they talked in 'dems' and 'dose,'" Sam recalled. "Lots of them had no college education, but they made a lot of money considering their backgrounds. A good broker could make a couple of hundred thousand a year, back when that was real money. The lead guys were like Mafia dons. You had to pay your respects to them or you weren't going to get into the specialists' booth. Upstairs was completely different. It was suits and ties. The guys on the floor were real street guys. But I loved it on the floor. I would stay late to do the work nobody else wanted to do, making sure the accounts were straight and all the tickets for the trades were clean and accurate. Everything was done on paper in those days, so it was tedious work, but it was a way for me to ingratiate myself. Just because my name was Israel, and I was known as a rich kid, I wasn't above doing the grunt work."

At home in Westchester on the weekends, Sam moved inside circles of enormous wealth and prestige. The Israels were fixtures at the Century Country Club, perhaps the single most exclusive golf club in the country. The crowd at the Century Club included many of the world's most powerful people. Sam read about their exploits as he rode the train to the city every day. "They were the crème de la crème," Israel recalled. "My father's friends were captains of industry. Presidents of investment banks. The heads of major multinational companies. Alan Greenspan before he took over the Federal Reserve. Sandy

Weill, who became the chairman of Citibank. Larry Tisch, who became a billionaire as the CEO of CBS.

"All of them were good friends with Larry Israel. Everybody loved my father. He was funny, smart, outgoing. He was overweight but a great athlete—nearly a scratch golfer. He was like Jackie Gleason—a larger-than-life character with a loud voice and a bad temper. As a kid I thought my father was a trader, like his father and grandfather. As I got older I found out that he wasn't a trader. He ran the business side of the company, not the trading side. His job was to schmooze and get along with people, and he was very good at it. The cats my father ran with had more money than anyone else. And I don't mean in New York, or the stock market, or even the United States. I mean in the whole world."

The dinner table at the Israel home was no place for the faint of heart. Conversation was fast-paced and barbed as Sam's father led a sophisticated ongoing seminar on the realities and complexities of the commodities market. Sam was regaled with tales from the lore of the Israel family. Like the way his namesake grandfather and great uncles had cornered the cocoa market in the 1950s and 60s. The Israels had hidden barges loaded with cocoa along the Mississippi to create the impression there was a shortage in the market. When prices spiked, they sold their secret stockpile to a rising market and made a fortune, a subterfuge Goldman Sachs copied in the aluminum market as recently as 2011. Incredibly, Sam's forebears had used deception to corner the cocoa market not once or twice, but three times.

The Israel clan had traded "actual" commodities for decades. But as the market changed, they'd become skilled at trading the complex and fantastical abstractions created by modern capitalism. ACLI and J. Aron, the company run by their first cousins, were two of the most admired firms in the business. They would provide the world's leading investment banks with many of their best minds, including future Goldman Sachs CEO and chairman Lloyd Blankfein. At the time, the family firms operated at the nexus of power and politics. ACLI had more than a hundred offices scattered around the world, many opened by chairman of the board Larry Israel. The Israels and the Arons were traders, but they were also economic diplomats and insiders at the highest levels of commerce and government.

"My father traveled all over the Third World because that was where the commodities were," Sam said. "He met with heads of state, top ministers, captains of industry. He dealt with Idi Amin in Uganda when he was importing coffee from there. Manuel Noriega in Panama was another. Ferdinand Marcos was a close associate of my father. The Philippines was huge for sugar. Marcos's number one guy was named Don-ding Corleone Cojuangco. He had a monopoly on bananas and beer in the Philippines. Don-ding offered to take me there to work for a summer, but my old man said there was no way he was going to let me go because I'd end up dead. My father's work was also very closely tied to the government of the United States. He was dealing with all the bad boys the CIA put in power. He knew how things really worked. When he came back from trips to places like the Philippines he would be debriefed by the CIA. Controlling commodities was how the dictators stayed in power—and that was how America kept power."

On the train to the city each morning, Sam tried to divine larger meanings in *Wall Street Journal* reports about company earnings and takeovers. Graber had little to do with Sam, apart from getting him to run an occasional errand. He never offered to pay Sam, and Sam never asked about money. To make himself useful, Sam took every opportunity he could find to do favors, however small. Fetching lunch or running to the local offtrack betting shop to place a bet on a horse was a way to please Graber and get noticed.

As Sam gradually insinuated himself, he began to be trusted with more complex tasks. Despite his youth, Sam knew that discretion was crucial. He'd seen how his father worked. Sam knew to be careful about whom he asked questions of—and what he asked about. Good intuition was essential. One day, Graber called Sam from the floor and told him to go uptown to the Pierre Hotel to collect a package. Sam knew better than to ask what he was going to get.

"Freddy told me to go to the third floor of the hotel and knock on the door of a specific room," Israel recalled. "A Swiss man would answer the door. I was supposed to say, 'The weather is nice for this time of year.' The man would say, 'Yes, but today it looks like rain.' It wasn't going to rain. It was sunny outside. I was pretty naive, but I was learning. The Swiss guy gave me a satchel. I took the subway back down to Wall Street. But the subway stalled, like it used to do a lot in those days. The lights went out. I sat in the dark in a packed subway car for three hours. When I finally got to Freddy's office he was pacing around in the hallway. He screamed at me, asking where the fuck I had been. He pulled me into the bathroom and opened the satchel. It was filled with one-hundred-dollar bills. There was easily one hundred grand in the satchel.

"I knew something was wrong with it, but I didn't know what. I didn't know about insider trading and how Wall Street really worked. I didn't know about Swiss bank accounts. I didn't know the secrets. I couldn't believe he didn't tell me to at least get a taxi. I could have been mugged on the subway. But Freddy wasn't going to tell me—I was just the kid. He calmed down and saw it wasn't really my fault. The important thing was that I didn't snitch. I didn't tell anyone about the cash. I didn't talk to my father or mother about it. I said nothing to the guys working for Freddy. I was showing Freddy I could keep my mouth shut. I was showing Freddy I could be trusted."

CHAPTER TWO

Upstairs

S am Israel spent three years slacking off at Tulane University in New Orleans, occasionally studying English literature, mostly smoking dope and carousing in the bars of the French Quarter. The only work Sam took seriously was his summer job in New York with Frederic J. Graber and Company. Finally, in December of 1981, in the middle of his senior year, Sam got a call from Graber. Phil Ratner, Graber's clerk, was going to retire. Ratner had agreed to stay on for a year to train his successor, and Graber needed someone he could trust to take over. Sam could have the job, but he had to come to New York immediately.

"I dropped out of college that day," Israel recalled. "I didn't care about getting a degree. I knew this was my chance. I packed up my bong, put my TV in my car, and left. From then on, everything started moving in fast-forward."

For a year, Ratner became Sam's full-time mentor. Decades after he had retired to a golfing community in Arizona, Ratner recalled well, and with great affection, the young Sam Israel from the early eighties. "He was a sharp kid. He didn't know what the hell was going on, but no one did at first. Everything went quickly on the floor. It was scary. But Sam behaved very well. He was a good student and he had no problem learning. He had an aptitude for the clerical work. You'd never know that his grandfather down in New Orleans was worth six hundred million."

Ratner was a chain-smoking character drawn from the pages of Damon Runyon—short, tough, Brooklyn born and raised. In the early seventies, Graber had given Phil a $2,000 stake to start trading on his own account. By the early eighties, Phil had parlayed the money into more than $1 million in cash, a small sum to Graber's way of thinking but more than enough for Phil.

"I never wanted to be rich," Ratner said. "Rich people think about their money too much. They can't sleep at night. I wanted just enough money to retire, and I figured a million was enough. I was only forty years old, but I was ready to move someplace sunny and take it easy. I figured a million bucks wasn't bad for a working-class kid from Brooklyn."

Ratner arrived at work every day at five-thirty and stayed until seven in the evening. Sam began to shadow his movements. A street-level realist who was aware of the many temptations that can lead a trader astray, Phil had two axioms that he lived by. One was *Never take a big loss*, by which he meant that it was crucial to recognize a loss quickly and sell the position before it began to lose even more. Admit defeat and live to fight another day, Phil told Israel. The other guiding principle was *Never turn a winner into a loser.* It was Phil's way of saying that a trader should take a profit when it was available, not wait and hope for an even greater windfall.

"Discipline was the key," recalled Ratner. "When I made a bad trade I would write the word *discipline* on my forearm so I wouldn't forget it. I urged Sam to find a niche—to find what he was good at. My niche was buying and selling stocks in fifteen-, twenty-minute blocks of time. I usually never held a stock longer than that. I didn't fight the market. I used to say, 'Let the trend be your friend.' If the stock is going up, follow it. If it is going down, sell. I also specialized in the stocks I traded. Some stocks I couldn't get a good feel for, so I didn't trade them. That was part of the discipline, I told Sam over and over—find your strengths and stick to them. One morning Sam turned up at work and told me he had figured out what he was good at. I asked what that was. 'Inheriting money,' he said. That was Sam. Always with the joke."

Freddy Graber and Sam Israel had many characteristics in common. The similarity was the result of their dispositions but also Sam's conscious effort to emulate Graber. "Sam got his sense of showmanship from Freddy," Phil recalled. "Sam modeled himself on Freddy. Both had very strong personalities. There was nobody that didn't like Freddy. The same was true for Sam. They were both very lovable. Everything had to be the biggest for Freddy. He wanted to be his own man. Sam was the same way."

For Graber, life was grand—even grandiose. In the upstairs office, he worked behind a huge white marble desk that had all the modesty of King Tut's golden throne. Sitting in his high-backed red leather swivel chair, Graber was surrounded by the latest trading gadgets, circa 1982—the Quotron and Instinet machines flickering like the set of the first *Star Trek* series. Graber had gone to Princeton and then received an M.B.A. from Harvard. But he was not an Ivy League stuffed shirt. The atmosphere was like a boys' club—the days filled with jokes, gambling, cursing, and smoking as a cassette player in the corner provided a Motown soundtrack.

In a decade as a trader, Graber had turned himself into a highly unconventional and inscrutable one-man financial institution. On Wall Street the perception was that Graber was running a large amount of money, perhaps more than $100 million. Because it was his money and hedge funds were unregulated, with no disclosure requirements, there was no way for outsiders to know. It was one of the myriad ways Graber was able to use leverage through deceptive appearances. The reality was that he traded far less than the market thought, $23 million at his peak. But Graber was a master of illusion. He also understood the venality lurking in the heart of Wall Street— the kickbacks, the self-dealing, the secret sweetheart deals. He knew how things really worked—and how to exploit every advantage.

"Freddy was the largest 'two-dollar broker' in the market," Ratner said. "That meant Freddy traded more stock than anyone else. He traded for his own account and he traded for other accounts. In those days it wasn't fashionable to have your own broker, so Freddy was the broker for Goldman and Lehman and the big firms. The big firms would charge their clients to make the trade and then get Freddy to execute the trade. It hid the order flow so no one would know what Goldman was buying. In return, Freddy kicked back five or six million dollars' worth of commissions to those firms every year—which made him the biggest payer in the market. Brokers were only paid a nickel a share, but it added up over the years.

"The guys at those banks made a lot of money out of Freddy—he paid them to send him their business. That was how Freddy wanted it. He wanted them owing him favors. He wanted to be the first to get the call from Goldman or Lehman when they were going to buy or sell stock. He loved getting that first call—the one where he knew first what the big players were going to do. Once he knew how the big boys were going to trade, he could buy shares a few minutes ahead of Goldman and then sell into the rising market. He would only own the share for fifteen minutes and then get out with a tidy profit. Freddy was always ahead of the crowd. He was able to front-run the market all day."

Over time, the distinction between "upstairs" and "downstairs" took on a new complexity for Sam. Upstairs was where the important decisions were made; downstairs was where traders kicked and scratched for every penny. At the time, an electronic program called Autex allowed buyers and sellers to identify potential counterparties, enabling a trader to measure liquidity in a stock before making a trade. Because of Graber's reputation, and all the money he spread around, specialists running the different listings didn't mind giving Phil Ratner a sneak peek at pending orders. This was the miniature version of Graber's foreknowledge of order flow. Being ahead of the market by even a few seconds gave Ratner a crucial edge. It was a primitive form of the computer program trading that would dominate the market in decades to come.

"Once you know the orders and the liquidity, how smart do you have to be to buy that stock?" Phil recalled. "You buy and buy and buy, and then at the right time when the other buyers come into the market you turn into a seller. It all happens in a matter of minutes. This kind of trading I taught Sam. We traded like that all day, scalping points all the time. We didn't give a shit about what the company did, or how it was run. We weren't interested in what would happen three months later. We cared about the next eighth of a point—is it up or down? Are there more sellers than buyers?"

Upstairs, Graber was on an amazing winning streak. In the early eighties the so-called fourth wave of mergers had begun. So had the accompanying wave of insider trading scandals. Oil companies were in heavy play, with commodity prices depressed. In rapid succession, the shares of Gulf, Exxon, and Citi Services took off on speculative runs based on impending takeovers. Miraculously, Freddy Graber managed to be ahead of the news every time. Even the green young Israel could see that it was impossible for Graber's success to be the result of chance.

"I saw how Freddy built positions in stocks," Israel recalled. "Then I saw how those companies got bought out. Freddy would make ten, twelve, fifteen points on each deal. Not a fortune. But put the trades together and Freddy made millions. He had eleven deals in a row in one year. Eleven wasn't lucky. How can you always be in the right place at the right time? You have to have good information. In that era, the Mafia was all over the news. You had the five families of New York and *The Godfather* and gangsters strutting around Little Italy. That was supposed to be organized crime. But those guys weren't organized compared to Wall Street. As big as those gangsters were, they weren't a pimple on the ass of an elephant compared to what Freddy and his crowd were doing on the stock exchange. And Freddy didn't have to kill anyone. Freddy didn't meet up afterwards to whack up a couple of hundreds of thousands with some wiseguys. Freddy whacked up millions and millions with *his* wiseguys—really the smart guys."

But there were paradoxes to Graber that he would pass along to his acolyte. He was effectively running a con on Wall Street, enriching himself by illegally trading on inside information. But at the same time Graber was himself susceptible to con artists. It was as if all his dissembling and deception made him oblivious to other people's lies and machinations. Or perhaps it was a measure of his ego that he didn't believe he could be fooled. Or perhaps it was recklessness. Graber, like Israel in later years, was prone to taking wild gambles, in the market as well as in life. The stakes didn't matter: Graber was addicted to risk. Everyone on the Street knew Graber had balls, big balls, balls made of steel.

"Freddy was a great trader and he made a lot of money, but he was also the easiest mark in the world," Phil said. "He was gullible. Like an overgrown child. He got conned all the time. He walked around with wads of cash, spending it left, right, and center. He would bet on anything—two ants walking across the floor, like they say. His settle point with his bookie was fifty thousand dollars. If Freddy went over or under fifty grand, they would meet to settle up. Worked either way, up or down. When Freddy would get near the fifty thousand point in losses he would start betting like crazy. He was trying to avoid hitting fifty grand in losses. And it worked. But in reverse. His losses would go from forty-eight thousand to a hundred grand in one day. Once he came to work with a brown briefcase filled with cash. He asked me to count the money. He told me there was a hundred thousand in it. I go to a room and count it and there was $152,000. He had no idea. I could have just taken the difference and he would never have known."

The lessons Graber taught Sam would take years to fully sink in, as Wall Street's secrets were gradually revealed in all their sly splendor. Graber called Sam's education learning by osmosis: over time he would absorb Wall Street's ethos by watching, listening, developing his own sensibility. As a market insider, Graber operated in what was effectively a parallel reality to the market known to the public. To Graber, large institutional investors like pension funds and insurance companies were chumps and patsies. The supposedly sophisticated players had no idea how Graber actually operated, or if they did have an inkling they weren't able to stop him. The same was true for the government. The ineptitude of the regulators was an open joke. Laws were broken so often and with such impunity, Israel learned, that there were effectively no rules. Trades were done "on the sheets" for legitimate business, but the real action was "off the sheets," in side deals done on the phone, on street corners, in bars. These trades were done in cash. The proceeds were spirited out of the country, to Graber's Swiss bank account (he kept the account number on the back page of his daybook).

One scam Graber introduced Sam to early involved two brothers. One brother worked at a large institutional investor, the other at a brokerage. Graber called them the Smith Brothers, after the cough drop company, because of the amount of money they coughed up. "One of the Smith Brothers would call up every morning and whisper his deal sheet for the day," Israel remembered. "The sheet said what he was going to buy and what he was going to sell. The fund he worked for was one of the biggest in the market. In those days volume wasn't very large, and his fund's trades could move the market. So if he called and said he was selling five million IBM, I would load up on shorts for IBM while I was eating my bagel and drinking my first coffee. There was no guarantee that IBM would go down, but it was a pretty fucking good bet.

"I didn't know if it was against the law, and I didn't really care. It wasn't big-time inside information. It was small-time inside information. But it affected the market. With the Smith Brothers, we were in with the guys who were making the market—the big players like Fidelity and Alliance. So if IBM was at one hundred dollars I would watch it go to ninety-nine, then ninety-eight, then I'd close out my position. It wasn't a huge amount of money all at once. But it added up over time—and I mean really added up.

"The way we paid the Smith Brothers was simple. After I had the information from one brother, I did the trades with the other brother, who was the broker. Because Freddy was such a heavy trader, the volume meant serious money. I didn't know how the brothers divvied things up. I didn't care. But the Smiths were right on for Freddy. They made him a lot of money."

Israel was enthralled by Graber, the first intensely close father substitute relationship of many he would have in the future. It was easy to see why Sam was so attracted. The trader was a large man with a larger-than-life presence. Eccentric and brilliant, Graber was like a mad scientist in his laboratory as he rubbed his forehead and placed mammoth bets in the market. Graber was also beloved by his peers. If a man was down on his luck—going through a divorce, in trouble with the law, on a losing streak—Graber could be counted on to throw business his way. Graber moved in elite social circles, but he didn't aspire to fit in with the country club set. He liked hanging out with characters, men with stories, a sense of humor, a checkered past. When Graber was arrested for drunk driving and forced to spend a night behind bars, he emerged in the morning friends with many of the men in the drunk tank.

In the beginning, Sam always dressed sharp for work. He'd inherited half a dozen elegant handmade suits from his grandfather. They fit Sam perfectly. He was literally filling the suit of Samuel Israel Jr., one of the greatest commodity traders of all time. "I wanted to look great when I went to work," he recalled. "I worked for Freddy Graber, and he was the Man. They called Freddy the King on the floor. He would walk by and people would literally say, 'Hey, King.' Like Freddy was Elvis. Freddy would come into the office in the morning and pick up a magazine and point to a picture of a car in a magazine—a Mercedes sedan. He would say, 'I'm going to make that today, and we're going to buy it today.' And then he would do it. He would buy that Mercedes that afternoon and drive it home. He was like Babe Ruth pointing to the stands saying he was going to knock it out of the park. He would make seventy grand one day. Sixty the next. Then thirty. His losses were always smaller than the gains. He had that kind of feel for the market.

"Freddy was a pure trader. He was one of the guys who really traded. He didn't buy a stock and fall in love with it. He didn't invest. He traded. Traders gravitated towards traders. You needed to make sure your alliances were strong. Traders weren't rivals or enemies with each other, like some people thought. They needed to be friends because they were small compared to the big institutions. Traders like George Soros, Michael Steinhardt, Jimmy Harpel, and Freddy Graber—guys who were running the important funds—banded together. Once we found out what huge mutual funds like Fidelity were trading, all bets were off. We would start working as a team, buying stock, shorting stock, fucking with them mercilessly. We were small, fast, nimble. The banks and pension funds were big and slow. Dinosaurs. We were there to guide them to extinction, a nickel and a dime at a time. Freddy traded ahead of the market—front-running—all day long. In and out, in and out. Like a maniac."

Since he'd begun with Graber, Sam had been dying to make actual trades. But Graber had a strict rule. As a beginner Sam wasn't permitted to trade with Graber's money. Sam was a clerk, taking orders from Graber and Ratner—including fetching lunch or grabbing a pack of smokes. "You're not going to learn how to shave by practicing on my beard," Graber told Sam. In other words, to trade, Israel would have to risk his own neck. Israel was making only $16,500 a year, which left him with little discretionary money. But he could see Graber and Phil making money all day, and he wanted in on the action.

"I asked Freddy questions about his trades, but he didn't like to be bothered explaining things," Israel recalled. "He told me I had to learn on my own. There was the obvious stuff, like front-running. But when I asked how he knew what to buy and sell he just told me I had to learn for myself. Freddy said I would know after a couple of years if I could read a tape or not—if I had a feel for the market. You could either read a tape or you couldn't—it couldn't be taught."

One day, Graber told Sam, he would have to decide if he had what it took to be a trader, or if he would have to settle for the more mundane life of a broker. On the Street, traders took risks. Traders were the heroes—the men with balls, big balls, balls of steel. As a broker, Sam could make a steady living. He could do well, even very well, executing the orders of traders. Like Phil, he could make a million dollars. But he would always be acting on other people's ideas. He would be an order taker—a soldier in the wars of Wall Street, not a general. Such a prospect never entered Israel's head. Sam imagined himself to be a born trader. The surname Israel said it all. Sam was only twenty-two, but he understood that in choosing to become a trader he was competing with his ancestors—and outdoing his father, who didn't have the mettle to trade, at least in his son's estimation.

A trader named Chuck Zion took an interest in Sam. Known as

Brown Bear, Zion showed Israel how to be a "paper trader." Following a matrix of three hundred companies, Israel learned to track the price movement of shares so that he could recognize characteristics. "Brown Bear made sure I was doing it every day, not being lazy and wasting his time," Sam recalled. "He was giving me a gift. Once you know the price range of a share, you get a chart in your head. You know if the stock is streaking. You know if it is tanking. Each stock has characteristics in the way it trades. Knowing the price of a stock was like dating a girl. How well do you know her? What does she like to do? What's her mood today?"

In the eighties, Graber shared office space with some of the most cunning traders on Wall Street. The L-shaped suite of cubicles on the thirtieth floor of 1 New York Plaza was like the 1920s Yankees batting lineup, a Murderers' Row of heavy hitters. As Graber's acolyte, Sam was known as "the kid." The older men took him into their confidence and started to teach him the tricks of the trade. Byron Wien, for decades one of the most influential voices on Wall Street, taught Israel how to understand macroeconomic questions like the difference between gross national product and gross domestic product. The government had switched the leading economic indicator from GNP to GDP, Wien explained to Israel, as a way to make it seem that the economy was growing faster—official sleight of hand understood by very few. Charlie Irish, Mark Finkle, Bob Sussman, Peter Peterson, the trader known as the Prince of Darkness who founded the multi-billion-dollar private equity giant Blackstone—many of the best hedge fund traders in the world were arranged along the stretch of corridor Israel was able to travel during the trading day.

"I didn't study in college, so I had to learn on the job," Israel remembered. "All of these guys were from Harvard and the Wharton

Business School. They were the A-Team. Steven Peck was one of the first real chartists. Everyone looks at charts now, but back then no one really did, not like Steven. He had a cool program that let him bring up charts by pushing a button on his IBM computer. I would go into his office for hours and watch him price different blocks of trades. He loved to teach. Same with Jim Harpel, who ran Century Capital and had one hundred million dollars at the time. His style was to buy and hold, or short and hold. Ninety percent of the guys running funds were Jewish. It was like the Jewish Mafia."

In the evenings Sam regaled his parents with stories of Graber's triumphs. His father had retired from ACLI with millions from the sale of the family company in the early eighties. Listening to his son's tales of the money made by the King, Larry Israel decided to take a desk in the bull pit near Graber to trade his own money. Sam's father and Graber were casual friends, and soon the trio started to ride together to work every day. "My father was there trading right beside Freddy—and right beside me," Sam recalled. "It was a little weird at first. But after a while it didn't bother me because I didn't work for him. He was making money. It was a moneymaking environment, to say the least. My father and Freddy became close friends.

"I was known for being around the office a lot. I stayed late. I would never take more than one week's vacation a year. One day they couldn't find me at work. I just didn't turn up. Around lunch Freddy was getting worried. He was going to call the cops. My father was getting worried too. Freddy stood up to get his lunch and he saw me lying on the floor. I got so drunk the night before, I had passed out under my desk, as my place of sanctuary."

There was a saying in Graber's office: You can't be a winner until you learn how to lose. It was a lesson Sam struggled with from the beginning, as Phil noticed when he gradually began to permit Sam to make trades for Graber. "Sam was a good trader when he was winning," Phil recalled. "But he hated losing. He couldn't stand it. He didn't want to face the disgrace. He would hide his losing trades in his desk, in the middle drawer, hoping they wouldn't get found, hoping the trade would turn around. He would let the loss go too far. Freddy was the same way. But it was Freddy's money, so he could do what he wanted. I would find Sam's hidden trades. I tried to teach him. I told him that if you want to trade you have to take your losses. You have to look at them. You have to stare at them. I lost all the time. But I got out quickly. And I didn't try to forget them. I kept the tickets in front of me to remind me. For years I never had a losing month. The whole thing is discipline. I begged him to listen to me."

One night, Israel got a taste of the kind of moral quandaries that could confront him at a moment's notice on Wall Street. He was still only twenty-three years old, but he was already in a position of considerable power as a conduit to the commissions generated by Graber's trades. "I got my first experience of a broker trying to get his hooks into me and reel me in," Israel recalled. "I was supposed to be going out to dinner with this guy, but I got bamboozled. He said he was going to take me to his private club. It was on Fifty-seventh Street. We walked up to a black door with a camera above it and we were buzzed in. We were shown into a little anteroom with a glass window. I was thinking about how private and exclusive the club was when we were shown into a room filled with gorgeous women. There were men there too—middle-aged, overweight slobs. The women were unbelievable *Penthouse* beauties. There was a swimming pool and a spa. The broker told me the girls were three hundred each, plus tip. I had a girlfriend. But I wasn't going to back down. I knew that I was now supposed to be buddies with that broker. He had done that for me—taking me out whoring. That made you friends on Wall Street."

Over time, Sam developed his own persona. Inspired by Graber's idiosyncrasies, Sam imagined himself to be different, an outsider of sorts, the Israel who wouldn't trade on his family name or live by the conventions of Wall Street. Part of his personality was his refusal to take work or himself seriously—an echo of Graber's devil-may-care attitude. Israel had come to hate the dress code traders followed, so he rebelled by wearing khakis, short-sleeve shirts, and cartoon character ties—the Road Runner, Bugs Bunny, Yosemite Sam. When he came to work one day with a Fred Flintstone tie, Graber demanded Sam hand it over immediately—so he could wear it.

As a velocity trader, Graber constantly bought and sold the same stocks. He churned stock so much he created a mystique about the companies on his buy/sell list, as if they were his children. Graber called Colgate his "firstborn." He talked about the stock he traded with intense passion, passing around made-up gossip, false specula-tion, and occasionally real news—anything to stir up action. One of Graber's abilities was to "paint the tape," the illegal practice of trading with the sole purpose of moving the price of a stock. The agribusiness giant Archer Daniels Midland was one of the stocks Graber fooled with relentlessly. To paint the tape on ADM, Graber and Israel would call eight different brokers and put in buy orders simultaneously to run up the price—at a time when Graber was holding lots of the stock ready to sell into a rising market. It was a racket the Securities and Exchange Commission was hopelessly ill equipped to stop.

"The SEC questioned Freddy all the time," Phil Ratner recalled. "But they couldn't catch him. He traded so much that it was impos-sible to say that he'd traded on inside information. Like the Columbia

Pictures takeover. Freddy had started on Wall Street as an analyst in the entertainment business, so he was always trading stocks in movie and music companies. He really knew the industry backwards. So when Coca-Cola bought Columbia, Freddy bought a huge amount of shares just before the deal was announced—because he had the inside information. The SEC called him in. Freddy wasn't worried. Of course he had traded illegally. But he showed them his trading records. He was always buying and selling huge pieces of Columbia Pictures. How the hell were they going to prove that he had inside information? He traded so much, they couldn't keep up with what he was doing. They didn't understand that there was a method to Freddy's madness."

After Ratner retired, Sam took over as Graber's eyes and ears on the floor of the exchange. Even armed with all of Graber's inside information, Sam needed to hedge risk on his behalf. That meant short selling, which would protect Graber if the price of a stock went down. Israel aimed to make himself Graber's short-position trader. It was a way to be useful to Graber, as it was a kind of trading his boss didn't understand particularly well. "From the beginning, I was fascinated by the short side, not the long," Sam said. "That meant I was looking for stocks that were going to go down in price, not up. In those days, the public wasn't sophisticated about the markets. People thought that when the market went down everyone lost money. I knew that wasn't true."

Sam also started to bet his own money on short selling. As a short, Sam didn't buy stock, he purchased a "put" or borrowed the stock to sell to the buyer. Shorting was not for the risk averse. Because there was no limit on how high a stock could rise, in theory losses could be infinite. Sam was trading on margin, so he was betting with borrowed money he would eventually have to come up with if he lost. More than a few traders had taken enough rope to hang themselves by short selling.

Because of the hazards and complexities, short sellers enjoyed a certain mystique. The aura was part of the attraction for Sam. He had developed a mantra for himself. If there were one hundred people playing the market in one direction, Sam wanted to be the one guy who made money while the other ninety-nine were losing their shirts. The notion was based entirely on ego—or hubris. After two years on Wall Street, the education of Sam Israel was well under way. So was the growth of his cynicism. "Under Freddy I learned that Wall Street was an illusion," Sam recalled. "There were different magicians using different tricks in different ways. But everyone cheated. It shocked me so much in the beginning. I admired those people. And they cheated."

CHAPTER THREE

Front-Running

In 1984, Israel asked his high school sweetheart to marry him. Janice McKergan was a pretty and clever Irish Catholic girl from Yonkers who had followed Sam to Tulane University, where she graduated with an accounting degree. "Janice was a girl I could love," Sam remembered. "She was blond, with blue eyes, very attractive, very athletic. She came from a lower-middle-class family. Her father worked in a bank. Her mother was raising six kids. There was never anything extra in her family, so Janice worked for everything she got. Janice was a cheerleader and I played linebacker on the football team. She was a straight-A student. She was stable. I was the fuckup. I was the bad boy. I took drugs and fooled around and didn't take anything seriously."

Janice agreed to marry Sam—provided Sam got his financial

affairs in order. Despite his apprenticeship in the art of running money, Sam's life was in chaos when it came to his finances. Sam's days were spent obsessing over money, but he had adopted Freddy Graber's strangely passive-aggressive attitude to it. Money was everything to a Wall Street trader: a way to keep score, accumulate possessions, assert status. But money was also a matter of indifference to a great trader. The small people of this world—accountants, regulators, losers— sweated the details. Not men like Freddy and Sam. In fact, Sam hadn't paid income tax in four years, and his credit card statements and bank accounts were a mess. Janice had just returned to New York to take a position as an accountant with Price Waterhouse. She was fastidious and well organized when it came to paying bills. Sam was shambolic, adopting the pretense that the ability to summon money out of thin air by trading negated the need to take care of petty issues like debt or taxes.

Then there was the matter of the lifestyle of a trader. Graber was concerned that the sweet and innocent young woman who was going to marry Sam didn't understand the nature of Sam's business. "When Janice and I got engaged, Freddy said he wanted to talk to my fiancée," Israel recalled. "She came by the office one day after work. Freddy sat her down next to his big marble desk. He said to her, 'I've been doing this for twenty years now. I'm tired. I'm raising a family. I need to go home at night. So Sam is going to go out every night for me. He's going to be with these brokers getting drunk. He's going to be out late and he's going to get up early and he's going to work his ass off. I've already talked to Sam about this. If you can't accept it, don't marry him. Because you'll be divorced.' I think Janice respected Freddy for saying that."

On the eve of the wedding, Graber took him out for a night on the town. To Israel's surprise, they went to the same high-end whore-house the broker had taken him to a year earlier. "I didn't tell him I'd been there before," Sam recalled. "He said I could go crazy. The place was packed with beautiful women—each one prettier than the last. I said, 'Could I have two?' He said I could have three girls if I wanted. So I got two. It was the best thing ever."

Newly married, Sam and Janice moved to a small prefab town house in Bronxville. With Phil Ratner retired, Sam was now respon-sible for doling out Graber's commissions, so the modest Israel home quickly became packed with the gifts from brokers trying to get into Sam's good graces—cases of Chateau Lafite Rothschild wine, antique clocks and maps, Tiffany glassware. "They would try to get me to go out with them as much as possible," Israel said. "Janice wanted noth-ing to do with Wall Street. She hated the traders and brokers with their drinking and drugs and cheating on their wives. She knew I had to go out, but she kept her distance. The brokers wanted me to owe them. They wanted me to walk into work the next morning and feel like I should give them the business because they'd shown me a good time.

"I knew this broker named Eddie. I was smoking dope with him at his apartment one night when he said something about 'soft dol-lars.' I'd never heard the term before. He explained it to me, saying it was the biggest scam ever—and it was totally legal. It was basi-cally a kickback brokers would pay traders to get their business. In the early eighties, brokers were cutting commissions. Trading volumes were going up really fast because of computers. I remember the first day a hundred million shares were traded in a day. People thought the system couldn't take it.

"So brokers began to offer flat rates, like eight cents a share. The way soft dollars worked was that the broker would charge us eight cents a share to make a trade. Then the broker would pay four cents back to us to pay for all the stuff we needed to trade—telephones, IBM computers, office space. That was how it started. Brokers would cover the legitimate expenses of their customers as a way to attract business. But then brokers started to pay traders for other things. Like country club memberships. Then cars and trips to Europe and home renovations. It was called 'soft dollars,' but really it was a form of bribery. After a while soft dollars would pay for a private plane full of traders to go to Tahiti for a party. That was why Wall Street was so lavish in the eighties."

When Israel explained the ruse to Graber, he was amazed and delighted. Graber moved a hunk of his business to Eddie and began to reap the rewards. Whatever concert or Broadway show Freddy or Sam wanted to see, the best tickets were at the ready. Graber would take Sam to Knicks and Rangers games and have an entire executive box reserved for the two of them, simply because Graber didn't like being around crowds. Trips to Las Vegas to gamble were taken in ultra-luxe style, often at a moment's notice.

"Freddy would go to Petrossian and order caviar," Sam said. "Not the little itty-bitty servings most people ordered. He got four or five big bowls. He didn't bother with putting the caviar on a piece of toast, or in one of the fancy shells they gave you. He scooped out huge spoonfuls. He would order a bottle of vodka, two bottles of Cristal champagne. It was excessive. There were no limits."

During the mideighties, the Dow rose to more than 2000 and kept climbing. Graber started to commute from the suburbs to Wall Street in a private helicopter. Sam traveled with him as they swooped through the sky above the snarled traffic below. The views were breathtaking—and so was the excitement.

"In those years, I became an asshole," Israel said. "I was making seventy grand, plus getting handed a bonus of a hundred grand by Freddy, plus there was the money I was making on my own account. When I started out, my ambition was to make a hundred grand a year, and I was already beating that. I went from a low-key considerate kid to this rich kid who was a complete jerk. All of a sudden I had to have the best cars. If I was traveling someplace I had to be flying first class. If it wasn't first class, I wasn't fucking going. I would only stay in five-star hotels. I would throw money away, just like Freddy would throw money away. My moral education from Freddy consisted of learning how to keep secrets and spend money. I started acting like Freddy. My mother said she didn't know who I was becoming. My ego was out of control."

Sam's hair was thinning prematurely, as it did for most of the men in the Israel clan, making him look older than his age. But he worked out regularly, preparing to run in a marathon and keep in shape for the grueling nights on the town. Maintaining a boyish sense of humor, Sam developed an alter ego he called Captain Proton, a fearless superhero whose special powers were infused by vodka and cocaine. When Sam inhabited the character, he would turn an umbrella into his sword and a curtain into his cape as he set about crusading through the bars and clubs of Manhattan.

"We were hedge fund heroes," Israel recalled. "There were only fifty or so hedge funds that traded a lot at the time. As Freddy's protégé I was in the thick of it. Everyone called me 'the kid.' I was out of my mind having fun. I would get shitfaced and do outrageous things.

I didn't give a fuck. I would get my ear pierced on a dare. I would pull the tablecloth out from a table filled with plates and glasses like I was a magician—only everything would go flying. I used to jump out of limousines at intersections and start directing traffic on a big street in midtown Manhattan. But the downside was that always I wanted to please people. I had a horrible time saying no. I would get invited out to dinner by two brokers, and I would say yes to both because I didn't want to hurt their feelings. Then I would find an excuse for one at the last second. I wanted people to like me too much."

At the height of the takeover craze, Graber's methods were increasingly ingenious and devious. Grooming his charge, Graber began to trust Sam with some of his most sensitive sources, introducing him as his right-hand man and vouching for his reliability and discretion. "Gradually Freddy showed me the ropes with the real insiders," Israel said. "There were the Jewish guys who went to Michael's and Smith and Wollensky. The Italian guys went to Tiro a Segno, which was a restaurant with a gun club in the basement in the West Village. There was the *Mayflower* set at the Harvard and Yale clubs. We moved inside all the circles. His best contact was a guy named Alan Jacobs— Jake, as he was known. He ran a boutique investment bank advisory company. Jake's clients were investment banks and accounting firms trying to figure out the value of companies that were targets for takeovers. On virtually every big deal in the eighties, Jake was hired by one of the players to assess the merits of the transaction. It made him the perfect insider. I knew Freddy had someone but I didn't know who it was. By then I'd seen a lot and said nothing about it. One day Freddy said, 'Tonight, you're going to meet our guy.' He was letting me in on his biggest secret. It was like I was a wiseguy getting made by the gang—getting sworn into the secret circle.

"Jake held court at a bar called Michael's Too. He sat at the far left end of the bar. The place would be packed with Wall Streeters watching basketball. It didn't look like it, but Jake's circle was exclusive. That was how things worked. The lines and boundaries were invisible. The guys at the left end of the bar looked like a few guys unwinding after work. Jake didn't look rich. He didn't act rich. He looked like a drone—an accountant, a corporate lawyer. He sat there getting drunk. Which became one of my jobs—getting drunk with Jake.

"The first time I went with Freddy I kept quiet and watched. Jake wouldn't come out directly and say things. But he would give you enough circumstantial hints that you could figure it out. Like Shell Oil getting bought out in 1984. Then the airlines happened. Then computers. Jake did every fucking one of these deals. Jake was doing the analysis. Or he knew the guy that knew the guy. It was an incestuous world. That was how people put things together. Jake was just one piece of the puzzle. If Salomon was backing the deal, we had someone at Salomon. If it was Goldman Sachs, we had an in there. That bar was where the real money was being made.

"Freddy had a thing he called the brother-in-law rule. He believed there was no such thing as a secret. If a deal was coming, there was always a way of finding out about it first. Everyone inevitably talked to their wife or cousin or brother-in-law to let them in on the deal. We got a lot of information in ways that avoided making a guy come right out and tell you things. I would call up Freddy's guy in the M&A department at Morgan Stanley. I would shoot the shit for a little while, give him something he could use—a tip or a lead. Then I would say I'd heard they were working on a deal. I'd name the deal. But I didn't put him on the spot. He had to be able to say under oath that he never told anyone about the deal. So I'd say, 'You don't have to tell me anything. I know you're backing the Shell deal. Is it still going through in the next two weeks? I'm going to count to four. Hang up before I get there if there's something going on.' Then I would count. 'One. Two.' Click. The guy hangs up. Now I know Shell is in play.

"These were people I knew. These were people I was in business with. I wasn't talking to strangers. They expected payment in kind. Some guys wanted Yankee seats. Some guys wanted to go to the opera. Some wanted cash. We'd get one of our brokers to hire that firm and use the money from our commissions to pay them. There were schemes upon schemes upon schemes. There were layers of layers."

BY THE MIDEIGHTIES, it was evident to Sam that a paradigm shift was occurring on Wall Street that would alter the definition of what it meant to be a trader. The introduction of computers was radically transforming the entire securities industry. When Sam had started, there were no desktop computers, and teams of secretaries were required to enter data to create primitive trading charts. The first Bridge Data machines were so large they had to be shipped in trucks and wheeled onto trading floors on mover's dollies.

Over time, the technology began to evolve, slowly at first and then quickly. There were still position traders, men like George Soros or Warren Buffett who were concerned with large economic trends and the underlying value of companies. In the hierarchy of the business, position traders imagined themselves to be the elite. But high-velocity traders like Graber were moving from the periphery of Wall Street to the center of the business. The big players were gradually coming to understand that the tiny sums of money Graber accumulated by exploiting the cracks on Wall Street could add up to billions if the volumes were large enough. It was impossible for humans to trade at the necessary speed, but computers were able to trade in vastly larger amounts and at exponentially faster speeds. By the middle of the decade, Goldman Sachs had scores of young techies working on their secret proprietary trading programs. More independent hedge funds were also trying to create programs that would quantify and digitize what Graber did the old-fashioned way. The machines were able to process much more information than was otherwise possible, providing an incredible edge to the possessor of the fastest, most sophisticated systems.

The term *quant* was coined to describe traders who used mathematics and algorithmic analysis. Sam didn't have the education or technical expertise to become a quant. But he was convinced of the importance of computer trading. A friend of Sam's named Stanley Patrick was also interested. Patrick was a southerner, like Israel, who ridiculed the conformist conventions of Wall Street, preferring the self-image of the eccentric oddball. Obsessed with catching lobster on Long Island Sound in his spare time, Patrick wore brightly colored rubber fishing boots with his suits, not as a lark but as his daily attire; it was a way of thumbing his nose at the men dressed in Gucci and Brooks Brothers.

"I loved Stanley from the day he walked into Freddy's office," Israel said. "We were kindred spirits, even though he was fifteen years older than me. He'd been a trader with some of the biggest firms on Wall Street—Goldman Sachs, Dean Witter, Morgan Stanley, the *biggest* players. He was regarded as exceptionally bright and exceptionally flaky, and that was kind of how I thought of myself. He'd make the most insane trades, take the hugest risks—but he made the positions work. He would go on coke jags and disappear for days. He was much more successful than I was at the time, but we were very close."

For years Patrick had trafficked in insider information, like most everyone else. Now Patrick was trying to make himself expert at the new computer trading systems. Working as a trader for a hedge fund that specialized in technical analysis, Patrick attempted to create programs that would detect trading patterns in specific stocks. The hope was to develop triggers that would track the flow of money in and out of stocks. The computer calculated spreads, premiums, volumes, and price, enabling a trader to have a matrix of data inputs to enable fast, precise, and profitable trades at low risk. In theory. The reality was far more complicated.

Israel was mesmerized by Patrick's work. He quizzed Patrick incessantly about computer programming. Sam watched as the handwritten ticket was gradually replaced by digital transactions on the floor of the exchange, threatening to make his position with Graber obsolete. The human element of trading had always been fundamental to the market. Information had been the most valuable asset. But Graber's skill set started to matter less and less. A strategy emerged called "program trading." The premise of program trading was that computers could be trained to automatically make trades once predetermined conditions were met, such as a drop in a specific stock index.

"I made myself a computer nerd," Israel said. "I could see I needed to know the technology and how it worked. Freddy didn't have any computers. I tried to get him interested, but he just wasn't into them.

He was set in his ways. Freddy and I got our charts once a week, on the weekend. I'd go to his house on Sunday night, or we'd talk on the phone. That was all the technical analysis he did. Freddy wouldn't even have a computer on his desk.

"By this time I didn't want to go out with brokers at night so much. I would go home to eat dinner with my wife. Then I would drive forty minutes to Stanley's house in Connecticut. We'd work on the computer program we were building until three in the morning. I'd drive home, sleep for a couple of hours, and then go to work. I did that for years. Stanley and I were going to create our own charting system. Everyone was looking at patterns from the past. We weren't interested in the past. We wanted something to look into the future. I wanted the computer to tell me what was going to happen."

Israel became a follower of the physicist Jurgen Ehlers, who was examining a similar question from the point of view of synchronicity. The German scientist had founded the Albert Einstein Institute and studied general relativity. It was Ehlers's study of "hidden symmetries" and the predictive possibilities of "frame theory" that fascinated Sam—how quantum physics might enable him to anticipate movements in the market as if stocks were particles of light. It was heady stuff for a liberal arts major who had barely paid attention in high school algebra.

In 1987, Wall Street learned about the ghosts lurking in the new machines. "Portfolio insurance" was one of the strategies program traders used. Computers calculated the optimal stock-to-cash ratios for various prices in the market. With the computer programmed to trade the instant the set parameters emerged, portfolio insurance was supposed to be like buying a put option—a kind of guarantee that a stock could be sold at a specific price. In the fall of '87 there were stirrings in the press that the new preprogrammed trading systems contained an inherent flaw—a contradiction that could lead to a fiasco. The problem was so obvious it beggared belief that it hadn't been noticed by the supposedly smartest traders on earth. If all the program traders had set their machines to sell in a falling market, then it followed that when the market fell all the program traders would be selling at the same time, creating a crash.

All through '87, the market kept climbing, a bull with no apparent end in sight. By August the Dow had gone over 2700, an amazing 70 percent increase in less than a year. It was a streak that Sam considered unsustainable. For months he'd shorted the market, expecting a decline—but none came. The frustration was incredible. On Monday, October 19, 1987, Sam shorted the market on his own account, as usual. The previous week had been unusually turbulent, with a sharp downward movement. Sam sensed that the trend was going to continue. This time he was loaded for bear. He'd shorted the S&P, betting on the market dropping. He was also on the short side of United Airlines. He was about to get very lucky. On Black Monday the crash started from the opening bell as terror swept across the NYSE and around the world. It was the largest-ever percentage drop in the value of global stocks in a single day.

"I made a lot of money that day," Israel said. "It was my biggest day ever. I was short on everything. It was just fantastic. But I didn't gloat or brag. I couldn't even talk about it. Freddy lost a couple of million. My dad was down a million or so. I was selling my puts slowly and I was getting back prices I couldn't believe. A put would be selling for fifteen on the screen and I'd get a report back at thirty-eight. People were in a panic—even George Soros. Everyone around me was getting wiped out. But I couldn't look happy about it, so I kept my mouth shut."

The following day, the traders arrived at 1 New York Plaza in a state of shock. It was as if the prior trading session had been a hallucination. Sam could see that no one had a clue what would happen next. Israel believed the crash was part of a larger correction. The five-year run that began in 1982 had created an unrealistic sense of value on Wall Street. Sam continued to short. But over the following days prices stabilized and then started to rise as the market began to recoup the losses from the crash. Sam was miffed. Then he figured out what was happening. The Federal Reserve was supporting the market. Specialists were required to "make" a market in the stock they covered, which meant they had to keep buying even when there was no one to sell the shares to. Liquidity had vanished from the market as cash reserves disappeared. Stock worth $50 a share suddenly had no buyers—not at any price. Finding the bottom of the market in the middle of a computer- and panic-driven selling spree seemed impossible.

But there was a lender of last resort: the Federal Reserve. As the market fell, the Fed intervened by instructing banks to lend money to the specialists. So specialists pledged stock to the banks as security for loans to buy stock with no real market value. To pay for the massive rescue, the Fed was creating money out of thin air. The end of the gold standard in the seventies had turned the American dollar into a fiat currency, effectively giving the Fed the power to print money. It was a kind of Ponzi scheme, Israel thought, but at the highest level of abstraction—and secrecy.

Sam believed he'd discovered the central illusion at the heart of American capitalism. He had the dizzying sensation that there was nothing underneath the whole edifice of Wall Street, the dollar, the

American economy. The Fed acted like the Wizard of Oz, creating an ornate fantasy, with Alan Greenspan as the man behind the curtain. Growing up, Sam had seen how his family had been on the inside of market manipulations and political plots to prop up Third World dictators. Now he'd glimpsed how Wall Street really worked.

CHAPTER FOUR

Other People's Money

T he crash of 1987 broke Graber's spirits. The margin calls ruined many of the traders Sam most admired. A generation of hedge fund heroes had been badly damaged, many forced out of the business entirely. "Anybody could lose it all on Wall Street at any time," Israel said. "It was sickening to watch. Great traders were crushed. The crash really hurt Freddy. He lost confidence. Trades that used to be second nature to him suddenly became hard to make. Doubts crept into his trading. You can't trade from fear."

After Black Monday, Sam's sense of himself was becoming grand, even grandiose—like Freddy's in his prime. Sam believed, if only a little and secretly, that he'd traded like Jesse Livermore, the Wall Street legend who had shorted the market in the crash of 1929 and made $100 million.

After leaving Graber, Sam bounced around for the next few years. Trading his own money, he was able to build up nest eggs, only to repeatedly go broke trying to trade on inside information. RJR Nabisco, National Cash Register, Donald Trump's attempt to take over United Airlines—Sam was able to scavenge tips, only to be undone by bad timing. Every time he accumulated a good sum of money the same thing happened. Three times Sam went on a winning streak, and three times Sam went broke. But it was a trade on Kansas Southern Railroad that nearly ruined him.

"I got a tip that it was going to be acquired from a guy who was literally on the board," Israel said. "You couldn't do better than that. I went into the stock big. But the deal got delayed and delayed. It was finally going to be announced on a Monday. Then the deal went bad. I lost four hundred grand in one day. It killed me. It was the fourth time I'd taken a huge loss. This time I swore I was never going to let it happen again. I wasn't going to put any of my assets in my name. That included houses, cars, bank accounts. I was going to live like a mobster—nothing in my name. No matter what, I would never put myself in that position again. I would not go down. I would not do it. Never ever ever."

The Israels had a healthy baby girl in 1990. The birth was one of the happiest times in Sam's life. But the pressure of having a newborn led the couple to fight. As the arguments grew worse, Janice asked Sam to leave the house. "We started so young," Sam recalled. "We were adolescents when we got together, high school sweethearts. Our whole adult lives were together."

The split hit Sam hard—but it also set him free. Sam was in his early thirties, caught between his party years and the responsibilities of fatherhood. He moved to a bachelor pad on the Upper East Side of Manhattan. Weeknights, he haunted the city's nightclubs and bars. On the weekends, Janice allowed Sam to come home to see their daughter. Janice didn't ask about his life in Manhattan and he didn't tell her what he was up to. The schizophrenic existence began to tear him apart. Sam wanted to be a decent man, even as he was drawn by the lure of fast money and one-night stands. He wanted to tell the truth, even as he was surrounded by a culture that rewarded lying. He knew many things he was doing were wrong, but he couldn't resist temptation.

After finally reconciling with Janice, Sam moved back to the prefab house in Bronxville and set about trying to establish his own hedge fund. Sam was going to "trade the tape," market parlance for executing the tiny high-velocity transactions he used to do for Graber.

"But I didn't even know how to begin to start," Israel said. "I didn't know how to attract money. I didn't know how to sell myself. I wound up trading a few hundred grand of my own money. That was all I had. Janice had stopped working because of our daughter, so we were broke. Janice was worried. We'd bought a piece of property and we were planning on building a house. My fund lasted six months. I had to get back to making money. I had to get a job."

In 1993, Israel heard that Leon "Lee" Cooperman, the former head of research for Goldman Sachs who'd started a hedge fund called Omega, was looking for a trader. Cooperman had been one of the guiding intelligences for Goldman, which ipso facto made him one of the smartest men on Wall Street. At the time, Omega was undergoing rapid expansion, growing from $250 million to many billions in the space of a few years, so Cooperman was happy to hire a canny trader like Sam.

"At Omega, we were one of the biggest players on the Street," Israel recalled. "We traded high volume, high speed, high commissions. We could move markets. I spread our orders out to a bunch of brokers so no one person could know what we were doing. We were paying so much in commissions that the brokers fed us the best information. I knew how to make money out of that information. It was like having a nonstop supply of information to front-run.

"Lee wasn't interested. Making fifty, sixty grand didn't really matter to him. If you added it up over the year, it would only amount to 2 percent of the funds he had in Omega, and that wouldn't move the dial for him. It was nickels and dimes when you're running billions and you need to make hundreds of millions to make your performance.

"I didn't want to see that money go to waste—it seemed criminal to leave all that money sitting on the table. So I reached out to an old trader who had moved down to the Carolinas. Bert was still an active trader with his own money. We could trade in his name with my information. Every morning I gave him Omega's positions for the day, and he knew how to turn that into money on a big scale, for us at least. My base salary with Omega was only one hundred thousand dollars, plus bonus. But with Bert I started to make real money—fantastic sums. Bert would take out enough to pay income tax—40 percent—and then we'd split the rest fifty-fifty. I'd meet him in Washington, D.C., or in Virginia, or I'd go down to his house, and he'd give me cash—hundreds of thousands of dollars at a time.

"When I was a kid with Freddy, he'd sent me to collect briefcases filled with cash. Now I was doing it for myself. I wasn't just trading through Bert. I had guys all over the country front-running for me. I had bags and bags of cash arriving at JFK and La Guardia. Or up in the Pierre Hotel, just like Freddy did with me. I couldn't trade in my own name because I was required to disclose all the trading I did. But when I used Bert and the other guys there was no way to get caught. After a while I put two safes in the house, one in the attic for jewelry, the other chained to the floor in the basement for cash."

In little more than a year, Sam had accumulated nearly $1 million. He and Janice began to plan to build a new home on the land they'd bought. Sam's sense of himself was growing, as were his ambitions. He was tired of working for Cooperman, a taskmaster given to yelling—like his father. The ambition to start his own hedge fund had returned with a vengeance. The computer program he'd tinkered with for years was getting more accurate, Sam believed. He was ready to put his trading strategy into the market and forge his own fortune.

Bert was outraged at Sam's decision to leave Omega and its illicit revenue stream—a fact he recalled vividly years later. "I couldn't believe he was quitting," Bert said. "Sam had the perfect job. Maybe he was only making a couple hundred grand with Omega, but he was making a fortune on the side. It was like the story about the boy killing the goose that lays the golden egg. The boy starts to think maybe he's not getting rich fast enough with one golden egg a day, so he tries to get all the gold out of the goose all at once by wringing its neck. Then all he's got left is a dead goose. That was Sam—the kid who didn't know how good he had it. As far as I was concerned, Sammy should have offered to do the job for free. He should have *paid* Leon

Cooperman just to be able to come to work and trade for him. But you couldn't talk sense to Sam. He was in love with computers. He fell for computer trading hard, like a star-crossed lover."

BY THE MIDNINETIES, the small and incestuous hedge fund business of Freddy Graber's era had become a booming multi-billion-dollar industry. The types of funds were astonishingly diverse: macro, micro, global, quant. In this new age, running money came to be the ultimate goal for a trader. But there was one huge difference for the new breed of hedge fund heroes. Freddy Graber had traded his own money. The fate of his fund had mirrored his own. In the new paradigm, virtually all of the new hedge funds traded other people's money. This meant the risk belonged to investors, who in turn demanded returns that were often impossible to satisfy. This combination was part of the untethering from reality that sent the S&P balloon flying off into a clear blue sky.

For young, corrupt, and soon-to-be middle-aged men like Sam, running money was like becoming a rock star. Or trying to. As Sam prepared to launch his fund, he was bursting with great expectations, like any garage band hoping to hit the big time. Sam would be the public face of the fund. His friend Stanley Patrick was going to be the lead trader. But there was one small wrinkle—the matter of a felony conviction. A couple of years earlier, Patrick had pled guilty to insider trading. The SEC had banned Patrick from trading for life. For Sam, the conviction was nothing more than a legal technicality. The solution was simple. Sam would front the fund. Patrick would be in the background. No one would know that Patrick was trading again. It was just a matter of keeping things on the down low.

The deception didn't strike Sam as being at odds with his determination to run an honest fund. As he imagined it, his fund would be state-of-the-art. He wouldn't have a fund that specialized only in technical trading, like so many others coming into the market. Nor would the fund have a conventional position strategy. Israel and Patrick were going to combine their trading program with their hard-won street-level experience. They were going to create a quant-like long/short, market-neutral fund run by highly experienced high-velocity traders.

"I'd been in the market for more than a decade," Israel said. "I'd learned a lot of things about chart theories, wave theories, arbitrage strategies. I knew that charting for the whole day didn't make sense. The first and last hours of trading were the important times. That was when the volume got done as funds got into or out of their positions. I also looked at transactional charts—not just the volume of shares traded but the number of deals that had been made and when the trades were made. I had two or three trend lines with the highs and lows for all the stocks I was watching. I'd put the assumptions about the past into the machine. From that, I would get projections about the high and low and open for the next day. It was intuitive to me."

"Forward Propagation" was the name Sam gave to the computer program. The word *forward* spoke to the software's soothsaying powers. *Propagation* aimed to conjure wave theory, biological reproduction, and religious evangelicism, all with a whiff of mathematical mysticism. Like fractals, the multiplying self-similar geometric shapes that occur in coastlines and snowflakes and lightning bolts, there were shapes to be divined inside the seemingly incoherent data, Israel maintained. With some fine-tuning, the machine could give him the ability to see those hidden patterns in stock prices.

The heady egoism of Sam's days with Graber was mutating into something more dangerous. Many hedge fund traders were eccentrics, following a peculiar trading strategy they believed could unlock the keys to the magic kingdom. Many were narcissists. But even in that company, Sam's inner voice was starting to sound unhinged. He wanted his machine to "hear" the market, the way a conductor hears music a beat before it is played by an orchestra. If Sam succeeded—if he could divine how to decode the massive amount of information generated every minute in the market—his name would echo through the ages.

"I wanted a chart that was different from everybody else's. I wanted to be better than other people. I wanted to see what other people couldn't see. What's the advantage if everyone looks at the exact same thing? I didn't want to watch history. I wanted to *be* history. I didn't want to be in the game—I wanted to *be* the game."

IN 1995, the Israels moved into their brand-new house on Buckout Road, in the well-to-do town of Harrison, leaving behind the prefab town house in Bronxville. The house had been custom designed by Sam and Janice with understated elegance. Unlike many of the mini-mansions being built at the time, the house was perfectly proportioned to the lot. There was a low stone wall in front, with a driveway sweeping down to a newly constructed four-thousand-square-foot executive-style residence. The interior was decorated with the signifiers of wealth and refinement—modern art, antique furniture, stainless-steel appliances. In the backyard there was a large gunite swimming pool. A nature reserve was next door, ensuring that the two-acre property would never have a neighbor on the north side. A homebody by inclination, Sam had created a perfect retreat for his young family.

Sam's sense of accomplishment and contentment was given new depth with the birth of a son. Sam was elated. For generations, Israel men had followed in the footsteps of their fathers. Traders had become traders, gamblers gamblers, screamers screamers. Sam was going to break the pattern. His imperative was to make life different for his son. Sam would be all the things he felt he'd been denied: calm, kind, easy to please. Sam would give his children the greatest gift of all: unconditional love.

BAYOU WAS THE NAME Israel chose for the hedge fund. It was a reference to his New Orleans heritage and the irreverence he loved, so much about the Big Easy. Bayou wouldn't be a pretentious fund run by M.B.A.s with delusions of grandeur. Bayou would be like Sam: informal, unique, brilliant.

But as the launch neared, money issues began to press in on the Israels. Since leaving Omega, Sam hadn't been able to rely on a regular paycheck, or the bags of cash he'd made by front-running. Like many Wall Street high rollers, Sam had paid for his house up front in cash. Mortgages weren't necessary for a trader of his stature, not when he was on the cusp of real financial independence. But throwing down more than $600,000 had stretched his resources. He was quickly burning through his savings. To economize and get a tax write-off, Sam decided to run Bayou from his basement. There would be no boardroom, or pretty assistants, or high-priced art hanging on the walls. He purchased inexpensive desks and chairs and installed an Internet connection.

Days before the fund was going to begin trading, Israel got a call from Stanley Patrick. He was in Brazil, where he could trade legally. He told Sam he had decided not to come home to start Bayou. In a halting voice, he said he was done, out, finished. The odds of getting caught by the SEC again were slim, perhaps, but he wasn't willing to take the risk. Sam pleaded with Patrick to change his mind. Sam said he needed Stanley to help him run the trading program. Sam also needed him to figure out what stocks to buy and sell; Sam had no experience actually picking stocks to trade. He'd always followed the orders of Graber or Cooperman.

"I can't do it," Patrick told Sam. "I just can't do it. I can't trade anymore. I can't pull the trigger. I don't want to be responsible."

"I panicked," Israel recalled. "All of a sudden I was by myself. I felt like I couldn't turn back. I'd come this far. I was ready to go. But I'd never been by myself before. I'd always been the number two guy. I was great at pulling the trigger on a trade. I would figure out how to work the system. But I needed someone to come up with the idea on what to trade. I had no performance record of my own to sell to investors. My record was everyone else's record. I couldn't market Bayou as my own. No one was going to invest in a fund run by Sam Israel. I didn't know what to do."

Israel understood his chances of finding a top-flight trader were slim. He didn't have the money or the reputation to attract a player from another fund. The market was booming, and a good position trader could demand a big salary and fat bonus. Sam could offer neither. Only one person came to mind. In the eighties when he had worked for Graber, Sam had grown close to a trader named Jimmy Marquez. At the time, Marquez had been one of the biggest and best traders in the business. Marquez had run George Soros's Quantum Fund for two years. He'd traded for the great Michael Steinhardt. For years his trading record had been excellent. A decade younger than Marquez, Sam had been entranced by his contrarian style and knack for picking winners. Marquez called himself a "strong hand" investor. It ran contrary to everything that Sam had been taught. Instead of following trends and taking small profits, Marquez considered himself smarter than others.

"I don't assume that the market knows more than I do," Marquez told *Futures* magazine in a profile. "I don't give the market that much credit. Securities prices can move around for no good reason. In most cases, when I reevaluate a situation where I'm going against the market, I conclude it is a buying opportunity and I gradually increase my position."

But Marquez's career had taken a disastrous turn in recent years. In the early nineties, he'd opened his own fund, which he named Half Moon Rising. The first year it was down 7 percent, the second year, down 40 percent, the third, 25 percent. There was no fourth year. Sam had worked for Marquez at Half Moon Rising for a short while and had witnessed the fall at first hand. But Marquez remained a friend, and the failure made it possible for Bayou to hire a trader of real stature. Sam had no other choice. Marquez was still a brand name on Wall Street. He was still well known. With a little gentle résumé editing—with some elisions and ambiguous wording and tactical amnesia—Marquez's trading record could still be made to look sterling to investors who didn't know the truth.

"It turned out to be perfect timing for Jimmy," Israel recalled. "He'd just finished liquidating his fund—giving people back their money.

I thought he'd learned his lesson. Jimmy was very bright—one of the brightest people I ever met. He was down on his luck. This was going to be a fresh start for him and for me."

As conceived by Israel, Bayou had an unusual structure, based on how Freddy Graber had run his fund. There were two separate entities: Bayou Securities and Bayou Funds. Instead of using outside brokers for its trades, like most hedge funds, Bayou Securities would be an independent in-house broker-dealer. By keeping the brokerage business to himself, Israel would capture the revenues from the commissions from his own trades. He would also get commissions for making trades for other funds. Bayou Funds was the hedge side of the business; it would trade the money of Bayou's investors. The structure gave the hedge fund a competitive advantage. The industry-wide standard for paying money managers was called "2 and 20." This meant that hedge funds charged investors a fee of 2 percent per year of the capital for the cost of running the business. In addition they received a bonus of 20 percent of performance (profit) made by the fund. Sam's idea enabled Bayou to offer a discount to investors. Bayou Securities would generate enough income to enable Bayou Funds not to have to charge 2 percent to defray its administrative costs. The saving was an enticement to investors, but it also spoke to the ingenuity and cost consciousness that Israel was marketing.

"I started out with high morals," Israel recalled. "I was sick of all the cheating on Wall Street. Brokers were all trading on their own account, so they had a conflict of interest with the investors they were supposed to be advising. Then there was the new greed of initial public offerings. Internet IPOs were coming onto the market every day. But they were all fixed games. I didn't want to get into that world. Because I had my own broker-dealer I wasn't legally eligible to get stock from the IPOs. I didn't want it anyway. We were going to do our own work. We were going to do our own trades. We were going to be steady Eddie, hitting singles and doubles, not aiming for the fence. That was what Bayou was all about."

Israel was the sole owner of the fund, though it was understood that he and Marquez would be equal partners in pay, power, and prestige. As ante money for their enterprise, Israel put in $150,000 of his own money. Marquez did likewise. The books would be kept by Dan Marino—an accountant who had worked for Half Moon Rising. Marino was a short, squat, and shy man from Staten Island with a severe hearing impairment. Marquez had plucked Marino from obscurity and brought him to Half Moon with the promise that he could run the venture capital business Marquez would start with the profits from the fund. The trader had imagined his personal wealth would exceed $500 million—a hope that seemed preposterous in hindsight. But the awkward accountant worshipped the ground that Marquez walked on, even after he had failed so spectacularly.

In March of 1996, Bayou's incorporation papers were executed by the three main players—Sam Israel, Jimmy Marquez, and Dan Marino. To get started, Israel and Marquez set about the business of raising money. For a start-up hedge fund like Bayou, this meant exploiting every contact possible—friends, family, colleagues. It meant calling in favors, ingratiating yourself, inveigling, pleading. Marquez was able to convince a few investors to put modest sums into Bayou. So was Sam. Together with their own investment, the initial sum Bayou had to trade with was $600,000. It was a pittance but a start.

The early results for Bayou were promising. Sam worked hard, following the trading patterns dictated by Forward Propagation. Marquez decided what stocks they were going to trade. At the opening bell,

Israel went into the market with his buy/sell sheet and traded the positions with discipline. Price movement was how Sam made money. It didn't matter if they were going up or down. Sam went short and long; he bought stock and he bought options. It seemed like Bayou's plan was working. In the first three and a half months, according to an audit by the firm Grant Thornton, the fund's performance was 17.6 percent, net 14 percent profit for investors after the 20 percent management fee was taken out. Annualized, that would mean performance of more than a 50 percent return, an incredible feat.

With the first audited performance report in hand, Israel and Marquez had something tangible to sell. By this time, a man named John Squire had approached Bayou with the idea of selling the fund to investors. Squire worked for a small investment firm with offices on Park Avenue called Redstone Capital Corporation. In a memorandum to an investor, Squire made the case for Bayou in compelling terms. "While three and a half months is a short performance period," Squire wrote, "I think I've seen enough over the years to recognize the real from the unreal. Sam and Jim's trading program is real—and a little frightening in its accuracy."

Squire described how Forward Propagation operated in practice. With a complex market data stream feed from a satellite, the machine was able to predict trading patterns correctly 86 percent of the time. When the data aligned, three colored lines appeared on the screen to show how to trade. "I've seen the system work dozens of times," Squire said. "It's really fun to watch the two of them at work. The type of investment is irrelevant: They do commodities, foreign bonds, indices, U.S. securities, anything which gives them the right pattern. The type of market—rising or falling—is also irrelevant. Once you are familiar with how the three colored lines work, you can pick situations, too. Sam told me his daughter had a successful morning trading stocks earlier this year while waiting for her school bus. I think his daughter is about five years old."

By the end of August, Bayou's performance was running at 19.8 percent. In September it was up to 21.8 percent. In October the Dow passed 6000 for the first time. Even so, Bayou was beating the market handily. Sam's dream was coming true. Bayou was developing a good story. In a matter of months, the fund doubled to more than $1 million. "If you are looking for an interesting form of money-management, may I suggest checking this one out," Squire wrote to potential investors. "I feel very comfortable with it."

BUT LUCK WAS A FICKLE mistress for Bayou. As the end of Bayou's first year neared, Marquez decided Bayou should go into gold stocks. Gold was badly undervalued, Marquez believed. When Barrick Gold announced a pact with the Indonesian government to acquire the majority of the largest gold deposit found in decades, Marquez decided the company was a must-buy. It looked like a classic Marquez strategy. Barrick was in partnership with the Indonesian government, then a dictatorship under the decades-long rule of President Suharto. The entire country had effectively become a private resource for Suharto to exploit through his *yayasan*, or foundation—a scam that yielded the family $35 billion.

To Sam, Barrick looked like an excellent trade. As a boy he'd sat on the knees of his famous grandfather and learned how commodities like gold were controlled in Third World countries. The exotic names of the men his father had dealt with were part of the fabric of Sam's life—Marcos's henchman Don-ding Corleone Cojuangco in the Philippines, or Fung King Hey in Hong Kong, who had provided the Israels backdoor access to China's billions. In those nations, Sam knew, money and power and corruption were inextricably linked. Barrick had stacked its board of directors with high-level politicians, including former president George H. W. Bush, who had been a friend of Sam's father. Sam believed Barrick was assured of having the ear of Suharto and his entourage. Marquez poured Bayou's money into Barrick like a riverboat gambler pushing his chips forward in an all-in hand of Texas Hold 'Em.

But circumstances conspired against Barrick—and Bayou. One of Barrick's competitors sued, then allegations of graft and market manipulation slowed the deal. The forces that Sam had imagined to rule the world were thwarted, at least temporarily. Barrick didn't get the Indonesian gold. The company proved to be one of the very few stocks that went down in the bull market of 1997. To the horror of Marquez and Israel, the market capitalization of the company was cut in half. Gold sank to a twelve-year low of $295 an ounce. Years later, as gold prices soared to unprecedented heights, Marquez would prove to be right—but a decade early.

As the position unraveled, Israel and Marquez began to bicker. As a distraction, Sam began to construct a play set for his daughter in the backyard of the house on Buckout Road. It was modular, with swings and monkey bars. Sam dug out an area in the yard, spreading wood chips. "Then I bought eight railway ties, the heavy hardwood ones covered with creosote, to create a square around the play set," Sam recalled. "I put two along each side. I was on the last railway tie when my mother pulled into the driveway for my daughter's birthday. I was carrying a railway tie that must have weighed a hundred pounds. I turned to say hello and I felt my neck go pop. It was total agony. There was a lump on my neck and I couldn't get it to go down."

Incapacitated, Israel saw a series of doctors trying to get relief, but he was unable to trade the way he had because of the pain. Then, in late October, the market suffered a minicrash when an Asian financial crisis triggered a shock wave that ran through world markets. In a matter of days the Dow dropped by 12 percent. More than $600 billion in market value was erased. It was the kind of crash that Sam had been able to capitalize on in 1987. This time, the Asian crisis came like a tsunami, a seemingly random event anticipated by no one—including Sam. Nursing his sore neck, he continued to tinker with the program as he worked nights in his basement trying to find a fix for the computer, Bayou, himself.

At the time it was little understood that it was perversely easy for hedge funds to be dishonest with their investors. Because Bayou's investors were technically partners, regulators assumed that they had access to financial information in a way that a partner would expect. But hedge funds were secretive. The only time investors truly received disclosure about the performance of the fund was when the annual audit was done by an outside accounting firm. That process occurred only at the end of the year, so Bayou had time to make up the losses before the trading record had to be submitted to an objective third party. In the meantime, Israel and Marquez continued to tell Bayou's members and prospective investors that the fund was thriving—even when it was losing.

There was no way to date the first deception. Or know with certainty who lied first—Marquez or Israel. They both talked to investors all the time. E-mails were exchanged, phone calls made, reports circulated. Both of the traders told investors that Bayou continued to perform well. They assured their investors that the rate of return—ROR in the industry—was outstanding. Mild exaggerations became stretchers, as Mark Twain called half truths. Outright lies followed. Both men knew that transparency would kill the fund. Neither could live with that prospect. Marquez couldn't afford another failure. Sam couldn't stand the thought of having to go back to Omega, cap in hand, and ask for his job back. Exhorting each other to focus and work harder, they gambled that they could make up the losses before the looming year-end audit. Sam was convinced that Bayou just needed a little time, and a little luck.

But at the end of the year, Bayou had a net loss of $161,417—a negative performance of 14 percent. It was obvious that as soon as investors learned of the loss, what remained of Bayou's money would be redeemed. Their baby had been stillborn. The fund would have to close. But then the accountant Dan Marino had an idea—a brilliant idea, one that would provide the foundation for a massive fraud. Bayou's partnership agreement stated that the broker-dealer "*may* charge commissions" for trades done by the hedge fund side of the business. The word *may* meant Bayou had discretion. Why not forgo the commissions? Marino asked. Better yet, why not rebate the commission the hedge fund had paid to the broker-dealer? The traders had lost money, after all.

Bayou's auditors were unable to grasp the concept. It sounded like flimflammery at the same time as it made perfect sense. Grant Thornton was a reputable national accounting firm. They'd audited countless hedge funds. But Bayou's structure was different. How to properly reconcile the books of a fund with two companies inside it doing business with each other, like Bayou's hedge fund and broker-dealer? The usual fear would be that the broker-dealer would overcharge the hedge fund as a way of ripping off investors. Marino's suggestion did the opposite. The broker-dealer was going to undercharge the hedge fund.

Marino was trying to hide the loss, of course, but it was done with the dexterity of a black belt in jujitsu. He made it look like a boon to investors. It appeared that Marino was benefiting Bayou's members at the expense of Sam Israel as owner of the broker-dealer. Marino was displaying a nascent genius to take a perfectly obvious fact (Bayou had performed terribly) and distort the mirror to make the situation look entirely different.

"I proposed a lump-sum transaction to the auditors," Marino recalled. "I told them I could've rebooked the commissions without telling them and they'd never have known. So why not rebate the commissions to the fund and call it a day? I told them that we could be in and out of a stock two, three, four times in a day, which cost Bayou's investors a lot in commissions. I said that if the investor suffered a loss because of our trades, why should they have to pay the brokerage commission as well? It was unfair that we earned the commission if we'd accomplished nothing. It would mean the net cost to the hedge fund of doing the trades was nearly zero. It allowed us the flexibility to trade how we wanted—high frequency. It also supported the risk management concept. I told Jimmy and Sam that the idea could be used as part of the sales pitch by showing investors we rebated commissions from the broker-dealer so there was no way we would churn the account. We were being honest with our partners."

The commissions totaled $400,000, more than enough to compensate for the losses of the hedge fund. With the commissions rebated, Bayou Funds would look as if it had turned a tidy profit. Bayou

Securities was another matter. But that was owned by Sam Israel and was not the concern of the hedge fund's auditors. Or so Marino claimed. Grant Thornton's accountants scratched their heads and pondered the question.

Meanwhile, the deadline for release of the audited results came and went. Bayou was obliged to provide investors final confirmed results by the end of the first financial quarter. As the end of March passed, Israel and Marquez were furious with Marino. Each day made Bayou look more and more dubious. Investors were getting nervous. Casting any suspicion on Bayou's competence or honesty at such an early point was risky—especially when they were trying to hide real losses.

After an excruciating delay, Marino was finally able to convince the auditors to agree to his approach. Once that money was applied to Bayou Funds' performance, the trading loss of 14 percent was magically transformed into an adjusted gross ROR of 40 percent. The dollar amounts were tiny. But the impact on Bayou's prospects was epic. Israel and Marquez had been granted a second chance. Even better, Marino had convinced the auditors that no disclosure was required, not even so much as a footnote, so no one was the wiser.

"Sam and Jimmy congratulated me," Marino said. "I'd just created a means for them to goose the performance with the commission rebates without disclosing it to investors. I thought once they raised more capital and got back on track, it was away-we-go time. I was on the verge of making a lot of money, and it was all legal."

Marino's bubble was quickly burst. Marquez and Israel told him they were letting him go. The socially awkward accountant from Staten Island wasn't giving investors the level of comfort needed, they said. Before Janice Israel had children, she'd been a practicing accountant.

She was smart, organized, and inexpensive. With the office in the basement of the house it would be easy for Janice to keep Bayou's books. Marino was told Janice was going to wait until the summer holidays were over, and the children were in school, before taking over. He would stay for the interim. "I felt betrayed, like they'd stolen my idea about rebating the commissions and now they were throwing me out," Marino said. "I was going to lose out on a wonderful opportunity."

During the first half of 1998, the gap between the real numbers and what Sam and Marquez were telling investors continued to grow. Bayou bought Gulf Island and Friede Goldman in the oil sector, Micron and Seagate in tech, Nord in resources. The positions weren't foolish, but neither were they the huge winners Bayou now needed. Sam's trading program was profitable, for the most part. After months of hard work, the pair managed to get Bayou to break even in real dollars. The fund was supposed to be "market neutral," which meant it made money whether prices went up or down. But being neutral in the sense of making no money was untenable in a bull market.

The traders might have been able to solve the problem if they'd been modest in the claims they made to investors about profits. But Israel and Marquez were both drawn compulsively to telling extravagant tales about their trading prowess. It was an irony that would haunt Bayou. In terms of actual money, the fund wasn't doing awfully. It was the imaginary money—the pixie dust—that was impossible to keep up with.

"In the beginning we had to live low," Israel recalled. "We were going to fix the problem. The amount of money wasn't that big. We were in the basement working hard. We took small salaries—less than a hundred grand each. We were trying to focus on getting out of the hole. But I was taking steroids for my neck pain and it was affecting my mood. I was starting to get more and more angry with Jimmy and Dan. If I'd made the problem on my own that would be one thing. We thought we could trade our way out of it. But that wasn't happening. It was really becoming a fucking problem."

Marquez blamed Bayou's environment. The basement was noisy, uncomfortable, depressing. He resented having to work in Israel's house. There was a separate entrance to the basement, but it made Marquez feel intrusive to arrive for work at five in the morning while the Israel family was asleep. Marquez wanted the freedom to do his research and make his calls in peace so he could concentrate on the situation that was quickly becoming a crisis. Marquez insisted on a change of scene.

Sam could see his point about the basement. But Marquez's solution was absurd. There was an office on Long Island Sound he'd been eyeing for years. The four-thousand-square-foot space at 40 Signal Road in Stamford, Connecticut, rented for $18,000 a month. It was the same cost as a suite of offices on Park Avenue in Manhattan. The office was only a three-minute drive from Marquez's home in one of the wealthiest towns in America. Set along a stretch of residential waterfront dotted with mansions, Bayou's headquarters would be in a tasteful two-story structure that had once been used as a boathouse. To one side there was a large field, and in front there was a patio for barbecues. The property came with a large private dock, with a slip to house Marquez's boat, and sweeping views of Long Island Sound. It was in the heart of an area known as "Hedge Fund Row," which boasted wildly successful traders like Barton Biggs of Traxis, Steven Cohen of SAC, and Paul Tudor Jones II.

Israel griped about the expense but did nothing to change the course of events as the lease was signed and movers were hired. On

Memorial Day weekend of 1998, Bayou opened in its new prestigious address. Relocating Bayou to the boathouse was upping the stakes in important but unspoken ways. The location staked a claim for Bayou as a fund on the rise. A potential investor visiting Bayou in the basement of Sam's house would see the fund for what it was: tiny, fragile, dysfunctional. But a money manager or high–net worth individual taking a meeting at the boathouse couldn't help but be impressed.

In a strange way, Bayou was in fact succeeding. The broker-dealer business was making money. With Marino's commission rebate sleight of hand, the hedge fund also *looked* as if it were making money—at least if it was not inspected too closely. Ironically, it turned out that incorporating the broker-dealer into Bayou to avoid the scams of Wall Street had rendered it tailor-made for fraud.

In the boathouse, Dan Marino—who was doggedly staying with the firm, hoping for a stay of execution—continued to do the accounting for Bayou, coming to work a couple of days a week to enter data and review the ledgers. But for the most part Israel and Marquez were alone.

"Jimmy was my friend and we were in this thing together," Israel said. "But he would have these long philosophical conversations. They would last for hours. Jimmy believed that oil and gas were going to go way up. He said they were underpriced. He was very persuasive. He said we were in the darkest hour. Soon people were going to realize that he was right. But who cared about philosophy?"

In the summer the market became wildly unpredictable. The giant hedge fund Long Term Capital Management had to be saved by the Federal Reserve when it lost more than $4 billion in a matter of days. It was an exceedingly difficult environment to solve Bayou's problem. Looking for a windfall trade, Marquez began to hear rumors about the federal government's annual auction of drilling rights for the outer continental shelf. Every year companies bid for lots to drill in the Gulf of Mexico. The auction had not gone well, it was said. If the reports were true, the consequences for oil and oil field service companies would be severe. This was the kind of opportunity Bayou could use—a sliver of bad news about an industry that they could trade against.

"I wanted to check out the rumor," Israel recalled. "I knew a guy who worked for a company called Tidewater. The company owned boats that took things out to the rigs—pipeline, food, people. So I called him and asked if business was slowing down. I did that kind of thing all the time. I would call companies if I knew someone there—if I had some way into the place. Talking to me was technically not legal. But it was the kind of thing that went on all the time. So I asked my guy what the earning forecasts for the quarter were. I asked if there was a 'downside surprise' coming. He said there was a surprise in the earnings. But he said it was an upside surprise. This was great news. I put the phone down and told Jimmy. We loaded up on Tidewater options. We thought, 'We're going to make our year.' A few days later Tidewater announced its quarterly earnings. Guess what? There was a big downside surprise. I was shocked. The guy lied to me. To this day I don't know why. We got pounded. It was the last time I ever tried to work on our positions at Bayou. There was too much treachery in the market—too many two-faced people. It was impossible to know what to believe.

"Then Dan found an accounting error. He said we were short one S&P future. By this time, Stanley Patrick had come back from Brazil and he was doing some clerical work for us part time. He'd made an error in closing out our overnight position in S&Ps. Stanley said it was me who'd fucked up. We went back and forth but it really didn't matter. It wasn't worth arguing about. Who the fuck knew? What mattered was the loss. We were down another sixty grand.

"For the year that meant we were down 18 percent. The market was up nearly 30 percent. So now we were behind the market by fifty points. I said we had to buckle down and make the money back before the end of the year. But there wasn't enough time left. That was when the hole really started. The amount of money we were down was small—we'd laugh at that kind of money later on. We only had a million and a half in the fund. We were so tiny. I mean, you got to understand, it was not a large amount of money to me. In dollar terms, we were down two hundred grand. That was a drop in the bucket. That was the kind of money that used to be in my error account when I worked at Omega. But it could ruin us."

CHAPTER FIVE

The Problem

A ccounts differ on where and when the decision to falsify Bayou's audit for 1998 was made. The stories of Israel, Marino, and Marquez also vary on who had the idea in the first place. When it comes to admitting to hatching the plot to begin a massive fraud, the three co-conspirators shift blame, self-justify, and avoid responsibility to varying degrees. No subject was more sensitive or contentious.

Sam said the conversation took place in the basement of his house on Buckout Road, as he recovered from back surgery. Marino said it happened in the boardroom at the boathouse. Marquez angrily refused to comment. Israel claimed Marquez and Marino came to him with the idea of falsifying the fund's results. Marino said that the plan came from Israel and Marquez.

But there was no dispute about what happened—or why. All three of the men had bet their careers—their dreams—on Bayou. Israel could not face the specter of failure. He'd promised himself that he would never go down again—never ever. For his part, Marino was desperately clinging to the hope of a high-flying career running the business side of a huge hedge fund. He was terrified of a life as an obscure accountant doing taxes in a strip mall on Staten Island. Likewise, Marquez still imagined himself to be a big-time trader in the manner of George Soros. Financially strapped after a bitter divorce, Marquez was in his late forties, and spent as a trader.

As the end of the year neared and the losses mounted, Marino received the reprieve he'd been hoping for. Israel and Marquez told him they'd be keeping him after all. No reason was given. Marino had long been treated as a glorified bookkeeper. Now it appeared the two traders needed him.

"I could never put my finger on why they changed their minds about keeping me on," Marino said. "They just said they forgave me. I chalked it up to them coming to their senses about the situation with the audit for the year prior and rebating the commissions from Bayou Securities. Their worries about investors redeeming had been overblown. They were letting bygones be bygones. But who knows the evil that lurks in the hearts of men? Maybe they became friendly to me because they decided a fake audit was the only way out long. That's very plausible. Sam and Jimmy weren't stupid people. I would prefer to think it wasn't premeditated. I would feel less of a fool."

IN 1998 New York City had its first white Christmas in twenty years as three inches of snow fell on the tristate area. But the atmosphere in the Israel house was glum. The pain from Sam's shoulder injury had migrated to his back. There had always been a psychosomatic relationship between Sam's state of mind and his pain. Now it seemed as if there were a synaptic connection between the unfolding disaster of his hedge fund and the torment of his body. The postop painkillers he'd been prescribed weren't working. Nor was the alcohol he was downing in increasingly prodigious amounts.

Affecting devil-may-care bravado, Sam sometimes convinced himself he could trade Bayou out of trouble. But other times he wasn't so sure. In quiet moments, questions about the fund's survival turned into existential questions. He needed someone to talk to. He needed to share the burden. His wife Janice had no idea of the stress her husband was under. If he confessed to her, Sam knew she'd demand he tell his investors and close Bayou—and perhaps go to prison.

"I hid everything from Janice," Israel said. "I'd been hiding things from her since we were kids. It was part of the way our relationship functioned. She was the responsible worker. I was the fuckup. I smoked weed and snorted coke. It was our pattern. I couldn't talk to her about what was really going on because I couldn't confide in her. We got together when we were so young, we never had the chance to find an adult way to talk to each other. As far as she knew, everything was going well for Bayou. Inside I was dying."

Over the holidays, Sam replayed events in his head. Marquez's trading positions had been dreadful. Moving to the boathouse had created a facade of success, but that had made closing the fund even harder. If only Sam hadn't invested all his savings in the house on Buckout Road, he could have covered Bayou's loss with his own money. The big-shot gesture of paying cash for the house had locked all his wealth into an illiquid asset. He couldn't ask his father for a loan, as a matter of pride but also because it would inevitably lead to uncomfortable questions. With only days left in the year, the options facing Bayou had hardened into a single stark possibility.

Wherever the meeting took place—Sam's basement or the boathouse—on the last trading day of the year, Israel, Marquez, and Marino convened to discuss the looming audit. The mood was somber. If Bayou was going to survive, this was the moment of truth—or, rather, the moment to lie.

"We're fucked," Marquez told Sam. "These are the real numbers."

Marino handed Israel a document showing the results for Bayou. Israel sat in a leather reclining seat. Now that the subject of Bayou's failure had been broached, the men rapidly discovered they were in agreement. As Sam reviewed the depressing document, Marquez said they needed to buy more time. Not long. A couple of months, maybe a year, maybe two—long enough to get back in the game. The solution was to fake the audit. With a bit of luck, maybe they could make up the shortfall by the time the audit was sent out to investors at the end of March. No one would ever know they'd massaged the numbers.

Obviously Grant Thornton couldn't perform the audit. The accounting firm had been hugely expensive in any event, charging more than $50,000 to audit the tiny fund. There *was* a solution, however. The plan was the soul of simplicity. Dan Marino would do the audit. Not in public, of course. Secretly. Marino was adept with numbers, so he'd know how to create a convincing audit. The deceit would be temporary, harmless, a white lie. If Bayou made it to the three-year mark with good performance numbers, major investors would start to consider putting money into the fund. Three years was the magic number. They were only one year away. All of their hard work was about to pay off. There was only a small shortfall in real money. Sam and Jimmy just needed to focus, trade with discipline, get lucky—and all would be fine.

"The truth is that I didn't need much convincing," Israel said, insisting that it wasn't his idea in the first place. "I really had no hesitation. Bayou was everything I'd worked for. I was going to do anything and everything that I possibly could to make it succeed—cheating or not cheating. I didn't have a problem with fudging the numbers. I was confident. Everything was going to be okay. Every time I'd gone broke in the past, I'd gone on a huge tear and made the money back in short order. I knew I could do it again. I figured we had a problem, but I didn't think it was a big problem."

For Dan Marino, faking the audit was crossing multiple boundaries, legal and professional. The deceit ran contrary to Marino's most basic ethical obligations as an accountant. But Marino didn't hesitate, either. He had only one demand. He wanted Israel and Marquez to sign a document stating that the false audit was their idea and then videotape confessions saying that they'd asked Marino to perpetrate the fraud. The letter and video would be Marino's proof that he was the lesser conspirator. Marquez was the lead trader at Bayou; Sam was the owner. Marino wanted it clear to the authorities, should the day ever come, that he was only a functionary.

"What are you talking about?" Israel said to Marino. "That's insane. I'm not doing that."

"You both should do it," Marino said. "This is both your faults."

"Go fuck yourself," Israel said.

"Go fuck yourself," Marquez added.

"Let me put it to you this way, Dan," Israel said. "We could put the right number in the audit and you're out of a job. You have nowhere to go because you work for Jimmy and Jimmy's got nowhere to go. I have somewhere to go. I can pick up this phone right now and dial Lee Cooperman. He'll say I can start tomorrow. You don't have that, Dan, and you don't have that, Jimmy. So you can both go fuck yourselves if you think I'm going to make a videotape."

The subject was dropped. Mutually assured destruction was what they were left with. Marino would create a false audit. None of them would breathe a word of what they were doing. No spouses or siblings or drinking buddies. No confidants. Marino would tend to the technical details. Israel and Marquez would come up with the performance numbers—fake returns that matched what they'd already been telling Bayou's members in phone calls and e-mails.

In Marino's mind there would now be two sets of books. There would be "Performance: Actual" and "Performance: Published." Marino would keep track of both to ensure they were able to pay the right amount when Sam and Jimmy finally traded them out of the hole. For Marino, the first step was to sprinkle the magic powder of commission rebates over the returns. The money generated by Bayou Securities was passed back to Bayou Funds, adding 12 percent to the performance numbers. The sleight of hand was literally robbing Bayou Securities to pay Bayou Funds, but that kind of deception was minuscule compared to what came next.

"I decided to set up a fake accounting firm to do the audit," Marino recalled. "The first thing I did was come up with a name for the firm. I went with Richmond-Fairfield. I liked the concept of a company that covered a geographical area—in this case Richmond County on Staten Island, where I lived, and Fairfield County, where Bayou's offices were located. It sounded cool to me. After that I came up with the stationery design and obtained approval from Jimmy and

Sam on that. Then I set up the checking accounts. I made sure they were part of it all.

"Next I made arrangements with someone to use desk space at their office in Manhattan. In a way, I told them the truth. I was setting up my own accounting firm and needed some space to work, as well as a phone and a fax. Part of Richmond-Fairfield was a backup plan for me. If Bayou failed quickly, or if it succeeded and they kicked me out anyway, I had a firm that maybe I could build up for myself. Then I did the audit. That part was really simple. Bayou was a plain vanilla trading firm. The fund traded and didn't take long-term positions. Since the fund was small, no auditor would rely on internal controls to do the audit. An auditor would do what is called substantive testing of the trades to verify the transactions and make sure they are recorded properly. But I didn't have to do the work, of course.

"The interesting part, to me at least, was how easy it would have been to put my name together with the auditor. All you had to do was google 'Richmond-Fairfield' and my name would come up. The fake firm was registered with the New York State Accounting Society. If anyone had gone to the office I sublet, they would have seen my personal name in the directory. Any minor but persistent due diligence would have discovered my link to Richmond-Fairfield immediately. Why no one did it is simply beyond me to explain. I would have done it."

TO CREATE THE ACTUAL AUDIT document, Marino copied verbatim the format Grant Thornton had used the previous year. On the one-page "Statement of Financial Condition for December 31, 1997," Bayou's assets had been listed as follows:

Cash	$1,526
Securities Owned	$1,587,936
Due from Brokers	$3,105
Prepaid Expenses	$4,000
Organization Expenses	$32,504
Total Assets	$1,629,071

The audit for 1998 by Richmond-Fairfield had an identical format, with higher numbers to reflect Bayou's growth:

Cash	$526
Securities Owned	$351,750
Due from Brokers	$3,761,539
Prepaid Expenses	$5,000
Organization Expenses	$22,505
Total Assets	$4,141,320

The biggest difference in amounts was in the line "Due from Brokers." The sum had jumped from just $3,000 in 1997 to nearly $4,000,000 in 1998. Because Bayou had attracted a lot of investment for the year and total assets had increased at a rapid rate, the huge increase made sense—provided no one asked what "Due from Brokers" actually meant. In 1997, it had meant the sum of money that Bayou had on deposit with its clearinghouse; Bayou maintained an account, so the nominal sum was a real asset. In 1998, the total of $3,761,539 was a fiction. The cheat was there on the page for all to see—at the same time as it was invisible. Marino knew that people's eyes glazed over when confronted with columns of numbers. Inevitably, attention fell to the bottom line.

"Due from Brokers" simply meant the amount that happened to be in the account Bayou maintained with its clearinghouse, Spear, Leeds & Kellogg—a highly reputable firm that performed the execution of the fund's trades. Who would question such a simple change?

"I didn't discuss this with Jimmy and Sam," Marino said. "I just told them that it was the best place to hide it because we didn't have to make up any positions in stocks that could cause an issue in the future. It was just cash sitting with our clearinghouse in an account under Bayou's name. Money was either 'owed to' or 'due from' the broker. The fact that it was cash dovetailed with the way Jimmy and Sam were marketing the fund. Going to cash at the end of the day or week or month was a way to manage risk. We told our investors that we got out of our positions, especially at the end of the year. That was the time of year when there were a lot of antics to try to window-dress performance, or lower taxes.

"If the investors were smart enough to truly look at the financial statement of Bayou Funds, they would've asked me for an explanation. No one asked. If they did ask, I would've said we had two accounts with the clearinghouse because we don't want them to know all the trades we do. The regulators could've looked at the audit and asked for statements when they were looking at Bayou Securities. The regulators should've known that when they inspected Bayou Securities they were actually seeing all the trading transactions of the hedge fund. They could've looked through the broker-dealer to see how the fund was doing—and see that it was losing money.

"You could say it was elementary, or you could say it was sophisticated. The bottom line is that it worked. No one looked. Ever. It was an example of the soft underbelly of the business. There are many soft underbellies in the hedge fund business that can be exploited—and that's what we did."

THE YEAR BEFORE, the wait for the audit had made some investors uneasy. This year the audit was ready right on time—in fact slightly early. On March 23, Israel wrote to Bayou's members, enclosing the annual audited report. "In order to provide all members with timely information, we have made the decision to switch our auditors from Grant Thornton to a smaller firm named Richmond-Fairfield Associates," Israel wrote. He said the change avoided paying Grant Thornton's exorbitant fee, underlining Bayou's thrifty ways. "We have found that being a larger fish in a smaller, high quality pond is more advisable for us at this time."

Attached was a cover letter from Richmond-Fairfield. The logo for the firm Marino had invented was a small teardrop. The address given was 111 John Street, the building near Wall Street where Marino had sublet space. "In our opinion the financial statements present fairly, in all material respects, the financial position of Bayou Funds," the auditors wrote.

The adjusted gross rate of return for Bayou was 22.047 percent. The year before it had been 40.92 percent (a concoction of Marino's commission rebate). The tiny fund was developing an outstanding record. The market had boomed in 1998, but there had been considerable volatility as well. Israel and Marquez reasoned that it was okay to not claim to have beaten the bull. The numbers had to attract attention—but only the right kind. According to the audit, gross income was $519,314, less the 20 percent management fee paid to the managers—which amounted to $103,862.80. The net profit to members was $415,452. To the unpracticed eye looking over Bayou's financials, the fund was promising, intriguing even, not one of the flash-in-the-pan funds that had one or two excellent years and then collapsed. But Bayou's performance didn't portray Israel as one of the leading men of Wall Street—not yet.

Israel and Marquez set about trying to attract the money they all believed was needed to turn Bayou around. Third-party marketers were engaged to sell the fund to high–net worth individuals. The fake audit proved a great marketing tool. Bayou's story was getting easier to tell all the time. Marquez picked stocks. Sam ran the computer program. Bayou was neither a value investor nor a purely technical buy/sell fund. It was both. The hybrid was a thoroughbred.

"Obviously, I was lying and cheating," Sam said. "But in my life I was not a liar and a cheater. I was doing things that just weren't like me. It was like it wasn't even me who was doing all the cheating and lying."

The money started to flow in. The sums weren't huge. But hits of $50,000 and $100,000 added up. Bayou soon crossed the $5 million threshold, another encouraging milestone. The move to the boathouse had energized Marquez. Prone to upswings in energy, inevitably followed by depressive downswings, Marquez arrived at work before dawn and scoured trade publications for leads. Internet stocks were the rage on Wall Street. But Marquez was interested in less fashionable industries, like oil and coal. While fortunes were being made on Internet stocks, Marquez shunned the herd. Big thoughts were his forte. The kind of trading that Sam did at Bayou was beneath Marquez's dignity, he told Marino. Marquez had theories about the economy and society—about life—that were consequential and would yield the profits Bayou so desperately needed.

But Marquez's positions turned out to be nearly uniformly awful. Marquez was becoming borderline irrational, it seemed to Sam. Long-shot long bets had to be sustained against the day the market caught up with Marquez—if it ever did. But Bayou needed to make money immediately. There was no time to wait for Marquez's airy theories to be proven correct. The arguments were becoming bitter and personal—screaming matches in the trading room upstairs at the boathouse.

As Internet stocks soared, no matter the underlying value of the company, Sam could see that the Federal Reserve was pumping liquidity into the stock market, as if the only social good were rising industrial averages, regardless of the cost. In his own deceptions, Sam saw the deception of a market artificially inflated by speculation. The way he looked at it, the entire market was doing what he was doing, only on such a massive scale it was impossible to see the monstrosity.

"With the Internet boom, people weren't trading and promoting real companies anymore," Israel recalled. "It used to be General Motors and Procter & Gamble employed millions of Americans. Now there was eBay, which had a card table in a room with four chairs and a computer screen. So many of the companies coming onto the market were nothing. You could pass your hand through them—there was nothing to them. All my life I'd cheered for people to get ahead. I wanted these Internet scumbags to lose. It killed me."

As pressures mounted, Sam found oblivion in booze and cocaine, becoming a functional alcoholic, by his own reckoning. His desire to not think about his woes found a healthy outlet as well, as he started to train like a maniac for a triathlon. Seeking the endorphin rush of extreme exercise, Sam ran and biked and swam in every spare moment. In the spring, Sam traveled to Florida to compete in the Tinman Triathlon in Pensacola. After he completed the grueling event, Israel decided to celebrate by getting a tattoo on his hip. The design he chose was "Little Devil," the small red cartoon character cherub with a crooked grin carrying a trident—the secret manifestation of his new reality.

FOR MONTHS Dan Marino had been plagued by a dry cough. When X-rays and repeated doctor visits failed to find a diagnosis, Marino treated it like a bad cold, or chest infection, and continued to work. But then night chills began, and Marino lay in bed drenched in sweat and shivering. Since a serious case of mumps as a child, which had triggered a brain infection and left him effectively deaf without his hearing aids, Marino's health had been fragile. A heart specialist ran further tests and told Marino that it looked as if he might have Hodgkin's lymphoma.

"I was in a state of shock," Marino said. "When I told Jimmy and Sam, I could see the look of dread on their faces. It was like their faces were saying, 'We're screwed.' They had encouraging words, and maybe they really were concerned about me. But they were also concerned about how to deal with the ongoing fraud."

In June, Dan Marino's diagnosis of cancer was confirmed. He began a course of chemotherapy. Marino's mother, whom he still lived with, was also suffering from cancer. For the next six months, Marino came to Bayou only occasionally. This left Israel and Marquez alone together, apart from the small support staff. Months of cascading disaster ensued—poor trades, angry recriminations, drunken nights. But investors heard an entirely different story—one of hard work and triumph.

"The second quarter of 1999 for us can best be described as the thrill of victory, then the same old story," Marquez and Israel wrote in a joint letter to investors in July. Stock prices were grossly overvalued, they said. The market was being dumbed down as the Internet enabled pajama-wearing halfwit day traders to run up prices. "So, once again we find ourselves trying to find value to trade long stocks and picking our spots to be short," they wrote. "Oh yes, we were able to post a second quarter gain of 12.45%, bringing our year to date to +19.56%."

Word of Bayou's success was beginning to spread to the higher reaches of the money management universe. Even in the booming hedge fund industry, the steadiness of their returns stood out. First Boston and Tremont Advisers began an index of the leading hedge funds and Bayou was included, a fantastic marketing coup. "We are definitely the smallest fund in the index which is all the more flattering to us," Israel wrote to Bayou's members. "We have undergone an intense amount of scrutiny for over two years to fulfill the criteria of inclusion. We share the same vision of steady above average returns in any market condition as you do. As I have said to you, we win with grace and lose with integrity."

But the reality was the polar opposite. Bayou continued to lose money. Marquez and Israel had countless excuses for their failure. Marquez complained about not having enough capital to make his strategies pay off—or "muscle," as he put it. Both complained about the ineptitude of their growing staff. The traders said they didn't have the right equipment. Or the market was wrong. Blame was pointed in all directions—except at themselves.

By the end of 1999, the S&P was up an epic 21 percent. Bayou had actually managed to make money. Precisely how much wasn't clear, as it had become difficult to truly follow the fund's performance—

even for Marino. The real number didn't matter—not when results could be invented. Israel and Marquez weren't going to let the fund drift along with mediocre results. They had egos to sate. In their version of events, that year the fund beat the market soundly, providing an ROR—rate of return—of 33 percent.

"Jimmy and Sam couldn't control themselves," Marino said. "The actual number was half that. Jimmy and Sam should have managed it better. If they'd claimed we made 12 percent or 15 percent for the year, the extra money we'd actually made could have been put towards solving the problem. But they didn't. When they had a good month and made money they used that as the performance number. When they had a bad month, they used a made-up number. They claimed it had to be done because they were getting feedback from clients about performance. I stopped tracking the published numbers against the real numbers. It made me sick to my stomach."

Late one afternoon, Israel was sitting in the trading room when he felt Marquez staring at him. Looking up from his computer, he saw Marquez watching him with an air of sorrow. Sam knew that Marquez was seeing a therapist, receiving treatment for the sense of dread and helplessness that was overwhelming his life. Marquez said he felt sympathy for Israel. Sam was more than a decade younger than Marquez, with two young children and a whole life in front of him. Now Sam's entire future was in jeopardy.

"I knew I was fucked if Bayou blew up," Marquez said. "But now you're fucked too."

"What do you mean?" Israel asked.

"You can't get another job either now," said Marquez. "You're just as fucked as I am."

"Fuck you," Israel said, anger rising. "I cannot believe you just said that. You were the one who got us in this situation. It's your idiot trades that got us in the mess. It was your idea to change the numbers. It's all your fault."

"I'm just saying you're fucked now, too," Marquez said.

Israel wanted to beat the living hell out of Marquez. He went for a walk instead, cursing his fate. Israel decided he had to find a way to bypass Marquez. Israel had to make the investment decisions himself. How could he do any worse than Marquez? But Marquez wasn't going to be easy to get rid of—not with the problem unsolved. Sam started to write investors letters on his own. As if to compensate for the creeping terror he felt, the letters to Bayou's members became breezy, upbeat, even flip. The market was booming and Bayou was expertly keeping pace, investors were told. By October, Bayou was up 26.5 percent for the year.

"The proliferation of day traders in the market can no longer be summarily dismissed," Israel wrote to his investors. "The complete, instant access to stock information has made this group a force to contend with. But when the market declines, most day traders suffer the death of 1,000 cuts. In the meantime, this is the world in which we live, and fortunately for Bayou it is a world we understand well."

Undergoing treatment for lymphoma, Marino despaired. He seriously considered walking into an FBI office and giving up the whole charade. But then he came up with another plan, which he shared with Israel and Marquez. Bayou should engineer its own death, Marino said. By crafting trading losses in a specific way, Marino said, they could kill Bayou over a period of months. Just as they had constructed fictional profits, they could concoct fictional losses. So long as the losses were created in a way that could withstand basic scrutiny—though not close examination—no one would be wise to the scheme. After all, who deliberately made themselves losers?

The plan meant Israel and Marquez would have to swallow their pride and withstand the humiliation of admitting defeat. Sam would have to concede that Forward Propagation hadn't worked. Marquez would have to reveal that his "strong hand" strategy had failed. But there was no way Israel or Marquez was going to commit hedge fund hara-kiri. Not when Bayou was on the cusp of greatness—even if it was a fantasy.

At the end of the year, Sam told the staff that the fund's goal was to reach $100 million. Bayou now marketed itself as the "ONLY" safe harbor for the inevitable crash when the Internet bubble burst. Sam wrote that Bayou's cautious short-term, low-risk incremental strategy was a counterbalance to the hubris he saw enveloping American society. Bayou's profile was changing rapidly. Serious investors were increasingly looking for a fund like Bayou, which offered predictability in a market that was clearly overheated. "Each of us is ready for a large payday," Sam wrote to Bayou's staff. "Assuming we do this correctly, we will realize the dream."

For a while, Sam seemed prophetic. The NASDAQ had plunged in the first half of 2000, and Bayou was able to take advantage of the trend. Sam shorted scores of Internet companies and made steady progress. If he'd been starting with a clean slate, Sam's record during the correction would have been outstanding. But he wasn't. Bayou was in a deep hole, and even Sam's streak wasn't able to solve the problem.

As the market tanked and Sam's predictions came true, in a matter of months Bayou grew to $10 million and then $20 million. The cognitive dissonance of great success coupled with catastrophic failure was sickening. Behind the grinning facade of sudden success, Sam was in free fall. On the way home one night he was pulled over for drunk driving. Cocaine was found in the car. Always expert at talking his way out of trouble, Israel insisted it wasn't his cocaine and managed to avoid a felony conviction—which would've imperiled the fund. Alcohol and drugs had become Sam's way to cope with anxiety, depression, low self-esteem—the counterweights to his bouts of grandiosity.

As Bayou's woes multiplied, and the fund continued its meteoric rise, Israel's back problems multiplied and intensified. Weakness in his neck and numbness and tingling in his fingers forced him to wear a support collar. Adrift on a sea of prescription drugs, Sam was quick to fly into rages—as his father had, something he had hated as a child.

Sam's wife Janice insisted he seek help. Days later, she walked into Sam's home office to discover him bent over a pile of white powder on his desk with a rolled-up twenty-dollar bill in his nose. Busted, Sam went for the big lie: The white powder wasn't coke. He was outraged by her intrusion. How dare she suggest he was taking illegal drugs?

The Israels began to see a marriage counselor. Sam believed he was sincerely attempting to repair their marriage. He confessed to things that he'd done that had harmed their relationship. But he couldn't say what was really troubling him. His conduct was becoming increasingly bizarre. Once, when Janice arrived home from a short trip with the children, they pulled into the driveway to discover Sam outside the house to greet them. He was naked apart from cowboy boots, a pair of his wife's bikini underwear, a lacrosse helmet, swim goggles, a life jacket, and a cape. When Janice didn't laugh, Israel grew angry. What was her problem, he demanded. Where was her sense of humor?

Trying to save his marriage, Israel sought help from a psychiatrist.

His need for mental counseling had to be kept secret from Bayou's investors, though. Any whisper of instability would lead to a rush of redemptions. As soon as the psychiatrist met Sam, he diagnosed him as bipolar. The condition was not uncommon among Wall Street traders. The doctor put Israel on a bewildering mix of drugs, including Depakote (for seizures), Neurontin (an antiepileptic), lithium (an antipsychotic), Wellbutrin (for depression), Zoloft (for anxiety), and Synthroid (a hormone)—all on top of his fistful of painkillers. The drugs made Israel even less predictable, loosening his already tenuous grip on what was going on around him.

"My shrink zombied me up ridiculously," Israel recalled. "This was when bipolar was the new diagnosis. Suddenly everybody was bipolar. It was the adult version of attention deficit disorder. It turned out there was a dirty secret with the doctors. The more drugs doctors sold, the more points they earned with the pharmaceutical companies. They were sent on trips. They received gifts. The whole thing was a scam. Pharmaceutical companies were just like Wall Street traders. They fixed the game. Only they were fucking with my mind. Everywhere I turned, I kept looking for something real. Something where people weren't cheating. I kept saying to myself, 'Please show me something real.'"

CHAPTER SIX

Boy in the Bubble

The morning of September 11, 2001, was glorious in New York City. The sky was cloudless, the warmth of the late summer sun softened by a gentle breeze carrying a whisper of the coming fall. Driving his son to school in his new Porsche Cayenne, Sam was feeling the best he had for months—maybe years. The year had been difficult, with the market in flux. The total losses at Bayou had grown to $12 million, so the problem persisted. But Sam was optimistic. Jimmy Marquez had finally agreed to permanently leave Bayou, decamping to a tiny office across the parking lot formerly used by Dan Marino. But the biggest news was that the fund had grown to $70 million, an incredible feat, leaving Sam with a queer mixture of elation and fear.

Then there was the promise of this fine fall morning. The previous

Friday afternoon, Sam's Forward Propagation program had lit up like a slot machine with a row of cherries. Normally, the computer offered contradictory data points—some pointing to buy, others to sell. But that Friday, all ten lights on the computer had pointed in the same direction: Go long. It appeared to be a massive opportunity to take advantage of an unprecedented buy signal. Since the fraud began—really since he had watched Freddy Graber trade on inside information—Sam had been trying to figure a way to make a lot of money quickly. The pressure of filling the hole had turned that urge into an urgent demand. And here it was, at long last: a chance for Sam to vindicate his trading system and solve the problem.

On the previous Friday, Sam had put 95 percent of Bayou's money into long positions. He'd then doubled down, using leverage to ramp up his positions. If the market followed the predictive powers of Sam's program, Bayou would make $15 million or more.

"I was way long," Sam said. "I had tech stocks—Microsoft, Motorola, Micron Technology. I'd loaded up on S&P futures. Monday morning the preopening noise was screaming. I was going to make great money. I felt fantastic. Then the radio said two planes had flown into the World Trade Center. When I got to work I found out that the market had closed. There was no trading. Nothing. I couldn't get out of any of my positions. It was obvious the market was going to tank. I couldn't do anything until trading started again.

"When the market finally opened the next week I got slaughtered. Margin calls meant we had to liquidate the positions, no matter the loss. We didn't have the money to hold on for a week or two until things stabilized. We had to sell into the panic. In just a few days, Bayou lost thirty-five million dollars. That was nearly half of what was in the fund. The situation was impossible. I was trapped."

Marino wanted to close the fund. The disaster could be seen as a blessing in disguise, he believed. With so much tumult, Marino thought Bayou's losses could be hidden. He wanted Bayou to post a huge loss, which no one could sensibly blame on them. The loss would include the $12 million—in real money that Marquez and Israel had lost, as well as the fictional performance. Bayou would return the remaining money to investors with an apology. Investors would be upset, but there were many other hedge funds suffering the same ignominy.

Sam refused. He would have been left with at least $2 million in personal liabilities. It was a sum that would have forced Sam into personal bankruptcy, costing the Israels their home as well as his reputation.

"Going bankrupt in the hedge fund business is a death sentence for a trader," Marino said. "Don't even think about trying to manage money again. Sam didn't want to do it. He begged me to give him a chance. He felt entitled to the opportunity Jimmy had been given to trade his way out of the hole. He said it wasn't his fault that the loss was so big. When was the last time two planes hit the World Trade Center? When had the exchange closed for five days? There was no way for his trading system to account for an absolute random event like a terrorist attack.

"Then Sam pointed out that if we did report a big loss to investors it would mean that we had to have broken the fund's rules about limiting risk. We were only supposed to have overnight exposure of 10 to 15 percent of the capital of the fund. How could we explain taking such a massive loss? The act of reporting a loss would be the same thing as closing the fund. I thought Sam made good arguments. I said yes. We felt obligated to the investors to recover the money we had lost."

"Dear Member," Israel wrote in a letter to investors on October 17,

2001. "Our inevitable duty here is to remember that business, like life itself, must go on in the face of the tragedy of September 11th." Israel didn't claim he had entirely escaped the consequences of 9/11. Bayou had lost 4 percent, he wrote. The fund was up only 1.21 percent for the year. Given the circumstances, Bayou's performance was miraculous—on paper. "We feel lucky to be in a position to close the year in a strong manner," Israel wrote. "We will attempt to stay as liquid as possible, and will be even more vigilant about always maintaining downside disaster insurance."

THE EVENTS OF 9/11 permanently transformed Bayou. Trading out of the hole was no longer a realistic option—unless a miracle occurred. The terrorist attack had turned Bayou into a Ponzi scheme. Not technically: Charles Ponzi had never actually traded the International Reply Coupons he used to lure investors, while Sam traded constantly at Bayou. But the essence of a Ponzi scheme was its pyramid-like shape. To pay existing investors who redeemed, Bayou would need to bring in money from new investors. In such uncertain times, with the entire nation fearing another attack, Bayou needed to attract money—a lot of money very, very quickly.

For Sam the disastrous losses proved to be the opportunity for him to discover his genius. Over the years, he'd become a student of human nature. His difficult childhood had given him unusual emotional intelligence—when he chose to use it. As a rule, grifters come from modest backgrounds and have to spend years learning how to dress and behave among the rich. Sam had grown up with money; he'd dated wealthy girls, played football with wealthy boys, and smoked dope and driven home drunk from smart Westchester parties. He knew the realities lurking behind their seemingly ideal families. He understood their insecurities and anxieties. He moved among them with serpentine ease precisely because he was one of them. Sly flattery, self-mockery, humorous boastfulness—Sam's rhetorical arsenal was formidable because it was preconscious. He was able to convey the most comforting message—we are alike, we are friends, we can trust each other—in a thousand different ways. He knew what they wanted because it was what he wanted—and what he'd invented for himself.

"When an investor came in, the first thing I wanted to know was how much they knew about the market," Israel recalled. "Before they interviewed me, I interviewed them. I got people to talk about themselves. I asked questions. There is nothing people like more than talking about themselves. If someone was talking about themselves they weren't talking about me. Then I'd say that I could tell them an extraordinary story about how my machines work, how my programs run, the genesis of the trading program. I could tell them all about my life's work. But first I needed to know if they understood charts.

"I was deferential to some of my investors, but usually I wasn't. I was in a position of strength. The narrative of Bayou was powerful enough that it spoke for itself. I'd grown up around people who were extraordinarily wealthy—like Sandy Weill and Larry Tisch. I knew how to stroke them. I knew how to get what I wanted from them. But I discerned that family money was shitty money. If someone came from big money, they invariably had time on their hands to harass you. They wanted to be directly involved because it was cool. They were given money by Daddy or Mommy, aristocrats with family who came to America on the *Mayflower,* and they wanted to make their parents proud. So they meddled. It wasn't stable money—rich kids were flighty.

"I liked people who had market experience, who understood trading, but didn't have the time to do it themselves. The best money came from the big funds that invested in smaller funds like Bayou—'fund of funds' is what they were called. There was no direct relationship with the investors, only the manager of the fund of funds. I didn't have to bother with forty different people. They could put in large amounts of money all at once. I also didn't want people who really shouldn't be putting money into a hedge fund. From the start, I didn't want anyone whose life would be changed by my success or failure. I didn't want anyone's college funds. It had to be discretionary money. At the start the minimum was a hundred grand, then we raised it to $250,000, then half a million."

After the initial meeting at Bayou's boathouse, Sam would invite investors to come upstairs—"to see where it all happens." Up a flight of stairs there was a second floor with one grand office. This was Sam's domain. The aerie was carefully staged to convey a sense of boyish eccentricity. Memorabilia were arranged around the room—an antique rowing shell, signed footballs from the days the Israel family partly owned the New Orleans Saints. Pride of place was reserved for an old GI helmet from World War II that summoned the heroics of Sam's grandfather and namesake. Sam always had the latest version of every imaginable gadget and high-tech doodad. The fratlike exclusivity was part of the sales pitch.

To qualify, the would-be member of Bayou had to fill in forms acknowledging himself to be a "sophisticated investor"—a kind of self-flattery most often belied by the facts. The view of the Long Island

Sound was spectacular. Like Freddy Graber, Sam blasted music—Paul Simon's "The Boy in the Bubble" was a favorite song—as he barked orders at his clerks like a demented General Patton. When he was in the flow, Sam sent four assistants scurrying as he bought and sold shares with mind-boggling speed in head-spinning amounts. On the wall were sixteen computer screens he could manipulate with toggles. On the screens, masses of data pulsed with the various stocks and sectors that he was following—oil and gas, automobiles, futures. As a lark, Sam would often have one screen devoted to a live shot of NASA's launching pad when a rocket was about to be sent spaceward.

There was one special screen Sam always pointed out. This was Forward Propagation. He told investors he made his money on the small movements of the market—a quarter and an eighth of a point, just as Phil Ratner had done for Freddy Graber in their halcyon days. Every morning, Sam said, he put millions into the market; every night he liquidated his positions and he was back in cash. Israel's program was supposed to give him the power to foresee the future—not for long, but for a "tick," as it was called in the stock market, the split second it takes for a stock to go up or down a point. Forward Propagation was accurate 86 percent of the time, Sam said. The machine was not infallible—such a proposal was absurd, Sam knew. But in Wall Street terms 86 percent was a fantastic rate of success. The precision of the number, a statistic plucked from the sky by Sam, seemed to infuse the machine with godlike powers.

Israel now promised investors absolute returns; he didn't need to resort to relative indicators to prove the value of his fund. Sam's letters to Bayou's members grew longer as he wrote about the kind of macroeconomic trends that ordinarily shouldn't concern a technical trader like Sam. By inclination and experience, Israel was skeptical about the economic prospects for the coming decade. The fraud he was perpetrating, with such astonishing ease, had convinced Sam that the United States was in the midst of a bubble. The markets were all crooked, he'd long believed. He was living proof of the hidden truth.

"The Emperor Has No Clothes" was the title of one of Sam's investor letters. The four-page letter was remarkably prescient about broad trends for the coming years. The value of stocks was greater than the value of the gross domestic product, a disproportion that far exceeded the decadence before the crash of 1929, Sam wrote. The ratio between price and earnings for shares was hopelessly out of line. Real estate was in a bubble. Government and personal debt levels were unsustainable. Severe energy problems faced the United States. A worldwide recession loomed. Like a few of the smartest people on Wall Street, Sam could see that the end was nigh. It was much harder to turn that realization into money. As Sam weaved in and out of stocks—Ariba, PepsiCo, Vignette—he was consumed by trying to figure out how to use his insight to save Bayou. The United States was going to tank— Sam just needed to come up with a way to make a killing when it did.

TOILING AWAY in his tiny one-room office across the parking lot, Jimmy Marquez was witness to the great good fortune occurring in the fancy boathouse. Marquez knew about the millions pouring into Bayou's coffers. He still owned half of Bayou, and he wanted to be paid for his stake. He sent a proposal to Israel. Marquez didn't directly threaten Sam with exposure, but it was understood—take care of me, or else.

Carried interest was the industry term for Marquez's ownership of the fund. Marquez began the negotiation by saying he would take payment for "only" 20 percent of Bayou as a goodwill gesture, effectively dropping his equity interest by more than half. It seemed a modest concession, given his role in Bayou's failure. "But what is the correct methodology for valuing my carried interest in Bayou?" Marquez asked. "Depending on who you are talking to, or what point you're trying to make, 20 percent of Bayou is worth a whole lot, or nothing. We can both win or both lose depending on how matters are dealt with from this day forward."

The bottom line: $3.7 million was Marquez's price. Israel refused—then caved. He had no choice, after all. As part of the settlement Israel also invested $3.6 million of Bayou's money into a clean coal company Marquez was promoting called KFX. The stock of KFX had long languished as the market doubted its claim to be able to deliver commercially viable clean coal. Marquez was being paid as a consultant to KFX, so he was profiting both ways in getting Bayou's money put into the stock. Israel bought the shares solely to be rid of Marquez.

As the end of the year neared, Bayou was closing in on $80 million under management. The ease with which the fraud was working preyed on Marino's mind. What if the fund grew to $500 million? Or a billion? Bayou was more than a fraud, Marino concluded. It was a brilliant business model. By rebating the commissions from the broker-dealer to the hedge fund, Bayou Funds could legitimately claim annual returns of 9 percent after paying salaries and expenses. If Israel was able to make only 1 percent a month as a trader, the fund would report 21 percent annual returns. As long as investors didn't withdraw their money all at once, Bayou would have the cash flow to maintain itself indefinitely. The only thing that could destroy the fund, Marino believed, was the extremely unlikely event that Bayou's members would suddenly decide to redeem their investments all at once. But why would they do that with such excellent performance numbers?

Such were the calculations of Bayou's accountant. Paradoxically, the bigger the fraud became, the easier the sale became. All Sam had to push was his story about technical trading. Value investing was a thing of the past, he told prospective members. The future belonged to short-term traders working the tiny inflections in price. In a bizarre way, Bayou was becoming a miniature Federal Reserve. The accounting trick Marino came up with gave the fund the fiat to print money by rebating the commissions and inventing returns. Like the Fed, the system functioned perfectly—provided no one looked behind the curtain.

THE BAYOU BOATHOUSE had become what con artists in the 1930s called the "big store." Everything looked exactly like a legitimate trading floor. Bayou's premises were art-directed with the care and precision of a movie set. Like the betting shop in *The Sting*, the impression was pluperfect. But in *The Sting* the people who populated the world were in on the joke, while at Bayou none of the employees knew about the scam. None knew they were bit players in an elaborate charade. This only made the performances of Bayou's employees all the more convincing: They weren't acting.

As the fund grew, Sam's manner with investors began to change. Instead of being friendly, he became aloof. After briefly acknowledging the presence of potential investors, Sam often ignored them. It was understood that he was too important and too busy for small talk. Every moment Sam wasn't trading, he let it be known, was a moment Bayou wasn't making money. If he wasn't trading he was hurting the existing investors in Bayou. Then he would suddenly declare in the middle of the morning that he was finished trading for the day. The reasons were characteristically inscrutable. Sam would say that his metrics for "normal" market activity had not been met. Or his machine predicted a lull in trading. Or he felt the market was going sideways. It was behavior that bordered on baffling. But that was the point.

"Pay no attention to the man behind the curtain," Sam would mutter to Dan Marino as Bayou's investors left the premises.

"We'd laugh," Sam remembered. "You had to keep your sense of humor about the thing. You had to keep a semblance of your humanity."

"I laughed when he laughed, and I was sad when he was sad," Marino countered. "I played politics. But it was all to get him to focus on the business and solve the problem. I liked Sam, in a limited way. He was smart and he had a lot of potential. I wanted to see Bayou work. It was my ticket to wealth. Sam already had money from his family. I had to keep the relationship working or else I would end up with nothing. I had nowhere else to go."

At the end of 2001, according to the audit of Richmond-Fairfield, Bayou had $85,354,183 in net assets. This included $10.7 million in cash on deposit with Bayou's clearinghouse, as well as $10 million in securities—SPDRs, Texas Instruments, National Semiconductor. The sum "Due from Brokers" was $64,499,627—a measure of the meteoric rise of the fraud.

Almost $7 million of the capital belonged to Sam, a number Marino invented to make it look as if the principal had a lot of his own money at risk. It was understood in the industry that hedge fund managers who put a lot of their own money into their fund provided another level of assurance of financial probity. Who would steal from themselves, after all?

If anyone had cared to look, there were signs that Bayou was falsifying its results. According to the records of Bayou's clearinghouse, Spear, Leeds & Kellogg (SLK), Bayou had actually lost $17.5 million in 2001. SLK received Bayou's audited results, so they could have seen the discrepancy between the reality of its losses and the preposterous performance reports—if they had bothered to look at the numbers, as Marino correctly wagered they wouldn't. What did SLK care? SLK and its parent company Goldman Sachs were making millions clearing Sam's trades, and that was all that mattered.

The same bewildering lack of oversight was evident in the conduct of regulators. As part of its year-end due diligence, the National Association of Securities Dealers inspected Bayou. A series of violations were discovered, but the infractions were tiny matters like failing to keep up with continuing education requirements and not maintaining proper copies of customer confirmations for trades. The only financial impropriety discovered involved the statement of net capitalization for Bayou Securities. The NASD found that Bayou had understated the capital in the broker-dealer by $4,730. "The difference is not material," a letter from the NASD said.

Deftly turning the reprimand of the regulator into a marketing advantage, Bayou made the NASD letter part of its sales pitch. The silly little misdeeds the NASD had caught illustrated how closely the business was scrutinized—particularly compared to other hedge funds that had no broker-dealer.

As the months passed, Sam began to believe his own lies, at least in part. He knew Bayou was in a deep hole. But the employees at Bayou believed in him. The investors believed in him. Why shouldn't he believe in himself? There were many good days. Sam was often an excellent trader capable of getting on a roll. When Bayou was making money, Sam didn't feel like a pretender. Forward Propagation actually did work, Sam knew, particularly when he was disciplined and followed its dictates. In those times, the hole shrank and a comeback seemed possible. Standing in his trading room at the boathouse, Sam was living out his boyhood dream.

"I was the swami," Sam recalled. "I made the money. I made something out of nothing. I could turn perception into reality. I did it every day. I was able to create an impression about a stock and leak out that perception and then make that perception a reality. There were lots of ways to do it. Like volume. A lot of the so-called soothsayers on Wall Street build their computer programs around volume. The computers tell them when to buy or sell. So I would buy a particular stock, like Intel or Archer Daniels Midland, to make it look like there was action.

"Once I'd created the impression in the market, I'd call one of my contacts in the media and tell them that it looked like there was a new chip coming out that was going to be great. Or that Archer Daniels Midland had some new pesticide coming out. I'd call Bob Pisani or Dan Dorfman at CNBC. The TV people would go on the air with the tip like it was the word on the street. I never asked the reporters to go on TV and talk about my tip. It was their choice. But it seemed like I was doing them a favor by making them seem smart and in the know.

"I did this thousands of times. I created a good rumor, or a bad rumor. Take your pick. I was always careful to make sure my lies had a modicum of truth to them. They had to be believable.

"Every day I was making history. I would take a company like McDonald's or Stride Rite shoes and for that day I would control that stock. My actions had far-reaching implications. I affected employees, pension funds, stockholders. I could bring down Coke one day, then

Bud, then Hershey. I would create the perception that something was wrong with the company. Perception was nine-tenths of reality. And I was one little guy doing that. It felt great. I wasn't some broker parroting other people. But there was a horrible downside. I created nothing—only money. I couldn't show my son a building I had created. It was an illusion."

CHAPTER SEVEN

Scumbaggery

S am was not a successful hedge fund manager, but he knew how to
 look like one. It was a role that came to him naturally. In hindsight, by comparison Bernard Madoff was an obvious fraud. Secretive, mysterious, obviously conniving, Madoff behaved like someone
with something to hide. Not Sam. Sam didn't conspire. He didn't
demand secrecy. He didn't whisper or insinuate. Sam Israel was an
open book. He acted like himself—an increasingly exaggerated and
unpredictable self. He was eccentric, unpretentious, half crazy. He
refused to take himself too seriously, or anyone or anything else for
that matter. He dressed casually, often turning up for work in shorts
or sweatpants. He arrived late for meetings. He fidgeted with boredom

and then bolted from rooms without explanation. Instead of being a poker-faced banker type, Sam would do anything for a laugh, using slapstick humor to break the ice—or distract attention. The most distinctive characteristic Sam possessed was his likability. There was no way to not like Sam—his grin, the glint in his eye, his uncanny ability to make money. He had a term for the lying and conniving he was doing, a term that described the toxic cocktail of self-loathing and arrogance that he personified.

"I called it scumbaggery," Sam said. "I was the biggest scumbag of them all. From day one on Wall Street I'd learned to cheat. You either played the game or you didn't play at all. Wall Street was built on cheating. It is nothing but cheating. That is what it was—pure, unadulterated scumbaggery."

For all his ironic pseudo-self-awareness, there were real consequences to behaving so badly. For years Sam had been tormented by back and neck pain from multiple surgeries, and he'd often disappear for days and be totally unreachable. Holed up at home like a rock star on a bender, he'd vanish into a cocoon. But even that was taken as further evidence of his tormented genius. Keeping up with Sam was exhausting and mystifying, as Marino and the staff at Bayou learned through his daily antics.

In a weird way, Sam's behavior was not unusual for a hedge fund manager. The business was populated by nutballs and megalomaniacs and idiot savants. His scruffy appearance and goofball attitude were typically atypical. Like the few thousand men—and they were nearly all men—running successful hedge funds, Sam belonged to a tiny and peculiar group who had mastered the mysteries of money. Perversely, the stranger Sam acted the more it enhanced his reputation. Sam used the image of SpongeBob SquarePants on his personal checks. He would suddenly suspend trading to go fishing in Long Island Sound. He was gregarious one moment, hermetic the next, irrepressible then depressive, a maniac then a megalomaniac.

"I didn't like to socialize," Israel said. "When I was with a bunch of people I didn't know I'd disappear. Janice would have people over and I'd literally leave. I'd be polite. I'd cook dinner. Then I'd go downstairs to make calls. Or take a walk to smoke a joint. People always wanted to talk to me about money and the market. Like one guy named John who was a friend of Janice's. At dinner one night, John asked me what he should do with all these tech stocks he'd bought. I said to sell everything. Sell, sell, sell. Then when the Internet bubble burst he complained to me. I told him he should have sold when I told him to. But he didn't because he got greedy. I said to him, 'Don't ask for my fucking advice if you're not going to follow it.' I got in a lot of trouble with Janice for that."

As a young man, Sam had been entranced by Freddy "the King" Graber. In the years since, Graber had fallen on hard times. Divorced, broke, now in his sixties and drinking far too much, Graber had been reduced to calling up old friends to borrow money. Over lunch, Graber would explain that he was about to undergo surgery and that he needed $4,000 to pay for medical tests—a sum calculated to be sizable but not so large as to provoke an answer of no. Graber's scam was transparent: The money wasn't for medical care, and it would never be repaid. Dressed in suits too tight by two sizes, the once-great Graber preyed on the mercy of the circle of men from his glory days. The descent was painful for Sam to witness. But the lessons exemplified by Graber's woes—the excess and delusion and ultimate ruination—escaped Sam. Graber had treated the world like a ship of fools. Sam was doing the same thing. But he didn't see the parallel—or the peril.

NEW INVESTORS ARRIVED regularly at the boathouse to meet Sam. The caliber of people he was encountering was rising with the stakes. Funds with buy and hold strategies were suffering in a stagnant market. The notion of what being a "trader" meant had changed. For old-school figures like Israel's former boss Leon Cooperman, being a trader meant understanding the fundamental value of a company. For Sam, it didn't matter what the company did. All that mattered was the next tick up or down. When the Hennessee Group asked Cooperman for his opinion about Israel, as part of their due diligence in considering investment in Bayou, they were told that he didn't know how to pick a stock but that he was a good "trader" in the sense of knowing how to buy and sell stock. In the market, there was no higher authority than the superstar Cooperman. Hennessee began to recommend Bayou to its clients—yet another huge coup for Bayou.

To raise even more money, Sam flew to California. In L.A. he met with Jeff Singer, who controlled $300 million for his high–net worth investors. Singer remembered Sam from the eighties, when he'd briefly apprenticed in Freddy Graber's office. In those days Israel had been part of a charmed circle, it had seemed to Singer. Now Israel's hedge fund sounded great. Singer was looking for a strategy with low "beta" (the measure of risk of a portfolio against the market) and high "alpha" (the value added by the manager's strategy). Sam's pitch was perfect. So was his analysis of the market. Singer placed $1 million of his client's money in Bayou.

Sam then returned to L.A. to meet with a group of Singer's

investors—a car dealer, a blue jeans distributor, a dentist, the representative for Matt LeBlanc of *Friends*. Israel suggested that he and Singer take their wives for a holiday in Cabo San Lucas in Mexico to discuss his joining Bayou full time.

"Sam knew how to keep me laughing," Singer recalled. "He knew how to keep me intrigued. He also knew a lot about the markets. He'd gone broke when he was younger and he'd learned his lessons. He had these sayings he called 'Sam-isms.' Like 'I don't tell the market what to do, the market tells me.' He said his goal was returns of 1 percent a month, maybe 2 percent. That added up to 15 percent annually. The story was great. I ate it up."

Bayou had never had an effective and focused employee doing nothing but raising money until Singer went to work for the fund. When he joined Bayou, Singer added a new dimension to Sam's efforts. Every month for the next three years Singer raised at least $1 million, many months far more—as much as $20 million one month. He was the biggest money raiser Bayou ever had, bringing in more than $200 million. The job was easy for Singer. When he arranged for Sam to meet with investors, the performance was beautiful to behold.

"I pitched myself as someone who was safe," Israel said. "I explained a short sale to the more naive investors. I told them that most hedge funds weren't even hedge funds—they didn't truly hedge like we did. I told them they couldn't trust their brokers. Wall Street was their enemy. Brokers didn't provide valuable research. Brokers and investment bankers were our competition. They hoarded stock. Goldman Sachs told their clients to buy stocks they knew were going to tank. They traded ahead of their own customers. That was why we had our own in-house broker-dealer. You couldn't trust Wall Street. But you could trust Bayou. It was us against the world."

. . .

AS BAYOU THRIVED, Sam didn't indulge in the typical excesses of Wall Street highfliers—Hamptons beach houses, private jets, art collections. Sam's luxuries were intangible. Since he was a teenager, Sam had been a fan of southern rock. His favorite bands were Lynyrd Skynyrd, Marshall Tucker, and the Allman Brothers. Sam leapt at the chance to be introduced to Butch Trucks, the drummer for the Allmans.

"At the time Butch was looking to get funding for a record label," Sam recalled. "A mutual friend got us together. We met at a steak house for lunch. It was supposed to be a one-hour meeting, but we went from 1:00 PM to 1:00 AM. We just couldn't stop talking, like brothers split at birth. Butch gave me my first set of really good drums. I started practicing all the time. It was a way for me to relax. Late at night in my basement I'd play for hours. After that Butch arranged for me to have backstage tickets at the Beacon Theater in New York whenever I wanted. I played with the Allmans a lot. I played with B.B. King, the Neville Brothers, Dr. John. When the Allmans were in town, I was up on stage with them."

Trucks was promoting a business he called Moogus, which was how his toddler son pronounced "music." The idea was to set up a virtual blues club online so fans could watch live acts at different clubs around the country on their computers. Israel invested $150,000 of Bayou's money up front, followed by sums that amounted to $790,000. Whatever the merits, the project never materialized into a meaningful business.

Word of Sam's success traveled along Buckout Road and through the town of Harrison. Sam was the subject of admiration and wonder.

Friends, neighbors, perfect strangers knocked on the front door of the Israel house and asked for investment advice. "People started to turn up with bags of cash," Sam said. "There would be five, ten thousand in cash in the bag. They wanted me to trade it for them. They said their son needed a new car, so they wanted me to turn it into twenty thousand. They wanted me to make them enough money to pay for their kid to go college. It was incredible—fucking incredible. I was the moneymaker."

But Sam's marriage was in trouble. His erratic behavior and appetite for illegal substances disturbed his wife. To Sam's dismay, Janice joined a women's support group. Sam argued that a group gripe about the various failings of their husbands would only undermine their marriage. Janice insisted. So at the suggestion of his psychiatrist, and as a retort to Janice, Sam joined a men's support group. Sam's men's group convened every Monday night. The men were Sam's peers—wealthy businessmen, white-shoe lawyers, surgeons, venture capitalists.

"The guys were all smart," Israel recalled. "I was okay rich, but some of those guys were really rich—like $150 million rich. The ones who were the biggest geniuses had the biggest problems. There was a doctor named Jack who'd prescribe himself fun stuff on the weekends, like Valium or liquid heroin. He had family money. When we met at his place, we played on his basketball court. The games would get serious sometimes—dishing out elbows, shouting. But mostly it was middle-aged white guys letting off steam.

"The group wasn't elitist. For dinner we'd order pizza. Some of the guys thought they were fancy, but the group would knock the fancy out of them. I enjoyed it. Men opened up with each other in a way they usually wouldn't. Men don't want to be vulnerable or to cry in front of other men. Of course I couldn't talk about what was really bothering me. But I talked about my back pain and how I had horrible issues with painkillers. I said I was having a hard time at work, controlling the staff. By then Bayou had a dozen employees or so. A guy with an Internet company who had one hundred employees gave me management tips. He was trying to figure out what to do with all the money he was making—up to a billion. It was all beyond his wildest dreams. Every time his stock went up one hundred points, he'd do something stupid, like kill a bottle of vodka and crash a car—which didn't matter because he'd just leave it there and get a new one.

"The men were the American establishment. They were supposed to be living the American dream. But guys would talk about how they hit their wives, how they went over the edge and didn't come home for two weeks because they were holed up in a hotel with a hooker and a handful of eight balls. Most of us were divorced or separated. One blond guy, maybe thirty, was a trader who came home to his wife every night and shot heroin and then got back up off the canvas in the morning and went to work. I knew from my own experience there were a lot of functional alcoholics and junkies who went to work, who were legitimate people, who were truly fucked up.

"For me, no matter how much medication I took I couldn't get my back to stop hurting. Eventually that creates a wound in your brain. But there was no way I could share with anybody what was really going on with me. There was no way I was going to say that I was committing a felony. It would destroy my reputation. It would destroy my life. Who are you going to tell that to?"

In the fall, Sam's neurologist injected dye into his spine and saw that he had a severe disc bulge. Bedridden, Israel was occasionally able to trade from home by calling in his orders to the office. But his control over events at Bayou was slipping. So was his ability to pretend that he was achieving the results necessary to keep the scam going. Then Dan Marino told him about a computer trading system that yielded 100 percent annual returns. Marino said he'd seen the system work. It was foolproof.

Sam should have been the first to doubt such a claim. But he was desperate and incapacitated. Marino traveled to L.A. to meet the trader who ran the program. Basil—he gave only his first name—was an exile from Iran. When Marino asked how the program worked, Basil refused to explain. Even so, Marino put $5 million into an account for Basil to trade. In a matter of weeks, Basil lost $4.1 million—further deepening the hole.

"I told Dan the trade was ridiculous," Israel recalled. "But I wasn't trading well and we were in a big hole."

Sam decided he needed to quit drugs cold turkey if he was ever going to regain control of himself. He checked into a Hilton hotel to detox. At marriage counseling the next day, Janice was alarmed by Israel's physical state. Stopping all his meds at once had turned Sam into a mumbling mess. After the session, Janice followed him to the hotel and urged him to get medical help. Sam's doctor said he could have a heart attack if he suddenly stopped taking his drugs. Sam was trapped in a vicious cycle: The meds were driving him mad, but the meds were the only thing that made life tolerable. The hole yawning at his feet, threatening to suck him into the abyss, was all he could stare at. But no one else could see it.

"There was a black hole in my heart," Israel said. "Every day I was in the hole. I had one hundred million to trade with. I was telling people I was beating the market. So I would trade and trade and trade and I would do okay. I would make some money, say 3 percent. But I was still seven million down because I had to show a 10 percent gain. The actual losses weren't that big most of the time. But the disparity between the real money and the performance was killing me. I was actually making money—just not enough. It weighed on me all the time—on my shoulders, my heart, my mind. I was always surrounded by blackness."

CHAPTER EIGHT

The Trump House

In January of 2003, Sam had back surgery—in fact a series of life-threatening surgeries. The first procedure involved decompressing his lumbar spine and fusing screws to his vertebrae. After a week in hospital, Sam was flipped over and another procedure was performed to address nerve damage. The next day yet another surgery was done to remove bone fragments—this time accessing the surgical area through Sam's chest. The prospect of Israel's death terrified Marino—but Sam viewed the possibility as a way to be released from his torment.

Bayou's results for the previous year were catastrophic—yet again. The fund had managed to lose another $27.7 million. But the audited statement that Marino prepared painted a different picture.

Richmond-Fairfield stated that Bayou now had nearly $150 million in assets. The fund had attracted $55 million in new investment. The "Due from Brokers" line in the financial statement had exploded to $103,923,506. But as in the past no one asked what was behind the number or what it was supposed to mean.

As far as Marino was concerned, the "plan" was working. Bayou was now a sustainable business, Marino believed. The key was cash. In a conventional Ponzi scheme, new money was used to pay old investors off. But Bayou didn't have to pay off old investors. Only $11 million had been redeemed in 2002, none of it because of displeasure with Bayou's performance. Investors were delighted to keep their money in the fund and watch it increase with every quarterly net asset value report.

Marino had unearthed one of the deepest—and most disturbing—truths about modern finance. All that was required to keep a con going was cash flow. It seemed to Marino that the entire system could be like Bayou. The implications were incredible. If Israel and Marino had seen how to maintain a facade like their hedge fund, who else had figured it out? How many other funds were doing the same thing? Dozens, hundreds, thousands?

The fraud could be expanded exponentially in size, Marino believed. So long as Bayou had enough cash and was able to maintain the appearance of a busy and prosperous trading desk, the ledger legerdemain functioned properly. Once Bayou's capital base reached $300 million, Bayou would legitimately throw off more than $20 million in pure profit a year, Marino reasoned, and that was before the 20 percent incentive fee on the (invented) performance of the hedge fund, which would be millions more. Marino's reasoning didn't make sense—but neither did much of the financial system in the bubble economy.

AS ISRAEL CONVALESCED from back surgery, Marino took advantage of the lull in activity to restructure the fund. Because of financial laws, the maximum number of investors Bayou could have was ninety-nine. But as with most things hedge fund related, getting around the rule was laughably easy. All Bayou had to do was open another hedge fund. The new fund could follow the exact same trading system as Bayou, using the same staff and office space. The new fund would be just as unregulated and inscrutable as the original Bayou.

To increase the amount of money the fund could attract, Marino decided to split Bayou into four different funds. For the scheme to be discovered, four funds would have to be cross-referenced and their returns integrated. It made the fraud harder to detect. But there was risk in making any changes. Marino was most worried about providing the supporting documents to the clearinghouse SLK. In the past, SLK had been incredibly lax. But the company had recently been acquired by Goldman Sachs for $6.5 billion, causing Israel and Marino to fear that higher diligence standards might be applied. They needn't have worried. When Bayou started to open the new accounts, SLK requested the offering documents that were going out to investors. But providing them would have been suicidal. The performance numbers Bayou claimed were wildly different from the sums in SLK's accounts. Even the lowliest clerk would notice the disparity. Marino played for time.

"I was able to see patterns in how people behaved," Marino said. "I saw how people followed routines and how those routines were filled with flaws. I knew from my own experience that when I received a FedEx package on a Friday afternoon I'd often toss it on a pile for Monday morning, and then when I got in on Monday I'd be busy getting the week started. Often I wouldn't get to the package until a week later. When I was an accountant I saw how often this happened when I sent out financials or tax returns. It was almost comical how predictable it was. So when SLK called to ask for Bayou's financials, as they were required to do, I told them that I would mail it to them. Of course I didn't. When they called a week later to ask again, I told them I'd mailed it. The process went on for a month and a half. Finally I'd sent it FedEx to arrive late on Friday afternoon. I knew that it would be put in a pile and not looked at until the next week, and that it would only get a cursory look."

As predicted, the false financials were glanced at and filed. Even the mighty Goldman Sachs, imagined to be omniscient by many, was fooled by Bayou—or allowed itself to be fooled. While one branch of Goldman (SLK) failed to perform even perfunctory due diligence, another branch of the firm (Pedigree) began to consider Bayou as a potential fund to promote to its clients. Normally, getting Goldman's attention was a coup. But Marino didn't want anything to do with them, no matter how much money they had.

"I knew at some point Goldman would want some detailed information that I wouldn't be able to give to them," Marino said. "So when they called, I didn't call them back. When they persisted, I answered questions only if they were directly asked. I was very slow in responding to requests for documents and setting up meetings with their clients. Everyone was confused by what I was doing, including Bayou's salespeople and advisors. They couldn't understand why we weren't pursuing the leads with Goldman. But I knew we couldn't deal with them."

On the rare occasions when securities regulators asked questions about the hedge fund, Marino and Israel flimflammed, using lingo about puts and swaps and derivatives. Regulators didn't understand how the market was supposed to work, let alone the reality. Nor were the regulators able to admit their ignorance. Sam was acutely aware of these truths. It provided him some comfort when financial regulators in Boston required that Bayou provide records related to the broker-dealer side of the business. Sam knew the SEC was checking to ensure that Bayou Securities wasn't overcharging Bayou Funds to bilk the hedge fund investors. If the real numbers were sent, no overcharging would be found. But the documents would also show Bayou had lost massive amounts of money—if the record was examined properly. Marino wanted to falsify the numbers. Israel said there was no need to take the risk. Leave the numbers as they are, Sam said. The SEC will never notice.

"I called the regulators up in Boston and asked if they were sure they wanted all the documents," Israel said. "I said it was going to be a lot of boxes. Dan was freaking out, but I told him to calm down. We shipped all the trading records up. They had no clue how to look at the numbers. Because they were looking for that one thing, I knew they wouldn't see anything else. The numbers showed that the amount of money in the fund didn't match the amount that was supposed to be there. All they had to do was look. But they didn't know how to look. Even if they did find something wrong, they would think they had made the mistake—not Bayou. They wouldn't say anything because they didn't want to look like fools—like they didn't understand what was going on. So I just hid in plain sight. There was no reason to do it any other way."

THE SANGFROID AT WORK wasn't matched by Israel's shambolic personal life. Now addicted to new powerful painkillers from another failed back surgery, Sam finally agreed to go to rehab. The Retreat was a deluxe facility set in the leafy grounds of a large hospital campus. There were only five rooms, each set up like a luxury hotel suite, with a concierge and gourmet room service. It was the perfect hideaway for a hedge fund trader like Israel to quietly slay his inner demons—and not be discovered by his investors.

Israel lasted twenty days. After checking out voluntarily, he immediately relapsed. Cocaine and codeine and marijuana were found in the urine tests he'd agreed to take. It happened that the Israels had tickets to see the Allman Brothers. On the night of the concert, Sam walked into the master bedroom to ask Janice if she was coming. She told Sam she didn't want to go; she didn't like the Allman Brothers. She asked if he'd gone for his urine test that day. "You want urine?" Sam asked. He undid his zipper and proceeded to take a leak on the bathroom floor.

The situation was hopeless. Janice demanded he leave the house. Sam didn't want to go. Janice insisted. He finally agreed to move out, though with the express agreement that they would try to reconcile. Seeking a temporary place to stay, Sam checked into the Doral Arrowwood Hotel in White Plains. He took a penthouse suite with sweeping views of the Hudson River.

"I'd been with Janice since high school," Sam said. "Now I wanted to meet as many women as I could get. I tipped the bartenders and bellhops really good. I told them to be on the lookout for pretty girls, to talk me up, to say I was a big-time hedge fund trader. They loved doing it for me."

Janice went with Sam to see his psychiatrist. She wanted a safe environment to tell Sam that she was going to seek a protective order to keep him away from her and the house. When Janice was done, Sam exploded, just as his father had done when he was a boy. "I took you out of the gutter," Sam screamed. "I made you and now I will break you. I'm going to send your ass back to Yonkersville."

Thanksgiving was a disaster for the Israel family in 2003. Hoping for a reconciliation, Sam and Janice hosted a gathering. Wasted, Sam passed out while trying to eat his turkey. Janice took the children to her sister's house. Sam's conduct had become completely unacceptable. Sam was still trading from an office in his basement when one day two policemen came to the house to see him. The officers were fathers of kids he'd coached in soccer. Sam greeted them in a friendly fashion, but their mood was somber. They asked Sam to take a seat and remain calm. For a second, Sam had a pang of fear: Was he about to be arrested? Had the Bayou fraud been discovered? The police said they had bad news. A protective order had been issued. Sam had to leave the house immediately. Sam had twenty minutes to pack his things. Israel refused to submit to the demeaning ritual of filling suitcases with his belongings. He had money. He would buy himself a new wardrobe—sneakers, sweatpants, baseball caps.

"My marriage didn't fall apart, it got cut off," Sam said. "Janice had looked up to me. I was the father figure, the rainmaker. But she lost faith in me. She saw me infirm. I was high on opiate doses because of my back pain and the surgeries. I fell off the pedestal. Instead of doing things that she thought were funny, now I was being an asshole. She saw fault in everything I did."

Sam decided he needed to start the next chapter of his life. He needed a place to live permanently. In the phantasmagoric world Sam inhabited, he couldn't live in just any house. He was a hedge fund hero. Sam wanted a home that reflected his position in society—a mansion where he could live out fantasies of a being a Bruce Wayne–like playboy millionaire.

Winding up the driveway of 52 Oregon Road in Mount Kisco, Sam knew he'd found the spot. The house wasn't so much a mansion as a monument to excess. The owner was Donald Trump. The self-promoting tycoon had lived there himself. Like Trump, everything about the house was comically over the top—so impossibly huge for one person to live in that it signified only massive insecurity. Set on a hill overlooking acres of woodlands, the grounds consisted of an apple orchard on one side and a meadow on the other. In front of the house was a courtyard with a large stone peeing-boy fountain. The eight-thousand-square-foot Tudor-style manor had been built in 1913 for the Heinz family. Donald Trump now rented it out for $22,000 a month. Trump had renovated the house in his uniquely garish style. Inside there were oversized chandeliers, and the bathrooms were done in marble and glass; the giant kitchen was stocked with the latest stainless-steel appliances. Next door, across a small walkway, was a chapel that the Heinz family had used for formal balls.

Sam turned the chapel into the adult version of a boys' club room. Always a music buff, with a passion for playing the drums, Sam bought high-end instruments for jam sessions—enough equipment for an entire band. When the Allman Brothers came to New York, the band's drummer jammed with Sam. Sam also built a trading room in the chapel to exactly replicate his trading room at the boathouse. Sixteen screens were set up in the same array as he had at the office. A direct video feed was established between the chapel and Bayou, but it functioned in only one direction, allowing Sam to watch his clerks. The rest of the chapel was turned into a party room, with pinball machines and a giant flat-screen television and a well-stocked bar. He bought an eight-hundred-gallon saltwater fish tank and stocked it with exotic species. He also acquired a menagerie of reptiles. Israel had chameleons, bearded dragons, geckos, South American horned frogs, and two giant African turtles that he kept in a pen.

"My favorite was a fourteen-foot-long reticulated python who would ball up on my keyboard while I traded," Israel recalled. "His name was Herman. He was my man. I loved reptiles. They strike quickly and they kill quickly. They don't prolong death like a spider might. And they don't eat more than they need."

But all was not well in the Trump house. In the span of three weeks Israel went to the emergency room three times when his right leg and foot became paralyzed. His lower back was hurting so much he could no longer stand when he urinated; he was forced to sit on the toilet for long stretches of time as he tried, often in vain, to pass water.

Romantically, things weren't going well either. An ongoing flirtation Sam had with an attractive young female literally ran into a brick wall when they fought over her involvement with another man.

"As you know, I am exceptionally good at reading and assessing people and situations," Sam e-mailed her after the argument. "I have to gauge and assess the markets each day, wagering hundreds of millions and having to be right consistently. I believe I do a pretty good job."

Sam wrote that his intuition had told him that the woman was going to see her ex-boyfriend. "I was quite upset, but I resigned myself to not asking you about him no matter what," Sam wrote. "So I decided to go for a drive in my new Porsche. Not fast, mind you, because it had begun to snow. I took the weather to be a bad omen for me. About ten pm I had one of my real absofuckinglutely unmistakable clairvoyant realizations that you'd done the dirty deed with him. That was certainly your right. That was when a truck pulled in front of me and I lost control and drove the Porsche into a brick wall."

CHAPTER NINE

Adventure Capital

B y the end of 2003, the problem had become the Problem. The tattoo of the Little Devil Sam had put on his hip seemed to have been brought to life as a gremlin sitting on his shoulder constantly whispering in his ear. All Sam could think about was solving the Problem. Somehow, somewhere, there had to be a way to make $100 million very, very, very quickly.

Bayou was now sitting on nearly $150 million in cash. There was more than enough cash flow to keep the fund afloat indefinitely, according to Marino's "business plan." But Sam didn't share Marino's confidence that they could keep up the fraud. All it would take was one employee or one investor or one regulator to stumble onto the truth. Sam wasn't able to physically cope with the stress.

Israel knew he had to do something radically different if he was going to solve the Problem. He didn't tell Marino of this dawning realization. Sam could see that conventional trading was never going to yield the kind of miracle windfall Bayou now needed. Sam had to up the stakes. He had to find a way to roll the dice. He began to look at the money invested in his hedge fund as his pile of chips in a high-stakes poker game. He was playing for his freedom, Sam knew—and possibly his life.

Venture capital (VC) was one way to garner extraordinary returns. It would take time, Sam knew, but it was better than doing nothing. Sam had a friend who worked in VC. John Ellis was the father of a boy in Sam's son's class at the Hackley School. Like most parents at Hackley—like Israel—Ellis came from a privileged background. But Ellis's pedigree was particularly impressive. His uncle was President George H. W. Bush. His first cousin and close personal friend was President George W. Bush. Ellis belonged to the trusted inner circle of the president. The Israel and Bush families had crossed paths over the years, through the oil business and Wall Street connections. Sam believed Ellis belonged to the tiny elite who really ran the world—the chosen few.

"If you're going to bring me a company, make sure it's going to go up tenfold, not by a few points," Israel said to Ellis. "I want businesses that can turn $20 million into $200 million."

KYCOS was a company with that kind of promise, Ellis believed. In the wake of 9/11, the Patriot Act required banks and corporations to perform due diligence on their clients to ensure they weren't laundering money for terrorists. KYCOS (Know Your Customer Outsourced Services) was going to sell access to a database for companies registered on the Isle of Man and the Cayman Islands, two tax haven jurisdictions. On Israel's instruction, Ellis told Marino the start-up had global potential. A similar company had recently sold for $775 million. For a mere $10 million, Israel and Marino could acquire a majority interest.

Sam was intrigued. But he didn't deal with VC proposals directly; he didn't have the time or energy. Israel had picked Dan Marino to run alternative investment strategies for Bayou. Marino had taken to the job with gusto, forming a company called IM Partners, the initials taken from the initials of their last names. The first $1 million investment in KYCOS was followed by another $4.5 million. As a new investor, Marino traveled to the Isle of Man to attend a board meeting. It was the first overseas trip of his life. The company was operated by a group of Englishmen with upper-class accents who fawned over Marino.

At an evening reception, Marino was approached by an American businessman who said he was promoting a company called Debit Direct. The man was literally a giant—six-six, with massive hands and the distinctive features of a person who had the disease of gigantism. He said his name was Jack O'Halloran. The nature of the business O'Halloran was promoting wasn't entirely clear. He said Debit Direct was going to use the Isle of Man as a place for online gamblers from America to keep their digital "wallets." He was also going to compete with Western Union and MoneyGram. Like the man himself, the ideas were gigantic. Marino said he didn't have time to talk, but O'Halloran should contact him the next time he was in the United States.

A few weeks later, O'Halloran called from New York. Marino invited him up to the Bayou offices in Connecticut. Israel generally left VC meetings to Marino. But when Sam dropped in on the meeting with O'Halloran, he lingered. O'Halloran was not just another supplicant in a suit. O'Halloran was larger than life—literally. He had a bone-crushing handshake and a booming laugh that he let loose constantly. As Sam listened to O'Halloran talk about his various business ideas, it seemed to Sam that he looked uncannily like the Hollywood villain Jaws from the old James Bond movies. The lantern jaw, the wide-set eyes, the overhanging brow—his face was somehow familiar.

When the meeting broke up, Israel invited O'Halloran upstairs to see his trading room. With a look of wonder, O'Halloran wandered past the computer screens with their pulsing data streams.

"This is like being inside a rocket ship," O'Halloran said. "Your office looks like the set of a movie I was in."

"What movie is that?" Israel asked, amused.

"*Superman*," O'Halloran said.

"You were in *Superman*?"

"I was the big dumb guy who couldn't make his laser eyes work right," O'Halloran said. "The character named Non."

The penny dropped. Israel *did* recognize O'Halloran—not from the James Bond movies, but from similar roles as the archetypal giant evildoer.

"You were in *Dragnet*, too, right?" Israel said.

"That was me," O'Halloran said. "With Tom Hanks. I spat on Dan Aykroyd in that one."

Sam hooted in delight. O'Halloran said he'd also had a bit part in *King Kong* in 1976, playing a sailor thrown into an abyss by the giant gorilla. O'Halloran's stories were amazing, each more improbable than the last. An expert name-dropper, O'Halloran told Sam about the actresses he'd bedded, like the French beauty Catherine Deneuve. He told Sam he'd been a heavyweight boxer, fighting as "Irish" Jack O'Halloran. A rising contender, he'd been slated to fight Muhammad

Ali in the early seventies. The match didn't come off. But O'Halloran had fought George Foreman in Madison Square Garden in 1970, getting knocked out in the fifth.

"I'm a huge fight fan," Israel said. "I've met Ali a couple times."

On and on O'Halloran went with improbable tales that had the unlikely virtue of appearing to be true. Israel and O'Halloran soon found points of connection as the giant slowly pulled the hedge fund trader into his orbit. O'Halloran said he'd played professional football for the Dallas Cowboys in the early sixties. Sam's family had owned a minority share in the New Orleans Saints for decades, and his father was friends with many famous NFL players. O'Halloran had a grandiose manner, an affect that Sam could relate to. It was impossible to tell when O'Halloran strayed into fiction. Sam didn't much care. The stories were worth the price of admission. Like O'Halloran's claim to be the secret love child of Albert Anastasia, boss of the Gambino crime family and leader of the notorious Murder Inc. The assertion was preposterous on its face: O'Halloran looked nothing like the swarthy mobster known as the Mad Hatter. But it was also impossible to disprove. Anastasia had been shot in a barber chair in New York in 1957—an iconic murder alluded to in *The Godfather*. No one could confirm or deny O'Halloran's claim—and who cared anyway?

Sam suggested they have dinner that night. He took O'Halloran to the Willett House, an expensive steak and seafood restaurant. Israel ordered lobster, along with jugs of iced tea. O'Halloran continued to pitch Debit Direct. Away from the KYCOS group, O'Halloran came on strong. Online gambling could make billions, he said. Israel was dubious. But he was having a great time. Sam relished any chance to think about something other than the Problem.

Over dinner, O'Halloran told Sam he was writing a book about the assassination of President John F. Kennedy. Not just any book, either. The book was O'Halloran's first-person eyewitness account of the day of Kennedy's assassination. O'Halloran said he'd been in Dallas in November of 1963, sent as a secret emissary by the Mafia. Sam was extremely excited. Like so many others, he'd been fascinated by the various conspiracy theories surrounding the death of President Kennedy. It remained one of the great unsolved mysteries, Sam believed.

Sitting in the steak house, O'Halloran told Sam he knew the truth about Kennedy's death. For decades he had kept secret his knowledge of that day, he said, for fear of losing his life. But now he was finally going to solve the mystery and challenge the most basic assumptions about American history. O'Halloran said he knew who killed Kennedy—and why.

"I'd read forty books on the Kennedy assassination," Israel recalled. "I was an animal for those books. My grandfather was tight with Hale Boggs—the only one to dissent from the Warren Commission and the single-bullet theory. Boggs died in an 'airplane crash'"—here Israel made inverted commas with his fingers to show quote signs. "The last job Lee Harvey Oswald had before Kennedy was killed was working for my uncle's company—Reily Coffee Company. Six of the employees at Reily Coffee wound up working for the CIA, so tell me that was coincidental. My family was very connected in New Orleans, which was tied up to the whole conspiracy to kill Kennedy."

That night, Sam sat down to read the outline of O'Halloran's proposed book *Mosaic: The Definitive Account of How and Why President John F. Kennedy Was Assassinated, by One of the Six People Still Living Who Knows the Full Story.* The tale put O'Halloran at the center of events on the day Kennedy was murdered. O'Halloran wrote that the famed gangster Meyer Lansky had personally sent O'Halloran to Dallas. To provide cover for his mission, O'Halloran related, he'd tried out for the Dallas Cowboys. The day before the assassination, the coach of the Cowboys invited O'Halloran and a group of players to a party at the team owner's mansion. "Night in Egypt" was the theme of the gathering. The guest of honor was J. Edgar Hoover, then head of the FBI. Richard Nixon was in attendance, along with a young oilman named George H. W. Bush. A late-night arrival was Vice President Lyndon Baines Johnson, arm in arm with his mistress. The notables secretly convened in a back room. When Johnson emerged he appeared flushed, excited.

"After tomorrow those goddamn Kennedys will never embarrass me again," Johnson whispered to his mistress. "That's no threat—that's a promise."

O'Halloran claimed he was there to overhear the remark. The next morning, according to his narrative, he was out for a predawn run when he happened to see a mobster named Johnny Rosselli slip through a manhole into Dallas's sewer system. O'Halloran claimed that Rosselli went underground to set up in a sniper position in a culvert in Dealey Plaza where he would have a clear shot at the president's motorcade. Decades of accumulated questions about what really happened that day would be answered by O'Halloran's magnum opus. Lee Harvey Oswald was a patsy. The shots heard from the Texas School Book Depository were blanks. Rosselli had first shot Kennedy from the culvert, then a mysterious second shooter had finished the job. The murder was the result of a conspiracy by the group of men who secretly controlled the world—a cabal of criminals from the underworld in alliance with elites from the "Upperworld."

History had recorded that a man named Abraham Zapruder had

captured the scene with his home movie camera. O'Halloran claimed that the Zapruder film released to the public had been doctored. Seven frames had been removed. In those frames, the Zapruder film showed conclusively who killed Kennedy: Secret Service Special Agent William Greer. It was Greer who was driving the limousine. After the first shot from Rosselli struck the president, Greer turned in the driver's seat and pulled out a gun with a silencer attached to the muzzle and fired a single shot. "That was all that was needed," O'Halloran wrote. "As Abraham Zapruder's film would record for all time, that single mercury tipped bullet exploded inside the President's head, blasting out a shower of blood, brain tissue, and pieces of fractured skull."

SAM LOVED THE STORY. The next day, Israel told Marino that IM Partners was going to invest $2 million in Debit Direct, starting with half a million in cash immediately. Marino refused to send the money. The accountant wanted to study the proposal first. But Sam circumvented Marino, instructing an employee to send $500,000 to Debit Direct with no contract or agreement about what precisely IM Partners was purchasing with Bayou's money.

O'Halloran then told Sam he could also buy 50 percent of the book and film rights to *Mosaic* for a measly half-million dollars. Israel took the idea to Marino. But when Marino read *Mosaic* he thought it was awful—and totally unbelievable. Sam himself didn't fully credit O'Halloran's yarn either. But it didn't matter. Another half-million dollars winged its way into the bank account of Sam's new acquaintance. As half owner, Sam now represented the book as a kind of quasi–literary agent. He prepared a submission letter to send to book editors in Manhattan. "Jack O'Halloran is about to change the way you look at the world," Sam wrote.

But the distraction of promoting the book didn't change the gloomy reality Sam inhabited. Christmas of 2003 was the first time Sam was forced to be away from the family, a fact he found hugely upsetting. Despite Sam's absence, the normal holiday traditions would continue at the Israel home. As usual Janice hired a local decorative artist named Debra Ryan to dress the Israel home for the holidays. Ryan had been making the house festive for the past four years. She'd also done extensive painting at Bayou's boathouse. Over the years, Ryan had developed a friendly rapport with the Israels. Tall, blond, and pretty in a tomboyish way, Ryan had an easy, joking manner that meshed with Sam's sensibility. This year, when Ryan arrived to start work, Janice explained that she and Sam were getting a divorce. But Sam would be coming by the house to pick up his son for a visit, she said.

It was freezing rain when Ryan and her assistant went outside to festoon the house with large red ribbons. As she worked, Ryan heard a distant voice calling her name. Sam was at the foot of the driveway, beckoning her. She walked to the street to say hello. Israel paced on the far side of the fence, accompanied by a large African American man—the court-appointed supervisor for Sam's visits with his son. Sam was smoking a cigarette and shaking from the cold.

"I'm not allowed on the fucking property," Israel said. "She wants to divorce me and make my life miserable. She thinks there's fifty million dollars hidden somewhere. She won't take ten million. Ten million fucking dollars."

"I'm sorry to hear that," Ryan said, moved to see Israel in such a pitiable state.

"I didn't threaten her," Sam said. "I swear I didn't threaten her. The only way for a woman to get a man out of the house in New York is to say they have been threatened."

Ryan sympathized. Sam had always been nice to her, and she hated to see anyone suffer so terribly. Two weeks later, she got a call from Israel's personal assistant. He wanted her to come to his house and do decorations for him for when the kids came to see him over the holidays. Ryan expected Sam to be living in squalor, like most men who have just split from their wives. As she drove up to the Trump house, she stared in wonder at Sam's new digs—the large Grecian sculpture in the water fountain, the chapel, the row of expensive cars. It was amazingly opulent, even to Ryan, who was used to working for wealthy clients. A maid ushered her inside.

"Hell, dude, you're supposed to live in a shack," Ryan said.

"I know," Israel said with a smile. "Donald Trump had a place for me, so I'm renting it."

"What do you need this place for?" Ryan asked. "It's huge."

"I can do it, so why not?" Israel said. "When you get to a certain status, when you have a hedge fund, you can't live in a little house because the world is not going to look at you as being successful."

Israel gave her a tour, explaining that he wanted a twenty-foot tree for the chapel, along with the best in trimmings and seasonal wreaths. Israel set a budget of $15,000. Working late into the night on the rush job, Ryan and her assistant ended up sleeping over at the mansion.

"There were four empty bedrooms," Ryan recalled. "I'd never been in a bed as comfortable as that. It was like floating on a cloud. There were big baths in each room, saunas, fluffy down comforters. I slept in a huge king-sized bed that belonged to Donald Trump. I didn't want to leave."

In his own goofy and lewd style, Sam constantly hit on Ryan. She was able to deflect his advances, but she enjoyed his company. Sam was unpretentious and down-to-earth, despite his obvious success. The German shepherd puppy Sam had just purchased was great fun, careening around the house and barking and nipping at strangers. Much of the time, Israel was confined to his bed because of his back pain. Ryan could see that her presence lifted his spirits.

"I could tell he was really sick," Ryan said. "He was a lovable guy. I felt sorry for him. The hours he kept were not normal. He was in a fog. We'd sit up in his bedroom and watch *SpongeBob SquarePants* together. Sam was like Elvis in a huge bed."

ON THE LAST TRADING day of 2003, Sam's computer program lit up the way it had on September 11, 2001. All of the indicators pointed in the same direction. The last time Forward Propagation had offered such a prediction, Sam had been thwarted by the terrorist attacks. This time he was not going to be denied. Sam loaded up on SPDRs—known as "spiders," they were bets on the S&P Index. He leveraged his position to the hilt. Then he waited. And waited. Days passed and the market didn't take the turn Forward Propagation had foretold. The margin call from the clearinghouse SLK had to be met. Sam had no option but to sell to meet the margin call. Another $20 million was gone.

According to Bayou's audited results for 2003, the fund had a total investment of $323,000,549. Net income was $34,527,736. The incentive fee Sam had earned was $8,631,935. The line "Due from Brokers" was $117,960,120. Not that Marino had bothered to calculate that figure precisely. There was the "real" loss of money, which ran to more than $50 million. The rest was "fake" money. Taken together, only a lightning bolt from the heavens could solve the Problem.

At the end of the year, SLK created a list of the clearinghouse's ten biggest losers. Three of Sam's funds were on the list, including Bayou Superfund, which had lost $35 million and thus earned the ignomy of top spot.

"Do these numbers reflect pure profit and loss or a combination with fund redemptions?" the managing director of SLK asked in an e-mail.

"Pure profit and loss," came the reply.

"Ugly!"

"No kidding."

But SLK took no steps to investigate how Bayou managed to stay in business despite the epic losses. In January of 2004 alone, the division of Goldman Sachs made $100,000 in commissions from Bayou. Speculation about the errant hedge fund led to an exchange of e-mails among traders at Goldman but no further.

"What is the dealio?" one SLK employee asked of Bayou.

"In out," said the reply, describing Sam's frantic trading style. "A real Wizard of Oz kind of place."

"Down on the BAYOU baby."

"We love them. Only question is if Bayou is a one hit wonder or real?"

As the losses mounted, Sam's mood swings were growing more violent. His sense of dread was deepening as if he were caught in quicksand. After struggling out of bed to see a psychiatrist as part of his desperate attempt to remain in contact with his children during the divorce, Sam suffered a full-blown panic attack in the doctor's office. Unable to breathe, unable to speak, Sam was convinced he was about to die. When he went to a heart specialist, he discovered he had a severe case of sick sinus syndrome. The anxiety from running the scam had slowed his metabolism down—the opposite of what might be expected. He was at risk of having a massive stroke.

"My body was falling apart," Sam said. "I couldn't tell my investors or else they would freak out and there would be a run on the fund. The doctors performed open-heart surgery and implanted a pacemaker. I took time off work, but I didn't tell anyone about my health. It had to be secret."

As Sam recovered from yet another surgery, his father called to say that the family was going to develop a tract of real estate they owned in New Orleans. The acreage was going to be turned into a residential subdivision. To get financing, all of the Israels had to fill out financial disclosure forms. Sam completed the document, stating that his income for the prior year had been $8 million. When Sam returned the application, his father immediately called his son in alarm. The elder Israel was concerned about how much money Sam was making. What was Sam doing to make $8 million? The sum was too big, Sam's father said—with well-justified concern. But all Sam heard was criticism.

"It was the biggest moment of my life," Sam recalled. "I was making it big-time. I was vindicated. I was finally showing my old man that I could really do it on my own. But he wouldn't give me any approval. All he said to me was 'It is too much money.' I was at the fucking peak, and my father still couldn't be proud of me."

CHAPTER TEN

Octopus

I nvesting in Bayou Funds entails substantial risks," the marketing material for Bayou released in February of 2004 stated. Investors were told that they were essentially entrusting their money to one person: Sam Israel. "Bayou Funds are single-manager funds," it was said. "This eliminates diversification of viewpoint and expertise. This risk is heightened by the facts that (i) trading strategies and tactics are essentially set by Sam Israel III; and (ii) such strategies and tactics are developed and implemented on the basis of his judgments about the market."

From the marketing material, tying your financial fate to Sam's judgment appeared to be an excellent decision. An investment of $1,000 in 1997 was worth $4,000 by the beginning of 2004. Like

Bernard Madoff's "split-strike conversion" strategy, Sam's Forward Propagation independently arrived at the pluperfect Ponzi performance: 18 percent. The number was calibrated to be incredible, credible, and irresistible all at once. There were other ways the men unconsciously mirrored each other. Both had legitimate broker-dealers inside their funds. The sight of a busy trading floor gave Madoff and Israel the invaluable ability to seem as if they ran functioning and normal businesses.

But the two men were fundamentally different. Madoff didn't try to solve his problem: The hedge fund was a fraud from its inception. Madoff gladly feasted on the entire life savings of many of his investors. Like Charles Ponzi, Madoff also never actually traded. Not Sam. When he was physically able, Sam traded and traded and traded. He constantly searched for a solution to the Problem—any solution. But the harder he looked the more lost he was. He wasn't just caught in a tangled web; he was wandering in a labyrinth of his own design, a maze as ornate as the one the legendary artificer Daedalus constructed in ancient Greece—a structure so cunning in its conception that even he himself could not find his way out.

Sam's torment was made infinitely worse by his brutal ongoing divorce. He could no longer safely indulge in illegal drugs. A single dirty urine sample would mean the loss of visitation privileges with his children. Now that he was forced to sit as he peed because of his back pain, the humiliation and peril involved in the simple act of urination perfectly illustrated the compounding impossibilities of his situation.

Debra Ryan watched in distress as Sam's mental health spiraled downward. Without knowing the cause of his misery, one evening she suggested Sam talk to her psychic, an English spiritual consultant named Bernard Ilsley. A telephone conference was arranged with Ilsley, who was based in London. Ilsley told Sam that as part of his craft, he communicated with a Native American spirit named Silver Cloud, as well as an Oriental avatar called Dr. Chan. On the call Ilsley said that the anger and recriminations of the divorce proceedings would not stop. "But in your career good things will happen in the next month or two," Ilsley said. "I see March or April being a time when you will have good luck. A financial opportunity will present itself that could make a big change for you." Ilsley said that a man named Robert was going to enter Israel's life and have a big impact. Ilsley couldn't quite hear all that Silver Cloud was saying about Robert—the spirit's voice was too faint. But Sam should prepare for Robert's looming arrival.

Afterward, Debra Ryan eagerly asked how the session had gone.

"It was a bunch of bullshit," Sam said, rolling his eyes.

DAYS LATER A MAN named Robert did enter Sam's life—and change it forever. Jack O'Halloran was the conduit to the foretold Robert. One evening Sam and O'Halloran were eating Chinese food in the chapel. Sam talked about Wall Street and the life of a trader. Running Bayou wasn't interesting anymore, he said. The hedge fund business was tedious and grueling. He was looking for a trading strategy that could change the game—and make him billions.

"There are paradigm shifts on Wall Street every ten years," Israel said. "When I started in the early eighties, it was insider trading and soft-dollar scams. Then it became IPOs and the dot-com bubble. Now it is high-frequency trading. The banks are front-running the market like crazy. I'm trying to figure out what's coming next."

"There's a technology I have heard about that might be good for your trading system," O'Halloran said. "But the guy who knows about it is really secretive. I shouldn't even be talking about him. He's very deep into CIA black ops."

Sam's interest was piqued. O'Halloran said the man's name was Robert Booth Nichols. He was a real-life Jason Bourne, a black ops national security asset who had worked on the dark side of America's covert activities for decades. According to O'Halloran, Nichols was a stone-cold killer, an agent who functioned at the absolute highest levels of government.

"Bob is a keeper of the secrets of the world," O'Halloran said. "He knows how the world really runs. That's the only reason he is still alive. Anything happens to Bob, the secrets get released."

After midnight, alone in the silence of the night, Sam turned on his computer and typed the name "Robert Booth Nichols" into his Internet search engine. Hundreds of links appeared. Nichols was an Internet celebrity, it appeared, his various operations turning him into a conspiracy theory superstar. There were references to "the Octopus" and multiple unsolved murders. Websites speculated about Nichols's ties to illegal black ops and organized crime. Sam clicked on a link to a book called *The Last Circle*. It was an unpublished manuscript written by an amateur author using a pseudonym to protect her identity.*

Exploring the intersection of organized crime and conspiracy theory literature, *The Last Circle* was written in dense, insistent prose.

---

* The author Cheri Seymour published the book in 2011 (Trine Day).

The chronology of events was overwhelmingly detailed, and it was often difficult to follow the complex, interwoven narrative. But it was evident the book required more than just suspension of disbelief: An entirely new way of seeing the world had to be embraced. Nothing was the way it appeared, the book seemed to claim. American covert foreign policy, the criminal justice system, the reach of computer technology—all of it was part of a web of deceit spun by a secretive murderous elite called the Octopus.

At the center of the story was Robert Booth Nichols. According to *The Last Circle*, Nichols was a CIA assassin, illegal arms dealer, mob associate, and con man. He carried himself with the air of an old-school Hollywood actor—Clark Gable, the book said, without the mustache. He was an international man of mystery with a smooth, sly, enigmatic manner, a cigarette dangling from his mouth, an American with the Anglophile habit of using words like *chap*.

According to *The Last Circle*, Nichols had been involved in virtually every nefarious covert plot carried out by the U.S. government for the past three decades. Iran-Contra, the October Surprise, the CIA's mind-control experiment called MK Ultra—Nichols was the Zelig of the conspiracy theory world. When the CIA dealt heroin to fund the war against Hezbollah in Beirut in the 1980s, Nichols was there. When Ferdinand Marcos of the Philippines smuggled billions of bullion into Swiss bank accounts, his "facilitator" was Nichols. When three people were murdered on the Cabazon Indian reservation outside Palm Springs in the summer of 1981, Nichols was there developing illegal biological weapons and machine guns to arm Nicaraguan rebels.

The unsolved triple homicide in Cabazon formed the premise for *The Last Circle*. It had become part of an investigation taken up by a freelance journalist named Danny Casolaro. In the early nineties

Casolaro had been reporting for a proposed book on the CIA's alleged theft of a computer program named PROMIS. The program had been developed a decade earlier by a company called Inslaw for the Department of Justice to turn the files of the federal court system into a searchable database. The program had been so successful that American intelligence agency apparatus had secretly stolen the software to put it to use covertly. The CIA had reconfigured the code and installed it in 32-bit Digital Equipment Corporation DAX minicomputers. The agency had used front companies to sell the new technology to banks and leading financial institutions like the Federal Reserve. Hidden inside the computer was a "trapdoor" that enabled intelligence agencies to covertly monitor financial transactions digitally for the first time. The highly classified initiative, known as "Follow the Money," had allowed the Reagan administration to trace the Libyan government's secret funding of a terrorist group that had bombed a disco in Berlin in 1986, killing an American soldier and wounding two hundred civilians. In Bob Woodward's book *Veil*, former CIA director William Casey said the secret money-tracking system had been one of his proudest achievements.

But it was done illegally by pirating the software—an act that led to a lawsuit by Inslaw. Casolaro believed the theft of PROMIS was only a small part of a vast conspiracy run by an extremist element inside the American intelligence community. The cabal killed, stole, dealt drugs, all with complete impunity. Nichols was part of this secret lawless group. According to *The Last Circle*, Nichols had been connected deep inside the White House during the Reagan presidency. Nichols had also acted as the go-between for the Gambino crime family in its dealings with the Hollywood studio MCA. Nichols had traveled the world as a hit man on behalf of the faction bent on world domination. Then there was this: *The Last Circle* reported that Nichols possessed the "real" Zapruder film, which showed who had really killed President Kennedy.

Sitting in the dark, Sam felt like his head was going to explode. There really was a "real" Zapruder film? Was it possible? Conspiracy theories appealed to Sam's sense of how the world worked. He believed Washington was just as corrupt as Wall Street; power was just as dirty as money. Danny Casolaro had given a name to this cabal. He called it "the Octopus" because of the way its tentacles were wrapped around so many aspects of society. The name made perfect sense to Sam. He had seen firsthand how the "giant vampire squid"* called Goldman Sachs manipulated the market. The Octopus was the same beast, only it was run by American intelligence agencies. Just as Goldman front-ran the market and created fraudulent derivatives, so did the CIA deal drugs and assassinate President Kennedy. It stood to reason that men like Nichols existed to do the bidding of the elite few who ran the world. To Israel, Bayou's fraud was his own secret manifestation of the deceit he saw everywhere.

So it was that Sam entered the lunatic world of Robert Booth Nichols—a house of mirrors in an upside-down universe that made the Bayou conspiracy look tiny by comparison. In *The Last Circle* Sam read how Casolaro believed he was about to expose a massive conspiracy that would solve the great puzzles of modern history. *The Octopus* was the title of the book Danny Casolaro planned to write. But Casolaro wasn't able to make his story make sense, not on the page or in his mind. It was as if the tentacles of the Octopus had

---

* The world's most powerful investment bank is "a great vampire squid wrapped around the face of humanity, relentlessly jamming its blood funnel into anything that smells like money." Matt Taibbi, *Rolling Stone*, April 2010.

wrapped themselves around Casolaro's imagination and dragged him to the bottom of the sea, where he drowned in paranoia.

As Casolaro descended ever deeper into the unfathomable Octopus conspiracy, he'd fallen under the spell of Nichols. The intelligence operative was an expert in mind control, according to *The Last Circle,* trained in hypnosis as well as the powers of intimidation he'd developed as a racketeer. When Casolaro said he intended to reveal the machinations of the Octopus, Nichols said he would be killed if he continued his investigation. The murder would be done in a way to ensure that no one was caught, Nichols said. It appeared to be a threat in the form of a warning. Terrified, Casolaro turned to law enforcement to ask about Nichols. He learned that Nichols was indeed CIA, at least to some degree. The nature and extent of his connections were classified, so the FBI agent and federal prosecutor who had investigated Nichols in the past didn't have access to the information. The prosecutor told Casolaro that Nichols had twice applied for Top Echelon status with the CIA. The status was granted only to the agency's highest-level informants. So Casolaro knew that Nichols had been a snitch—information that could get Nichols killed if his mobster friends found out.

The Last Circle described how Danny Casolaro was found dead in a motel room in Martinsburg, West Virginia, in August of 1991. He'd spent the preceding weeks in close contact with Nichols and had warned his brother that if something happened to him it wouldn't be an "accident." Both of Casolaro's wrists were mutilated by a dozen deep gashes—wounds that seemed inconsistent with suicide. There was a shoelace around his neck and a razor blade in the bathtub, along with a can of Old Milwaukee. On a side table there was a suicide note: "I know deep down inside that God will let me in."

Sam read *The Last Circle* with saucer eyes. The mystery of the death of Danny Casolaro had caused a media sensation at the time. "The Man Who Knew Too Much?" *Time* magazine asked. Features speculating on the circumstances appeared in *Vanity Fair*, the *Washington Post*, and the *Village Voice*. Lou Dobbs of CNN became obsessed with the story. HBO began to develop a television series. *Spy* magazine ran a three-part story strongly implying that Nichols had gotten away with the murder. The author of *The Last Circle* made it clear that Nichols was an extremely dangerous and violent man.

Dawn rose at the Trump house. Sam was enthralled. Had Casolaro committed suicide? Had he been "suicided"? Had he staged his suicide to look like a murder to posthumously justify his conspiratorial beliefs? Robert Booth Nichols had never been charged, despite obvious suspicions. Indeed, Nichols had never been charged with any crime, despite decades of apparent illegal conduct as an arms dealer and an international hit man engaged in shadowy financial activity. This was proof, Sam believed, that Nichols was connected to the CIA—and the Octopus. Sam decided he had to meet Nichols. Sam had to see the Zapruder film and judge its authenticity with his own eyes.

But there was another reason to seek out Nichols—one with a direct and urgent application to Bayou. Casolaro and the author of *The Last Circle* hadn't grasped the significance of the story they were chasing. With his devious turn of mind Sam had seen a way to use PROMIS to front-run the market trading stock. The computer program was tracking the movement of money inside banks all over the world. It was inside the Federal Reserve. It was inside the leading financial institutions. And none of them knew it. If Sam could get PROMIS, he realized, he'd be able to watch money transfers in real time. He'd be able to watch how the Fed secretly surged money in and out of the market. By integrating the program into his trading system, Sam wouldn't have inside information: He'd have signals intelligence. He would be a one-man National Security Agency. He'd be ahead of the market by minutes, hours, even days. He'd be able to actually do what he had long claimed Forward Propagation did. He would be able to see the future.

"A lightbulb went off in my head," Sam recalled. "The PROMIS software was the answer to everything I'd suspected about the markets. I'd seen how the markets were manipulated after the crash of 1987. But I didn't know how they did it—how the money actually flowed into the market. If I had PROMIS I could track the movement of money. I could see how the Fed operated. If money was going into semiconductors, then I could get there ahead of the market. The same for consumer goods, or oil and gas. I would be at the flux point. I would be able to see the volume going up before the stock moved. If I could get this tool, I knew I could kill it. I would slay the market. I was going to make so much money it wouldn't even be fun. It would be the ultimate inside trade."

Turning off his computer and retiring to bed, Sam resolved to track down Nichols and get PROMIS. The Octopus was dangerous, he could see. Danny Casolaro had been murdered because he threatened the cabal, Sam believed. Nichols was involved somehow. He was clearly a confidence man of some kind and extremely dangerous. But Sam was not going to be cowed. He would take the risk. He had balls—big balls, balls of steel.

CHAPTER ELEVEN

The Shadow Market

The Dorchester Hotel in central London was the setting for Sam Israel's first encounter with Robert Booth Nichols. Jack O'Halloran had made the arrangements. The pretext was to get Nichols's assistance in obtaining the CIA's latest technology on fingerprint recognition for the identity card KYCOS was developing. For half a million dollars in cash, Jack O'Halloran had told Sam, Nichols could arrange for a briefcase to be left on Bayou's doorstep containing top-secret biometric software—no questions asked. But Sam had insisted on a face-to-face meeting. Israel hadn't told O'Halloran that the real purpose was to get PROMIS from Nichols. It emerged that Nichols had had unsuccessful dealings with O'Halloran in the past, so he'd insisted on a fee of $25,000 to be paid up front. Sam didn't know it, but as he arrived in London he was about to step into a different dimension in the time/space continuum, an irreality filled with deception, double-dealing, and cascading delusions.

At the Dorchester, half a dozen men gathered around a long glass table in the lobby. Two engineers had been flown in from Prague by KYCOS to consult on the technical aspects of the fingerprint ID system. Jack O'Halloran was present, along with a young Irishman who worked for him. Sam represented the money, as the largest investor in the company. When Nichols arrived, O'Halloran greeted him as an old friend. Introductions were made. Sam took a seat on the couch at the end of the table next to the mysterious character.

In person, Nichols was much as Sam had imagined—only more so. To Sam, Nichols exuded an air of mystery and menace. As Nichols sat, Sam caught a glimpse of the gun Nichols was carrying in a shoulder holster—a very unusual occurrence in London, where arms are closely regulated. Nichols was six-three, more than two hundred pounds. He was now sixty years old, tall, pale, with a paunch and the deep, gravelly voice of a lifelong chain-smoker. The world-weariness of decades living as a real-world Jason Bourne was evident in the lines around his eyes, in his soft jowls, and in his guarded manner. He was dressed in a blue suit—not shabby but not well tailored, with frayed cuffs. "Clark Gable with big ears" was how Nichols had been described in *The Last Circle*. The depiction was accurate, Israel thought, though it didn't capture the air of danger surrounding the CIA operative. It seemed to Sam that under the wan complexion and cagey but correct manner Nichols revealed nothing—except the fact that he was obviously capable of extreme violence.

As the meeting convened, Nichols talked in general terms about how CIA computer systems could be applied to thumbprint identification. It was evident to all present that Nichols was far from tech-savvy. The young Czech programmers, sensing Nichols's lack of sophistication regarding computers, began to list the challenges. Nichols assured the group that he knew the right people in the intelligence community to talk to.

As the engineers talked about modalities, Israel leaned over to whisper in Nichols's ear. "I need to talk to you privately," Sam said.

"Aren't you part of this group?" Nichols asked.

"This has nothing to do with them," Israel said. "I'm here to see you about something different."

"What is it?"

"PROMIS," Israel said. "The computer program."

Nichols looked surprised—but he nodded in acknowledgment. He whispered that he would meet Israel outside. Nichols told Sam to wait five minutes and then excuse himself. Claiming he had another appointment, Nichols took his leave. Following instructions exactly, five minutes later Sam exited the Dorchester through the front door and turned left. On Park Lane, he spotted Nichols waiting in a cab. Sam got in. Nichols was talking on his cell phone. He gestured that the call would take a minute. Israel noticed Nichols was holding a piece of paper with numbers in columns. Sam could hear the voice on the other end, but he couldn't understand what they were discussing. Nichols hung up. He quickly returned the piece of paper to his briefcase.

"Where are you staying?" Nichols asked.

"Claridge's," Israel said.

"We can talk there," Nichols said.

"I want PROMIS," Israel said, too impatient to wait to speak. "I know you're involved in the computer program. I know about you, and I want PROMIS."

Sam didn't mention reading *The Last Circle*. He wanted to create the impression that he had access to confidential, even classified, information.

"Why should I give it to you?" Nichols asked.

"I'll pay for it," Israel said. "I don't give a shit. I'll do whatever it takes."

"What do you want it for?"

"To trade with," Israel said. "I run a hedge fund. I'll be able to keep track of the market. I'll be able to watch how the Federal Reserve is moving money and trade ahead. Volume precedes price."

"Who are you?" Nichols asked.

"I run a fund called Bayou," Israel said. "I'm a trader."

"No, I mean who *are* you?" Nichols asked. "Are you affiliated with an intelligence agency? How long have you been on Wall Street? Who are your relatives? What are your ties?"

"I've got my own questions," Israel said. "I'm going to ask you some nasty questions."

"Go ahead," said Nichols.

"Did you kill Danny Casolaro?"

"No."

"That's a lie."

"I'm not going to lie to you," Nichols said. "I've killed people. But not Danny. You can ask me questions and I will tell you. Some things I can answer. Some I can't."

Nichols's cell phone rang. He took the call, speaking in a low voice to avoid Israel overhearing what he was saying. After Nichols hung up, another call came in, and he again talked in a hush. Israel was able to make out the words "payout" and "the program" but not the substance of the conversation. When Nichols hung up, Israel asked what he had been talking about. Nichols was reluctant to say. All he would reveal was that he was doing business with a prince from Saudi Arabia—business that involved a trading program. London traffic was at a standstill. Nichols's cell rang yet again. This time as Nichols spoke he opened his briefcase to retrieve the document he'd consulted earlier. Nichols scanned the page and swiftly closed the briefcase. For a split second Sam caught sight of the columns of numbers.

"What is that?" Israel asked.

"Nothing," Nichols said.

"Let me see it," Israel said.

Reluctantly, Nichols clicked open his briefcase and handed over the document. "It's a payout sheet," he said. "From a trading program."

Israel looked at the figures on the page. On the left were numbers arranged to show amounts of money invested—figures in the low millions. On the right side was a column displaying the profits made. The returns were astronomical. An investment of $5 million in the "trading program" became $20 million in a matter of days. There was no indication of what was being traded, or where. But the results were astounding.

"These are the returns?" Israel asked, incredulous.

"I'm doing this with the Saudis right now," Nichols said.

"What are you trading?"

"Bonds," Nichols said.

"What kind of bonds?" Sam asked.

"This is something that could benefit you greatly," Nichols replied. "But it is very difficult to get into this market. Nearly impossible."

"What market?"

"High-yield buy/sell trading programs," Nichols said. "The market is only open to the biggest players."

"So how do I get in?" Israel asked. "I know how to trade anything."

"Do you have one hundred million in cash?" Nichols asked.

It seemed to Israel that Nichols had tossed out the huge number as a way to brush him off. But Israel wasn't deterred. He leaned forward.

"I do," said Israel. "I've got one hundred million in cash."

"Do you have $150 million?" Nichols asked.

"Yes."

"Do you have two hundred million?"

"That's pushing it," Israel said.

"You should forget about PROMIS," Nichols said. "I know how to put your money to work. I know how to make you a lot of money."

Turning onto Brook Street in Mayfair, the taxi arrived at Claridge's. Passing through the revolving doors and entering the lobby, Sam and Nichols stepped into the quintessence of London sophistication and money: The art deco hotel was frequented by royalty, celebrities, and socialites taking tea under the massive Chihuly chandelier. The Israel family had stayed at Claridge's for generations, and Sam moved with ease and entitlement through the plush surroundings. Sam had taken a suite on the third floor. The elegantly appointed sitting room had a coffee table with matching stuffed chairs for the two men to hold their meeting. They ordered room service and got down to business. For the next three hours, Israel and Nichols got to know each other. Nichols asked Israel how he knew about PROMIS. Sam talked about the Israel family and his history as a Wall Street trader.

Israel described his trading system at Bayou. Forward Propagation enabled him to be correct 86 percent of the time, Sam said. Bayou's strategy was market neutral, so it didn't matter if prices went up or down. Sam said that the whole system revolved around the combination of his proprietary computer program and his years of experience as a trader. Nothing was written down, Sam said. Nichols was fascinated by Israel's talents, although it was evident that he wasn't knowledgeable about Wall Street and the complexities of running a hedge fund. Nichols said that Sam's skills as a trader would be invaluable to their efforts to get into the secret trading program.

"I then asked if I could ask him some questions," Sam recalled. "He said he would answer as honestly as he could. I went through his history with intelligence—Iran-Contra, his weapons-dealing background, the Cabazon reservation. I didn't mention *The Last Circle*. He was unaware that the book existed, it seemed. He looked impressed and uncomfortable with how much I knew about him. I wanted to convey to him that I also had sources of information so I wouldn't be at a disadvantage. It turned out that we knew people in common. My family had relationships with powerful people that he knew as well. Like Ferdinand Marcos and Clint Murchison, the Texas oilman who had doctored the Zapruder film. I figured out that we'd met once before, in Las Vegas when I was out there with Freddy Graber in the eighties. Bob had been working with Robert Maheu at the time, the guy who was Howard Hughes's right-hand man. Bob and I had a lot of commonality."

Nichols explained how the secret bond market functioned. The world Nichols described dwarfed the conspiracy theories evoked by Jack O'Halloran and by *The Last Circle*. According to Nichols the basic institutions of the modern world—the U.S. government, the Federal Reserve, the International Monetary Fund—were all a front. The reality—if Sam could handle the truth—was far darker and more dangerous than anything he could imagine.

"There is a secret government operating within the world's government," Nichols said to Sam. "They run the secret trading program—the high-yield market. Only a few chosen people participate in the program. The returns are staggering. The proceeds are used to fund black operations, wars, to pay off foreign governments. The proceeds are also used for good works in the Third World—to build hospitals, construct water treatment plants, cure diseases. It is the way that order is maintained in the world. The programs are top secret—highly, highly classified. Getting approved to trade in the market is extremely difficult. I don't know if I can do it. But I know people who can give you a shot at getting in."

Nichols said the Saudi prince he had been talking to in the taxi was trading medium-term notes—or MTNs. But Nichols said the Saudi was not paying him properly. All he was getting was a small finder's fee, not the proper commission he was supposed to be paid for facilitating entry to the market. Nichols said he was tired of being taken advantage of by his clients. He was more than a simple broker. He was a guide for the treacherous trek into the shadow market. Nichols said he had the ability to lead Sam into the labyrinth of what he called the "Upperworld."

"Bob told me how the market really worked," Sam recalled. "The Treasury bonds of the United States were supposedly created at the Federal Reserve. That was the public story. The bonds were issued at a discount—88 percent, say. The Fed then sold the bonds to their few select banks—primary dealers, they were called. Goldman Sachs, Deutsche Bank, Nomura, Union Bank of Switzerland, BNP Paribas. The largest financial institutions in the world had access to the pre-market for the Fed's notes. The prime dealers were given a discount to incentivize them to buy the notes. The rates varied but they usually got a discount of a couple of points. Their returns were basically guaranteed and riskless. The prime dealers were the insiders who got the sweetheart deal. The big banks then put the bonds on the market priced at 93, 94 percent, and those were bought up by the little shit-box dealers—TD Waterhouse, Ameritrade. The bonds were marked up 1 percent or more. That was when John Q. Public got to buy Federal Reserve notes—after the banks had taken their slice of the pie, at no risk.

"That was the known market. People think the Federal Reserve is run by the federal government. But it isn't. The Federal Reserve is a private company, owned by the banks. It's a club. That's why everything it does is so secret. Everything is behind closed doors. The public doesn't know who really runs the Fed—or who owns the Fed. Bob said that if you understand the powers behind the Federal Reserve, you can see who is really running the world. Money makes the world go round, after all. The reality, Bob said, is that the United States government is bankrupt. When Nixon took America off the gold standard in 1972 the shit hit the fan. There wasn't enough gold in the Federal Reserve to pay for all the dollars that had been issued by the government. So America just changed the system. That was what created the so-called fiat currency. The American dollar isn't worth the paper it's printed on.

"I knew Bob was right. I'm never wrong about this kind of thing. This was the stuff I knew—the stuff I had been taught by the traders in Freddy's office in the eighties, the real Masters of the Universe. I'd grown up watching how things were manipulated. This was where the secret bond market came in, Bob said. To keep the system solvent the Fed secretly issued notes at a huge discount—under fifty cents on the dollar. The notes were then traded in the shadow market. The major banks had special departments that did this kind of trading. The margins were huge. The sums were huge. Billions upon billions. But the public wasn't told about the market because if it became known how flimsy the global economic system really is, there would be a huge panic.

"Bob said there was a catch. If you traded into this market, you weren't allowed to keep all the profits. If I managed to get into the market—which was a big if—Bob said I would be able to keep a cut. Maybe 20 percent. Maybe 10 percent. It depended on the structure of the deal. The rest would go to charities approved by the ruling families. The money would be spent curing AIDS in Africa or building water treatment plants in Pakistan. That was how the system worked—how the world financial system really functioned.

"I didn't understand everything Bob said at first. But the core of what he was saying made sense to me. I knew the Fed was fixing the stock market. All the 'quantitative easing' the Fed did was just to drive up the S&P to keep the little people happy and not asking difficult questions. I told Bob I wanted to learn more. If what Bob was saying was true, the implications for me were amazing. If I was going to get into the shadow market, I knew that I was going to have to stay in London to make the trades. Bob said he was going to introduce me to his colleagues the next day. They were brokers in the market who could explain the charitable part of the business themselves.

"Bob said he was going to stick close to me. From that day forward, we were together constantly. He kept me away from other people as much as he could. He was my handler. That was his word for it. From then on he was going to handle me."

AS A MASTER OF DELUSION, Sam had found a kindred spirit. Nichols told lies with such authority and frequency it was hard to tell if he knew he was lying at all. Nichols had told Sam to lie to Jack O'Halloran the next morning about their meeting and the secret bond market, for instance; Nichols didn't want O'Halloran interfering with their new project. As part of the project of developing *Mosaic* into a movie, O'Halloran had arranged a meeting with film producers in London. Israel went along with O'Halloran in the morning, as promised, but he was itching to leave. Sam liked Jack and he enjoyed *Mosaic* and thought it would make a fine movie. But all Sam could think about was the high-yield investments—the existence of which he had to keep hidden from his friend.

"From the very beginning Bob swore me to secrecy," Sam said. "Bob didn't want Jack knowing about the secret bond market. He didn't want Jack to know that we had met privately. Bob wanted to keep me away from Jack. He told Jack he was looking into the fingerprint technology. He would get back to him. But he told me he wasn't going to do anything about it. Bob wanted to convince Jack that I wasn't doing any business with him. Nothing could have been further from the truth. But Bob was a facile liar. He lied by misdirection. He lied by omission. He was an accomplished bullshit artist."

Before Sam's second meeting with Nichols, Israel and O'Halloran had lunch at Claridge's. Across the lobby, the movie star Tom Hanks and his wife, the actress and producer Rita Wilson, were checking in. Though he wasn't a great celebrity buff, Israel instantly recognized Hanks. So did O'Halloran. To Sam's amazement, O'Halloran walked across the lobby and shook hands with Hanks. Sam followed and was introduced to Hanks and Wilson. "Jack had been in *Dragnet* with Hanks," Israel said. "They knew each other well. It was great. Instead of me being a fan with nothing to say, standing in the lobby staring at a movie star, there I was shaking his hand, saying hello. They came over to our table and had lunch with us. Jack was fun in that way. I liked being around him."

Israel departed after lunch. Nichols had told Sam to meet him at the Grosvenor Park Hotel, another luxury hotel a few blocks away on Park Lane. On the seventh floor of the Grosvenor was the Royal Club Lounge, a private business center for the hotel's guests. It was a little-known fact that Gold and Platinum memberships could be purchased for a nominal sum by anyone, enabling nonguests to conduct business in the lounge at an extremely low cost. Hostesses were at the reception desk twenty-four hours a day, and members enjoyed free refreshments and newspapers and magazines. Flat-screen televisions showed cable news and financial networks. The space was quiet, clean, centrally located—the perfect meeting location for a traveling executive. It was also the perfect front for a grifter looking for a cheap place to give the impression of respectability.

Nichols introduced John Cassidy and Nigel Finch, men he claimed were veteran intelligence operatives. Cassidy and Finch were key to gaining entrée to the bond market, Nichols said. According to Nichols, Cassidy was a former CIA station chief in Hong Kong and had been a pilot for Air America during the Vietnam War. He was a descendant of Butch Cassidy, the notorious frontier outlaw of the Wild West. Nichols said that Cassidy belonged to a faction of intelligence operatives who had been close to Ronald Reagan and the first Bush administration. But in the early nineties Cassidy had fallen out of favor with the incoming faction attached to the Clinton administration. The new faction had vanquished the previous faction, sparking a rivalry that was still going on—a violent fight for supremacy inside the secret market. As a result, Cassidy had been forced into exile.

"Bob didn't really trust Cassidy," Israel said. "But he said Cassidy was the way to get into the market. Bob said Cassidy had put a lot of people into the high-yield bonds. Before the meeting Bob had warned me that Cassidy was very volatile and dangerous. Cassidy had been injured in a helicopter crash in Cambodia. I knew he'd been disfigured. Bob told me to be careful, to not look at him too much. But he was truly freaky looking. He had tattooed eyebrows. He limped badly. He was short. His teeth were fucked up. He was one scary-looking dude. He was hard not to stare at."

By contrast, Finch was a suave Englishman with a refined accent. According to Nichols, Finch was a veteran of MI6, the British secret intelligence operation. Finch also ran an antiques store and specialized in the restoration of metalwork and sculpture. A fellow of the Royal Society of Arts, Finch did work for royalty as well as major museums and dealers. Nichols joked about Finch's breeding and how unlikely it was for such a man to be involved in the rough-and-tumble of doing business with "the boys."

The four men took their seats in a private conference room. Half a dozen chairs were arranged around a small table with a window over Hyde Park. The meeting could have been taking place in any boardroom—such was the setting's resemblance to a mise-en-scène of a multi-billion-dollar transaction. But the conference room was complimentary, the coffee and pastries provided by the hotel, the air of high finance an optical illusion.

"We have a number of items on the agenda today," Nichols said, taking up the role as chair. "We are going to deal with the issue of the bonds. Plus, Sam wants to acquire the computer program PROMIS."

But the subject of the CIA's covert "trapdoor" digital surveillance system wasn't raised again. Sam had lost interest in it anyway. The shadow market was what he wanted to hear about. Nichols explained that the three men had squired wealthy people into the trades for years. But all they had received was broker commissions. They hadn't been able to trade on their own account. They hadn't been able to reap the billion-dollar benefits. Now, at long last, it was going to be different. With Sam's $150 million, they would have the chance to get into the game as principals. They would form their own faction. The group would consist of Sam, Nichols, Cassidy, and Finch. Making the trades would not be easy—far from it. The mission, should Sam choose to accept it, was nearly impossible. Just attempting to enter the shadow market meant that Sam risked being killed at any moment by a rival faction. Sam nodded solemnly.

The mechanics of the bonds were discussed. Nichols explained that investing in the high-yield market was risk free. Bayou's millions would be placed in a "nondepletion account." It would be a joint account in Sam's name, along with that of a designated approved charity. But no one would be able to access the money other than Israel. The only purpose for the cash was to provide capital to leverage the trades. It could be used only as collateral for the securities traded in the shadow market. If the trade didn't happen for any reason, Sam wouldn't lose a penny.

Nichols explained that Cassidy and Finch operated an organization called the Humanitarian Coalition. The charity was a necessary part of the structure. The Humanitarian Coalition was an approved charity, registered with the appropriate British authorities, tax exempt, and ready to distribute the hundreds of millions it would reap as a result of the trading program. The money would be used to cure AIDS, the men told Sam. Cassidy and Finch showed Israel a zinc-based mineral supplement they had developed. The liquid had been proven to drastically reduce levels of HIV, they said. The charitable donations from the bond market would be used to distribute the elixir in sub-Saharan Africa.

In a matter of minutes, Sam had gone from contemplating becoming a billionaire to getting killed for doing so and then on to the prospect of curing AIDS. The conversation was preposterous. What qualified Cassidy and Finch to cure AIDS? Wouldn't it have made the news? Wouldn't the Nobel Prize committee have noticed the breakthrough? Nichols and his colleagues were straight-faced, matter-of-fact. It was as if the leaps in logic they invited Sam to take made perfect sense. The HIV medicine wasn't available because pharmaceutical companies were making a lot of money selling antiretroviral drugs and were protected by powerful and violent factions inside the American government. The suppression of the cure was evidence of the ruthlessness of the forces they confronted.

Israel inspected the medicine with interest. The three men watched him expectantly. Israel could admit to the insanity of the proposition and depart, returning to Bayou and the Problem. Or he could suspend his disbelief and consider the possibility that Nichols was telling the truth—in fact, the Truth. Given the dysfunction and despair of the hedge fund, there really was no choice. Sam's family had always been heavily involved in charitable work; his mother's life had been devoted to philanthropy. The idea of making money and rescuing Bayou excited Israel. So did the prospect of helping so many people at the same time. The trio told Sam that the zinc compound also enhanced sexual appetite and performance. Sam took three drops of the magic medicine and grinned.

"Millions of lives could be saved," Nichols said.

Israel felt Cassidy staring at him. The look was long and hard and searching. Israel began to feel uncomfortable. Sam turned to him, but Cassidy didn't avert his eyes.

"Can I help you with something?" Israel asked.

Cassidy kept his gaze steady. Nichols was visibly agitated.

"Do you have a problem with me?" Israel asked.

"I know you," Cassidy said.

"I don't think so," Israel replied.

"I'm sure I know you from somewhere," Cassidy insisted, still staring.

"Maybe you're seeing me through the eyes of Butch Cassidy," Israel joked.

Cassidy didn't laugh. Nor did Nichols. Cassidy left abruptly. Once he was gone, Nichols told Sam to mind his manners. But Sam said he wasn't going to take crap from a psycho. After a few minutes Cassidy returned.

"I knew it," Cassidy said, rejoining them at the table. "You're Mossad."

Israel laughed at the notion that he worked for the Israeli intelligence agency. "You're out of your *cabeza*," Israel said, using the Spanish word for "head."

"He's Mossad," Cassidy repeated.

"It isn't true," Nichols said calmly. "I have vetted him thoroughly."

Cassidy sneered. "Have you had any recent heart trouble?" he asked Israel. "Have you had a heart attack, or a bypass, or had a pacemaker put in?"

Israel was flabbergasted. He had told no one about his heart troubles. *No one.* There was no way some stranger in London could know about Israel's condition. Not unless he had access to confidential information—the kind of secrets a spook would be able to obtain.

Cassidy watched Israel's speechless reaction. "I thought so," he said. Cassidy turned to Nichols and Finch. "He's Mossad," he said.

Israel looked around the room, disbelief turning to anger. "I'm telling you, I'm not Mossad," he said. "I am who I say I am. I'm a trader. I run a hedge fund called Bayou. You can look it up."

"I did look you up," Cassidy said. "I did a background check. You're on something called the Intellectual Threat to State list. The CIA poisoned you and made it look like it was heart failure. There are people who want to kill you. You're either very lucky or you're in great shape."

Israel started to panic. The Intellectual Threat to State list? Mossad? Could he have already captured the attention of the dark forces of the Octopus? Was Sam caught up in the same vortex that had killed Danny Casolaro? The doctors hadn't been able to explain the cause of his rare heart condition. Was this the reason he had nearly died?

Cassidy reassured Israel. There was no need to be afraid. Not anymore. Cassidy could arrange to have Sam's name taken off the Intellectual Threat to State list. Sam was now under the protection of Robert Booth Nichols, a highly skilled assassin. The important thing was to keep Sam alive so they could proceed with the high-yield program. Israel was now convinced he was in the presence of truly powerful men. To what end, good or evil, he wasn't sure. But Sam wasn't going to let fear stop him.

BACK IN HIS SUITE at Claridge's, Israel called Marino at the Bayou offices in Connecticut and excitedly said he had found the answer to their Problem. Sam wanted Marino to come to London immediately. Sam said he couldn't talk over the telephone. The news he had was too explosive. The line might be tapped. Marino was skeptical, but he flew to London on the red-eye. Over lunch, Sam gave Marino a thumbnail sketch of Nichols's background—the years as a CIA hit man, his connections to the NSA, the shadow market.

"It sounded fantastic to me," Marino said. "If what Sam was saying was real, I was going to be a billionaire. I was excited—if it was true."

At the Royal Club in the Grosvenor Hotel that afternoon, Nichols showed Marino a chart illustrating the returns on an investment of $150 million. Even if Bayou kept only a fraction of the windfall, the profits were amazing. Marino stared at the numbers with incomprehension. Nichols said that Bayou would receive $6.25 billion in the first year alone. The math made no sense to Marino. He couldn't follow the logic of Nichols's presentation. But Sam was convinced, so Marino kept listening and hoping. Sam was the trader, so perhaps there was something Marino was missing.

"The market is unknown, and only a few people are able to get in," Nichols said.

Nichols said it was classified top secret. Both Israel and Marino had to sign nondisclosure documents that specified thirty years in prison as the punishment for revealing the existence of the market. The agreement required absolute confidentiality. It failed to specify who would imprison the men—or where they would be detained—in the event that they talked. Perhaps the Octopus had a secret facility somewhere, along the lines of Guantánamo Bay.

"There are a lot of people pretending to have access to the program," Nichols said. "I can help you through the process. I am one of the facilitators that can bring the right people to the table. I can make sure you aren't cheated. There are a lot of cons out there that try to copy these trades. They are frauds. They aren't real. I can get you into the real market."

"I believe in you, Bob," Israel said.

"This market is extremely dangerous," Nichols said. "You can get killed trying to get in."

"I don't care," Sam said.

"I can protect you," Nichols said.

"I know you're a stone-cold killer," Israel said to Nichols. "But if you steal $150 million from me, I swear I will kill you."

"That is absolutely fair," Nichols said.

Israel and Marino left the meeting and rode the elevator down in silence. Marino's mind was spinning.

"What do you think?" Sam asked.

"Why would rich people do this?" Marino asked, sensibly. "Why would they let you make so much money?"

"Because they know the world is bankrupt," Sam said. "If they don't keep the financial wheel going it will come off the tracks. There will be revolutions all over the world. The masses will take over. By doing this they're able to control what is happening and to keep their status as the superwealthy."

Marino could see Sam's point, intellectually. What was really behind the Federal Reserve, after all? There was no gold standard, so the Fed didn't have gold to pay for all the paper money it printed. If all of the liabilities of the U.S. government were taken into account— the federal debt, Social Security, Medicare—the country was indeed bankrupt by accounting standards. The American dollar, the global economy, all of it could be seen as one vast Ponzi scheme. But still: It sounded too good to be true. What was the real proof that the market existed? What if it was all a con?

"So?" Sam asked.

"You want me to make a judgment call about people I just met?" Marino said impatiently. "I have done no due diligence on them. I don't know who they are."

The pair walked out the rear of the Grosvenor and turned toward Claridge's.

"I believe Bob," Israel said. "I want to pursue this."

"I don't know if it is real or not," Marino said. "I do know if it is real, then you are talking about a conspiracy that's bigger than the assassination of JFK."

"We have to do it," Sam said, stopping on the sidewalk.

Marino stopped as well.

"I can't trade my way out of the mess," said Sam, with a heavy sigh. "I just can't."

Marino stared at Israel in disbelief.

"Thanks for telling me that now," Marino said. "What choice are you giving me?"

Sam didn't reply.

"If you pursue this, make sure you keep the money in Bayou's name at all times," Marino said. "Do not put it in anyone else's name. You need to stay here and follow it all."

"I will," Israel vowed.

"I can't stop you," Marino said. "If you're going to try, just make sure you keep the money in an account in Bayou's name."

Israel and Marino walked the half-dozen blocks to Claridge's without exchanging another word. Marino felt uneasy. Nichols's tale was hard to believe. But what if Nichols was telling the truth? What if the Problem really could be solved so quickly? Israel and Marino had traveled so far together running Bayou. They'd reached a distant land only they knew existed. Perhaps the shadow market really did exist, Marino thought. Perhaps they could be saved. It was possible— maybe.

ON APRIL 14, 2004, Bayou Funds wired $150,999,847.42 to an account at Barclays Bank in London. Under the terms of the Beneficial Stewardship Agreement Israel had signed, he was now called the "Benefactor." Sam believed he'd read the terms carefully. Lawyers had notarized the documents, providing a veneer of legitimacy. "The parties agree that the financial return to the Benefactor shall be one hundred percent (100%) paid every ten days," it was stated.

But the precautions he'd taken were woefully inadequate. It turned out that the money wasn't in an account in Sam's name, as he'd solemnly promised Marino. More than $150 million was now deposited in the account of the Humanitarian Coalition. It was an ominous beginning. The saving grace, it appeared, was the fact that the money was in a "nondepletion" account. It meant Israel's signature was required for any withdrawals or transfers—unless Nichols or his cronies were sly enough to convince a clerk at Barclays to let the Humanitarian Coalition make a withdrawal. Sam was blissfully ignorant of the nature of the risk he was taking. He had confidence in his own vigilance and instincts.

"We went out for a celebratory dinner," Sam recalled. "Bob said we were now in business together—we were partners. Bob took me to the Ritz, a private gaming club he belonged to. A doorman in a red uniform with a top hat opened the door to the taxi when we pulled up. The stairs down to the casino were carpeted red with ornate brass rails. The decor was ornate but not ostentatious—it was a beautiful and impressive place. The woman at the desk knew Bob, and it was clear that he was close to the owners. Bob introduced me as a big financier from America who was going to join the Ritz. We walked down a hallway to a heavy brass door and entered one of the prettiest dining rooms I'd ever seen, and I'd seen a lot as a kid. There were two large crystal chandeliers, and the ceiling was painted like the Sistine Chapel. The chairs were plush fabric and decorated with flowers and silver trim. First class all the way. Bob told the maître d' that he expected me to receive the same care he got. We sat at a small table in front of a fireplace and ordered a good bottle of wine—the place had a superior wine list.

"I asked Bob what he had meant when he told me that nothing is the way it seems—to expand on what we'd discussed in my room at Claridge's. He made a huge deal about me being able to keep a secret. I said that we were in business together so we had to trust each other. I'd put up a huge amount of money and that showed how much I trusted him. He should have the same confidence in me."

"The government has been keeping things from the public for years," Nichols said. "The people you think are running things—politicians, bankers, diplomats—are not even halfway up the food chain."

"What are you talking about?" Sam asked. "The Illuminati? The Bilderberg Group?"

"What do you know about these things?" Nichols asked.

"I've heard that there are five families that run the world," Sam replied.

"Thirteen," said Nichols. "There are thirteen families that are in charge of the planet. The families are famous, but no one outside the inner circle really understands what they do. The De Beers, the Mai

Wahs from China, the Rothschilds. They are 'the boys.' The boys are the ones with the gold to back the Federal Reserve—the ones who really own the Fed. The structure is as old as time. Even the Americans who are the most wealthy are at best second- or third-tier players. It is the only way to control the planet. If humanity is left to its own devices there will be chaos. There are reasons for everything. There is order in what seems like madness. Presidents are appointed by the families. Wars are sanctioned."

"Bob said the Fed was nothing but a front," Israel recalled. "That was what the trading program was for. I told Bob that I was a Rothschild, on my mother's side of the family. Not the ones involved in the market. Those Rothschilds were solvent, like the other families—they had trillions of dollars' worth of gold on reserve. They issued the debt, backed the debt, and authorized the Fed to print money.

"As we drank, Bob started to tell me what happened when a head of state didn't do what he was told. Kennedy was killed because of his stance on Vietnam. After the Cuban missile crisis, Kennedy and Khrushchev met secretly and decided to de-escalate the cold war. The cold war was big business. There were a lot of people making a lot of money out of the arms trade. Bob told me about the Kennedy film— the one I'd read about in *The Last Circle*. He said it had been given to him for his own protection. I asked if I could see it and he said no—it was too dangerous.

"The notion that we're all controlled runs against what we've been taught and what we believe about how we live our lives. Believing that presidents are the pawns of the financiers seems like a stretch. But even FDR knew that the 'financial element' has controlled the United States since the days of Stonewall Jackson. I started to take notes as

Bob talked. He told me about a book called *Tragedy and Hope: A History of the World in Our Time*, by a professor named Carroll Quigley. The book showed how there is an Anglophile network that operates the same way the radical right wing claimed that communists acted. Basically as a conspiracy. But this group is secret. It's a cabal of global financiers who have created a world system of private financial control. There are secret agreements that are made at private meetings. The central banks of different countries control treasury loans and exchange rates to dominate the political system."

ISRAEL AND NICHOLS negotiated a side agreement granting the CIA asset 5 percent of the profits—a sum that promised to be hundreds of millions. To begin trading, all that remained was for Sam to meet the designated trader who had been assigned to the newly minted faction. Emily Hardwick was five-four, blond, in her early forties. Nichols said she was expert in the programs. The meeting was in the Royal Club Lounge at the Grosvenor—Nichols's base of operations. Hardwick spoke with an upper-class English accent and dressed in conservative business attire. But she had the blotched face and scratchy voice of a heavy drinker. Israel was told that her problems with alcohol had forced her to take a leave of absence from the market. She was back now, though, and she would be trading Sam's money. To Israel it was evident that she was well versed in the bonds. Hardwick explained her ground rules. She didn't want her real name disclosed under any circumstances. She wouldn't allow any photographs of her to be taken. Secrecy was paramount.

At midnight, Israel, Nichols, and Hardwick went to the offices of Barclays Bank at 54 Lombard Street in London's financial district. Nichols accompanied Sam as bodyguard, minority partner, and handler. Despite the late hour, the trio had to pass through security. Upstairs, there was a large trading room, with thirty or forty desks. The room was empty and the computers were turned off. They walked through to another room in the back. This was the secret shadow-market trading room, with high ceilings and dark wood furniture and the formal decorations of a boardroom. On one wall there was a bank of screens. Bonds were stacked on a desk—embossed and sealed and stamped documents with the U.S. Federal Reserve mark. Israel paged through the financial instruments. They appeared legitimate. Nichols pointed out the CUSIP numbers—the ten-digit security identification given to securities—and Sam concluded they were real.

"We were given a trading desk," Sam said. "There was a computer on the desk, showing how regular bonds were trading in the overnight markets. Then there was another computer showing where these other bonds were trading. Emily was a stand-alone trader. She'd been trading with the Fed for years. She was a secret squirrel. She didn't want to be known in any way. So Emily and I started to bid on the bonds. We were the only ones in the room, but I could see the other traders on the screen. The German bank Postbank was trading. HSBC. Mellon. There were sixteen or seventeen banks approved to do these trades. They were the night traders. Not because it was done at night—though it was. They were night traders because the business was invisible. No one on the outside could see what was going on. Emily introduced me online as a new night trader. I was trading for my own program—for my $150 million.

"It was like regular trading. There was a quote, a bid, an ask. The denominations ran up to billions. I was just a little guy in this market. But I was buying and selling. Prices were moving from forty-four points to fifty points. Because of the spreads there was lots of room to trade. Bob was with me in the room. He never left my side."

At dawn, trading ceased. Sam retired exhausted to his hotel room. He was pleased to be started on the new market. But he was impatient to see tangible results—actual profits that he could send back to Marino. The pace of night trading in the program bonds was slow. Trading took place only every third or fourth night. Sam wanted to hurry up, but Hardwick insisted on patience.

Under the agreement, Hardwick was required to give a weekly report on her trading activity. On April 29, one week after Hardwick began, she said that the profits from her trading program were $942 million. Israel listened to her with amazement—then joy. Sam was entitled to a third, after paying the Humanitarian Coalition and Hardwick. The sum meant that with the return of Bayou's $150 million from the Barclays account, Sam had $450 million. The money was more than enough to solve the Problem. Bayou was back in the black. Israel was ecstatic. The Problem was gone. The evil genie on his shoulder that had been taunting him for years had vanished!

"I knew no one would care about the fraud if I got the money back," Israel said. "This is America. No one cares how you make money, as long as you're making it. I knew no questions would be asked. As far as I was concerned, I was going to close Bayou and get the whole thing over with. There was the chance to make billions in this market. It was happening the way Bob said it would. I wasn't going to trade through Bayou anymore. I was going to do these trades on my own."

Eager to share the incredible good news, Israel called Marino. Bayou was saved, Sam shouted into the phone. The shadow market was real. Marino was skeptical initially. He didn't understand the details of the trade—how it worked, how the trades were cleared, how the money was transferred. But Israel was knowledgeable about trading and he was utterly convinced. Israel's enthusiasm was infectious. Marino could scarcely believe this turn of events. They could shut Bayou down and end the nightmare. In the meantime, the pair agreed that Sam should stay in London to see that the trades were completed and he received the money he was due.

"Sam said we were going to be wealthy beyond our wildest imaginations," Marino recalled. "We would start with one hundred million in cash each. Sam's attitude was very much 'I told you so,' mixed with giddiness. I became giddy too. I wanted to believe him so much. I went out and celebrated with a lady friend. We went to the Post House in Manhattan for steak. I bought drinks for people I knew at the bar. I bought cigars. I easily spent a thousand dollars on dinner that night."

Days passed. Hardwick failed to deliver the funds. Then she disappeared. Nichols and Cassidy and Finch were infuriated—or feigned being infuriated. Hardwick was ripping them off, the trio told Sam. She was making fantastic sums using the money in the Barclays account as collateral, they said, but she was refusing to share the proceeds.

Cassidy sent a sternly worded letter of notice to Hardwick detailing her breaches of contract. "You are hereby given FORMAL NOTICE to produce a detailed accounting of all transactions, including all private placement buy/sell transactions," Cassidy wrote. But there was no reply. The sense of elation Israel had felt began to dissipate. By this time, according to Israel's calculations, Hardwick had made billions. Cassidy told Sam that Hardwick had disappeared because she had a "woman's problem," namely a hysterectomy. Israel believed she had relapsed and was drinking again. There was no explanation for the disappearance of the money she had supposedly made. Sam was crushed. He had no choice but to call Marino and share the devastating news.

"When he said the trade hadn't worked out, I was so disappointed and confused I became inconsolable," Marino said. "He wouldn't tell me the details on the phone. He just said that the woman who was doing the trade had gone nuts. I never got the story straight—why she went nuts, why the trade was reversed, what was the next step."

Sam was stuck. But Nichols wasn't going to give up without a fight—not with Bayou's $150 million still sitting in an account in London. Nichols told Sam they could still trade in the secret market. With Hardwick out of the picture, Nichols suggested that Israel could do the trades by himself. The trading he'd done earlier had been under Hardwick's authority. But Nichols believed that Sam could qualify to become the designated trader for their faction. Sam took the bait. He'd spent enough time studying the shadow market to know how it functioned. He'd made trades alongside Hardwick. He figured he could trade anything.

"So I stepped into her place as a trader," Israel said. "I started to become the man—or I tried to. I knew it could be a fraud. I kept looking around at the trading room. It was a crème de la crème place—a real trading floor, not some bucket shop."

Because of the vagaries of the high-yield market, there were only two other active traders the night Sam started to trade on his own. One was in Germany, the other in France. Israel spoke to them on the phone as they made the market on the bonds. But they didn't exchange names—or at least real names. In the business with no name, no one used a real name. It was too dangerous. Code names were used instead.

"I called myself Daedalus," Israel said. "From the Greek legend. Daedalus was the father of Icarus—he made the wings for his son. I thought the name fit. I was flying too close to the sun. I knew there was a good chance my wings would melt."

CHAPTER TWELVE

The Big Lie

C onfidence men are not thieves, at least not in the conventional
meaning of the word. The true con man practices an art, a mixture of improvisational theater, mind control, and mimetic misrep-
resentation. His most basic insight into the human condition is that
it is impossible to con an honest man. It is the larceny lurking in the
soul of his victim that he must prey upon. This was true of Sam Israel,
who understood the irrational expectations of Bayou's investors and
satisfied them to perfection. So was it true for Robert Booth Nichols.
The confidence man offers a deal that is too good to be true and
makes the mark believe it to be the truth—the urgent, lucrative, top-
secret truth. The sophisticated long-con artist sets out in the manner

of a novelist, creating an entire universe for his mark—or Babbitt, as the victim is called in the business. The Savage. The Fool.

The modern American confidence game was created in the 1890s in frontier saloons and riverboats by grifters with names like Limehouse Chappie and the High Ass Kid. Their scams revolved around gambling on fixed horse races and prizefights—cons known as the Rag and the Wire. The con unfolded in a choreographed series of steps: telling the tale, putting the mark on the send, taking off the touch, the blow-off, putting in the fix. The Babbitt usually came from a wealthy family. Or he was a self-made man with little formal education. He had outsized opinions of his accomplishments and intelligence—as well as his facility for making money. The con artist hung out in the best hotels and bars looking to befriend a high–net worth individual with enough money to make the long con worthwhile. The best Babbitts considered themselves visionaries, even geniuses—the type who might run a hedge fund fraud.

It may seem as if only a fool could fall for a pantomime like the shadow market, but the contrary was true: The smarter and more cunning the mark, the quicker he was able to see the potential riches. The more greed lurking in his soul, the more likely he was to suspend his disbelief in return for the promise of a fast fortune. "Very shortly the victim's feet are quite off the ground," David W. Maurer wrote in his 1940s classic *The Big Con*. "He is living in a play-world which he cannot distinguish from the real world. He is living in a fantastic, grotesque world which resembles the real one so closely he cannot distinguish the difference. He is the victim of a confidence game."

Such was the fate that seemed to have befallen Samuel Israel III. The con man was being conned. It was the Hollywood-worthy twist of the tale. Sam's years of running his own long con had evidently made him extremely susceptible to being conned. The son of privilege, Sam truly did consider himself to be a talented trader: a natural, born to the business, hardened by years of experience on Wall Street. The inability to build his own hedge fund in an honest fashion had engendered in Sam a poor appreciation of the skill and diligence needed to become a true success—which in turn led him to believe that there were shortcuts available in life. Freddy Graber had taught Sam to treat the world like a ship of fools. Only the dim-witted lived by the straight and narrow. The smart set swapped inside information, ate caviar by the spoonful, and stashed their winnings in Swiss bank accounts. Sam had learned to play the game, because that was what it all was: a game—until you were being played yourself.

If Nichols and his circle were cast as con artists, the swirl of events surrounding Sam suddenly made sense. All of the elements of a classic con were present. Sam had been expertly roped into the secret market scam. Cassidy and Finch were able and experienced "shills"—bit players who populated the world of the con and provided texture and nuance to add credibility. The demand for secrecy was always part of the con. So was the dubious legality of what they were doing. Danger and intrigue and urgency created the hothouse atmosphere that separated the mark from his senses—and his money.

The "big store" was the setting for the con—the sound stage created for the performers to put on the show. Thus the private trading room at Barclays. Like the gambling parlor in the movie *The Sting*, or the trading room in Bayou's boathouse, it had the trappings of the real thing—flickering computer screens, security guards, oak-paneled walls. Sam did not know that at that time Barclays was in the process of moving its Lombard Street headquarters to new buildings in the

Canary Wharf section of London. Nichols and his crew could easily have slipped a night security guard a few pounds to look the other way. But there was no way to prove the suspicion—had Sam suspected.

Con men know which cities are "right"—where it is safe to function because the law is corrupt, or incompetent, or indifferent to their presence. For a white-collar criminal operating a high-yield scam there has long been no better city than London. As a global financial capital, London has always been the Wild West, a teeming metropolis populated by rich Europeans, Arabs, Asians, and South Americans unschooled in the black arts of international finance. These legions of the super-rich were drawn to London by an extraordinary loophole that allowed resident foreigners to pay tax only on income earned in the United Kingdom, effectively rendering money made in their homelands tax-free. It was a situation that perversely made the money-obsessed, tax-evading expatriates only more likely to fall for a con.

Then there was London's history. Capitalism was invented there—and so was its evil twin, financial fraud. When the first-ever securities were issued in London in 1694—Exchequer Bills devised to pay for the national debt run up by war—fraudulent forgeries began to appear immediately. The new profession of stock jobber found its counterpart in London's "alley men," well-dressed slicksters offering the timeless promise of fantastic profits.

By far the most important role of the long con was the star—the "inside man." As the master of ceremonies, the inside man "told the tale." He was the mark's handler and confidant. He had to hold the whole production together. In this part stood the once movie star–handsome Robert Booth Nichols. He'd sold Sam the idea of the shadow market and all of its associated conspiratorial counter-realities. From the first moment in the taxi outside the Dorchester, deftly teasing Sam with the payout sheet, Nichols had pulled Sam into his fantasy world. The fact that Sam was himself an accomplished con artist was unknown to Nichols. But the irony might not have shocked the NSA operative. Living a life of artifice made con men prime targets for other con men. The larceny, the greed, the belief in their own cunning—cons were perfect marks, a fact widely appreciated by the best con men.

The scam Nichols was working might be called the Big Lie. It was like the old-school cons, in essence, but with a postmodern twist. Instead of running a fixed horse race or stock market manipulation, Nichols appealed to Sam's deepest beliefs—and doubts. In an age of rampant distrust in government and social institutions, conspiracy theories have become an entire industry. Millions believe that powerful people control world events through devious machinations. The Illuminati, the Trilateral Commission, the Bilderberg Group—the list of groups who secretly run the world is virtually endless. Despite the Byzantine complexity of Nichols's tale, at its heart it was radically simple. Thirteen families control the world. There were no coincidences. Nothing was the way it seemed. The logic preyed on Sam's long experience on Wall Street. If Sam was sure of one thing and one thing only, it was that the world was constructed on a tissue of lies. Fortunes were built on lies. Wars were started with lies. Goldman Sachs, the Federal Reserve, they all lied and cheated—just as Sam lied and cheated.

"I kept asking myself if it was all a con," Israel said. "I was with Bob all the time. I saw everything that he saw. I knew how hard it was to keep up a fraud. It was extremely difficult. I could see that there were too many people involved in London. There were too many moving parts. He would get drunk and talk all night about the shadow market, but he never slipped up and made a mistake. I watched very carefully.

There was no way Bob could have constructed the whole thing. Bob was the real deal."

WHO WAS THE REAL Robert Booth Nichols? Was the man Sam was dealing with in London really the online conspiracy theory superstar, or an impostor who'd inhabited the role to defraud Israel? Claiming to be a CIA asset provided the perfect front for a con man: American intelligence agencies refuse to confirm or deny any association with their organizations. The policy has the perverse effect of creating a universe of impostors.

As the weeks passed, Nichols gradually narrated his life story to Sam. As they sat together in the Royal Club Lounge at the Grosvenor Hotel, played blackjack at the Ritz casino, or drank at the World's End or one of the other London pubs favored by Nichols, a self-portrait of the supersleuth emerged. In Sam's eyes, Nichols really was like Clint Eastwood in one of his spaghetti westerns: *Uomo senza nome*, the Man with No Name. "The boys" had battered, betrayed, and nearly killed Nichols on every continent of the earth for decades, Sam believed. The only reason Nichols was alive was that he kept the secrets of the world—like the existence of the shadow market.

The countless deceptions and myths that constituted Nichols's life made it impossible to distinguish between actual events and his own self-mythologizing—perhaps even for Nichols. He claimed he'd been apprenticed into a tiny elite of national security operatives who called themselves "the Chosen." The men were CIA and NSA operatives who carried out the covert policies of the United States—like the Phoenix assassination program in Cambodia. Nichols said he was a "facilitator"—spook-speak for jack-of-all-trades.

What could be established about Nichols's life story was limited, partly because of his dissembling, partly because of the veil of national security. Over the decades, he had left a footprint, however faint and open to multiple interpretations.* The son of a wealthy Los Angeles surgeon, Nichols had attended Hollywood Professional High in Los Angeles, a school specifically established to cater to movie stars. Nichols didn't become a professional actor like many of his classmates. But he did master the most American of all performing arts: self-invention.

By his early twenties, Nichols was a grifter in Hawaii, apprenticed to a vending-machine dealer associated with the Japanese organized crime group Yakuza. One evening at the Surfrider Hotel in Waikiki, a man who introduced himself as "Ken" asked Nichols if he'd be willing to pick up a woman sitting at the far end of the bar. Find out what she's doing, Ken said. Nichols's pay was $50. Ken said that he worked for the CIA. Nichols was soon going undercover for Ken regularly. It was easy for the young hustler: He created and discarded identities like a snake shedding its skin.

In 1978, a secret FBI report stated that Nichols was a professional confidence man—but with some undefined association with intelligence agencies. He lived in Los Angeles for three months of the year, spending the rest of the time traveling the world. The FBI said Nichols used a series of aliases: Robert Nelson, Robert Nioon, Robert Bert

---

* Extensive court testimony that remains under seal in federal court was obtained in the reporting of this book. A Freedom of Information search led to the release of formerly secret FBI reports on Nichols, though many pages were redacted. Scores of interviews with Nichols's associates were conducted. Law enforcement and federal prosecutors refused to comment on Nichols—refusing to even confirm his name or any association with the U.S. government.

Nichols. He also had code names: "Mongoose" was one, "Eel" was another. Nichols was licensed to carry a concealed weapon—a 9 mm Walther semiautomatic. He'd also been issued a license to manufacture the G-77 submachine gun.* According to the FBI, Nichols claimed he'd been sent to Switzerland for three years to be taught the secrets of high finance for intelligence agencies—the intricacies of how the CIA and NSA secretly funded black ops using billions of off-the-books dollars hidden in numbered Swiss accounts. The FBI report ended on an ominous note: "Nichols should be considered armed and dangerous."

By the mideighties Nichols was based in Zurich. He'd married Ellen Hopko, his third wife. He'd also acquired an undergraduate degree and a doctorate—both from a mail-order college in the United Kingdom. He had no visible means of support, but the list of homes he claimed as residences included a multi-million-dollar villa in the Italian resort of Acqui Terme and a chateau on the Côte d'Azur. He also had a flat on Half Moon Street in London's Mayfair District, and a house in the exclusive suburb of St. Lucia in Queensland, Australia. From these locales, Nichols claimed he controlled billions of dollars on behalf of the U.S. intelligence apparatus. It was in this role that he participated in covertly funding Nicaraguan rebels and Phalangist extremists in Lebanon—illegal ventures supported by extremist elements in the American military-industrial complex.

When the Iran-Contra scandal broke in 1986, Nichols claimed he'd been disowned by the CIA, like many others involved in Oliver North's dirty-tricks campaigns. Cut adrift, Nichols moved back to America and turned himself into the ultimate desperado: Hollywood screenwriter. *Acceptable Casualty* was the name of Nichols's first film

---

* The license was published in *The Last Circle*.

treatment. It depicts the HIV/AIDS plague as a genetically engineered bio-weapon deployed by rogue elements in the CIA to wipe out the homosexual population. *Decision of Conscience* involved a massive financial fraud, with the Soviets printing large amounts of counterfeit American money to destabilize the Federal Reserve.

The stories were based on real CIA operations, Nichols claimed. A master at inveigling meetings with important people, he was soon associating with legendary Hollywood lobbyist Jack Valenti and Howard Hughes's right-hand man (and former CIA operative) Robert Maheu. Frank Carlucci, former deputy director of the CIA and founder of the multi-billion-dollar investment firm the Carlyle Group, was another associate, Nichols claimed. Nichols held himself out as someone with access to sensitive information from the uppermost reaches of the government—"above the NSA," Nichols said.

Working on a secret investigation into links between organized crime and the MCA studio, the FBI watched in amazement as Nichols walked into a branch of the Union Bank in L.A. and opened an account, declaring he was expecting a wire transfer of $25 billion. The money was from a Swiss charitable organization, Nichols told the clerk. The funds never materialized. But what was he up to? Was he trying to scam the bank? Was he for real?

"Everyone we talked to in Hollywood thought Nichols was a CIA undercover hit man," FBI Special Agent Thomas Gates recalled. "In the entertainment business everyone was a name-dropper. But Nichols took it to a whole new level. He was a very convincing braggart. He was very astute. He also had a mean streak. Nichols alluded to his murder victims, but there were no bodies. He talked about disappearing people. But his stories were discombobulated. We talked to people he'd name-dropped from the White House. They all said Nichols was full of bullshit. They had maybe met him once. They didn't have dealings with him. It was all part of his con man persona. We finally subpoenaed all of his corporate records. There was no money in his company. We discovered that he was selling stock that was basically valueless."

By the early nineties, Nichols had managed to talk himself into the role of munitions expert advising the producers of the Steven Seagal film *Under Siege*. Nichols's credentials in weaponry were fictional, in all likelihood, making him the perfect foil for a fantasist like Seagal. Nichols turned up on the set carrying a primitive version of a satellite telephone—the first anyone had seen, so it wound up as a prop in the movie. As a lark, Nichols was given a tiny part, playing an NSA-like officer sitting in the Pentagon situation room as Tomahawk missiles closed in on Honolulu.

"What are we going to do?" a panicked general asked.

The camera panned to Nichols dressed in formal military regalia, looking like an alumnus of Hollywood High pretending to be a soldier.

"Approximately one million people will reach one thousand degrees Fahrenheit in less than a second," Nichols said. It was his only line.

"The secret spy shit Nichols talked about on the set was ridiculous," said a former Special Forces soldier who was actually a munitions expert and who also worked on the film. "He would say things like 'I can't tell you what I did, or else I will have to kill you.' He claimed he'd killed all these people. But none of his stories could be confirmed. Steven Seagal was swept up by Nichols. It was like Seagal was taking Nichols's stories and turning them into his own mythology—the martial arts, the tough-guy act, the connections to the underworld. No one who had really done what Nichols claimed to have done would act the way Nichols acted."

When a lawsuit Nichols brought against the City of Los Angeles came to trial, court reporters sat slack-jawed as Nichols testified. Nichols had sued because his gun license had been revoked after he got in a drunken dispute with the police in a seedy bar in West Hollywood. Nichols demanded $20 million, claiming the loss of the license had forced the Swiss financiers behind a proposed arms-manufacturing company to back out.

"Trial Offers Murky Peek into World of Intrigue," the headline in the *L.A. Times* said. "During four days of frequently heated testimony, Nichols presented himself as a dashing, globe-trotting businessman and intelligence operative," the *Times* reported. "Armed with letters on White House stationery and snapshots of himself posing with foreign political and military dignitaries, Nichols told jurors that he had toiled quietly and selflessly for nearly two decades on behalf of shadowy CIA keepers from Central America to Southeast Asia."

"Are you sure the CIA was paying you all these years?" Nichols was asked on cross-examination.

"I'm not sure, no," Nichols replied.

AS APRIL TURNED TO MAY, Sam gave himself completely over to Robert Booth Nichols and the denizens of the Royal Club Lounge in the Grosvenor Park Hotel. Like a character out of *Alice in Wonderland*, the dissipated, chain-smoking flimflam man led Sam down the rabbit hole, always holding the golden key just out of reach. Nichols's associates were also Lewis Carroll characters—the Queen of Hearts, the Cheshire Cat, Tweedledee and Tweedledum. To Sam, Nigel Finch really was a smooth-talking English antiques dealer who carried his MI6 background with the grace of a gentleman. The eerie-looking

John Cassidy had been part of a secret assassination team exiled from the United States by a rival faction. The Humanitarian Coalition was going to rid Africa of AIDS. Sam took the miracle zinc drops every day, certain that the minerals were strengthening his sex drive.

"I was the moneyman to Bob's people," Israel recalled. "While we were waiting for the trades to happen, I met a lot of folks in his circle. At night different guys would turn up with different deals to pitch to me. One was a guy who looked like he hadn't had a bath in a month. He was wearing a motorcycle jacket, he hadn't shaved, he had stringy hair. He reached into a courier bag and pulled out a rock and put it on the table—wham. It was one of the largest uncut sapphires in the world, he said. Jewelers were afraid to cut the stone because it might crack. He wanted three million for it."

To encourage a sense of paranoia, Nichols impressed on Sam the need to be vigilant. Danger lurked everywhere. Any passerby could be an assassin. Nichols had done the same thing to Danny Casolaro before his death—told him his life was in peril, encouraged fearful thoughts, uttered threats as if they were warnings.

"When you were trading, there were a lot of people coming after you," Israel said. "Other factions were trying to stop me from trading. The other factions were pursuing their own agendas. There were groups who used cutout corporations to funnel cash to the Taliban, for example. There were factions who were not friendly to the United States. The program wasn't only for the United States. It was a global trading program. The undertaking was very secretive. The different groups were funding black ops, or covert government projects. The danger would arise if we were found out to be making the trades. I couldn't divulge the existence of the program to anyone—and that meant anyone."

Nichols often used public places for meetings with Sam, spots where it would be difficult for their enemies to hear and record their conversation—such was the classified nature of what they were discussing. Israel was instructed to take evasive measures en route to their encounters, to shake anyone tailing him. The second bench south of the American embassy on Grosvenor Square was a favorite point of rendezvous. On the way to meet Nichols one overcast May afternoon, Israel stopped at a McDonald's on Regent Street to use the bathroom. As he entered the restaurant he stopped and turned to check if he was being followed, as Nichols had instructed him to do. Sam caught the eye of a man who seemed, perhaps, to be watching him. When Sam came back out a minute later, into the bustle of shoppers streaming along the sidewalk, he recognized the man still lingering. Sam caught his eye, but the man averted his gaze, conspicuously, it seemed to Israel.

"He was following me," Sam recalled. "I just knew it. For all I knew, he could have been trying to kill me. I had no choice. I had to run. I went back into the bathroom and found a window. I climbed on a toilet, went through the window, and got out into an alley. I fell into a garbage can as I landed. I was wearing a suit—a new Zegna I'd just bought. I didn't care. I ran down the alley and jumped over a spiked iron fence. I caught my leg on the fence but I got myself out of it. I ran all the way to meet Bob in Grosvenor Square. I was convinced I was going to be murdered."

Reaching the bench, Sam sat next to Nichols, panting.

"I was followed," Sam said. "I tore my fucking suit."

"Did you lose them?" Nichols asked.

"I think I did," Sam said. He glanced along the street. None of the faces were familiar. No one was looking their way, it seemed. Israel was drenched in sweat. His back had been wrenched.

"I told you to be careful," Nichols said, lighting a cigarette.

. . .

THE COUNTER SPY SHOP was located at 59 South Audley Street in Mayfair—a brisk five-minute walk from Claridge's. After the incident, Sam went to the store to purchase equipment to help him take countersurveillance measures. The Junior Attack System consisted of a powerful infrared camera with a long-range lens and microwave transmitter. The system was disguised in a plastic lunch box that Sam could leave wherever he liked—in a car, his hotel room, the business center at the Grosvenor—to record what was happening. The device had a remote trigger. The price was more than $5,000. But Sam was willing to spend any sum for peace of mind—an increasingly difficult state for him to achieve under the sway of his Svengali.

Nichols told Sam he never traveled without a gun. Carrying a concealed handgun was illegal in the United Kingdom, but Nichols was always armed with a Browning semiautomatic in a shoulder holster. If he had need for more weapons, Nichols had a contact in London who supplied him with whatever he needed. The man was Pakistani. Nichols called him Kumar. He was a cousin of President Musharraf of Pakistan and had high-level connections in the Pakistani military. Kumar was able to supply Nichols by using the Pakistani diplomatic pouch to transfer arms throughout Europe.

Nichols said Kumar was working on a water purification project outside Karachi. It was one of the projects approved by the Chosen to keep Pakistan on the side of the United States in the War on Terror. Nichols's man also had extensive contacts among the tribes of northern Pakistan and exclusive knowledge about the operations of Al Qaeda. Nichols intimated that Kumar knew the whereabouts of Osama bin Laden—and why the Pakistani army refused to hand him over to the

Americans. The claim that Kumar could locate bin Laden was typical of Nichols's grandiosity: The self-styled spy constantly told stories that placed himself at the center of world events. The entire American intelligence apparatus had failed to find bin Laden, but a sallow-faced drunk sitting in a bar in London knew his whereabouts?

Sam reveled in Nichols's intrigues. But the weeks continued to pass, and not a single trade came to fruition. The Hardwick initiative had come to nothing. Nichols said that the trading schedule for the shadow market was limited but reassured Sam that his opportunity would come soon. Still, Sam was growing increasingly frustrated. On weekends he flew back to New York to see his son. He returned to London on the red-eye on Sunday. He told Nichols that every day he wasn't trading, Bayou's investors were losing money. The opportunity costs for his investors ran to millions. The waiting and uncertainty were intolerable. So was the ongoing chance of Bayou's fraud being discovered.

Sam needed to create leverage. In frustration, on May 10 Sam wired $150,999,847.42 back to Bayou's account in Citibank in New York. The transfer was potentially disastrous news for Nichols. Keeping the money in play was a crucial component of the con. Nichols needed a new big store, and he needed it fast.

So it came to pass that the day after Sam wired back to the United States, Nichols announced that he'd discovered another way to enter the shadow market—a path that was even better than night trading. Over drinks at the Royal Club, Nichols introduced Israel to a man named George Katcharian. Nichols said Katcharian was highly experienced in alternative investment strategies—including high-yield securities. Katcharian was from Denmark, in his early fifties, five-five, with an intense but proper manner. His large nose framed dark eyes with large bags underneath, giving him the appearance of a jet-lagged international businessman burdened by heavy responsibilities.

Katcharian spoke perfect English, with a slight Danish inflection. He began to discuss the securities that he traded. Medium-term notes were arcane, Katcharian allowed. Israel struggled to understand the details of precisely how such fantastical profits could be made so quickly. The difference in the price—the arbitrage—was enormous, more than a 50 percent discount on the face value. Every bank and hedge fund in the world had rooms filled with traders scouring the market looking for assets that were mispriced. The adage on Wall Street was that there was no such thing as a hundred-dollar bill lying on the sidewalk— which was another way of saying there was no such thing as free money. Bonds issued at less than half of their real value would attract a swarm of traders, Israel knew. That explained the need for secrecy. But how did the market actually function?

Katcharian used a real-world example. He was currently involved with Deutsche Postbank AG, one of Europe's largest retail bankers. In Germany, Postbank was the essence of dull respectability, with 14 million customers and more than $250 billion in assets. But Katcharian said Postbank was also secretly one of the "prime banks" that traded in the premarket. Then he proved it to Sam. At Katcharian's suggestion, a regional director of Postbank sent a letter addressed to Sam regarding the purchase of bank "debentures"—another word for the medium-term notes, Katcharian explained. The letter purported to represent Postbank's firm commitment to purchase senior unsubordinated bank debenture bonds in the amount of $2 billion. The securities would be issued by a European bank with an AA rating. "Said instruments shall be seasoned, live and existing, and shall have a maturity of ten years and an interest coupon of 7.5% per annum," the director wrote. "Such instruments will be purchased for several of our clients and will be kept on deposit in their portfolios. Please provide us a quotation at your earliest convenience. Time is of the essence."

The discount on the debentures promised Sam a profit of more than $100 million in a matter of days. Katcharian explained that there were different ways of structuring the deal. Bayou's $150 million in Citibank in New York could provide the collateral for the whole deal, if he acted quickly. But there were complications to doing it that way—technical problems, the kind of thing encountered in the normal course of business. It wasn't the ideal structure. The approach Katcharian preferred was a joint-venture agreement. On one side would be Israel and the Humanitarian Coalition. On the other would be a company called Intercontinental Securities Limited—or ISL. The company was fronting for a clandestine intelligence agency, Sam was told.

"I definitely picked up the vibe that Katcharian was connected to intelligence agencies," Israel said. "It was clear that he'd dealt with British and Danish intelligence regarding the bonds. He had access to the bankers at Postbank. He had access to the program. Access was the key. I didn't really care about what structure was used—as long as the deal came off."

A meeting of the principals was called. Postbank's officer flew to London from Hamburg. Sam and Bob and Katcharian and the German banker gathered at the Promenade in the Dorchester Hotel, an ornate five-star restaurant decorated in gold and green. The German had managed money for high–net worth individuals for Postbank for years, Katcharian said. The banker had recently been promoted to run transactions in the shadow market, gaining entrée to the highest level of high finance.

The deal was straightforward, Katcharian said. The joint-venture agreement structure ensured ease and certainty. Sam said he was prepared to act with dispatch—he was "ready, willing, and able," in the language of the shadow market.

As the group finished eating, Katcharian said he had another meeting to get to. Sam watched Katcharian depart and waited a few moments before he said he had to leave as well. Quick-stepping through the lobby, he spotted Katcharian exiting through the revolving doors onto Park Lane. Sam followed. The Dorchester Hotel was near Nelson's Column, and the streets were packed with tourists. Katcharian walked for six blocks, wending his way through the streets of Mayfair. Near Grosvenor Square he hailed a taxi. Israel got in a cab and followed. The two cabs made their way through the afternoon traffic. In Chelsea, near the banks of the Thames, Katcharian got out of the taxi and entered a town house.

"He had his own key, so I figured it was where he lived," Israel recalled. "I waited outside for a few hours. Just lingering in the street. Then Katcharian came out of the house arm in arm with another man. It was obvious he was gay. He sure didn't seem like he was a family man, like he'd told me.

"I tailed him because I wanted to find out who all the players were and what was going on. I wanted to know who I was doing business with. I had to be paranoid. I knew from Bob that there were a lot of factions out there that were trying to get me. All the cloak-and-dagger stuff was driving me out of my mind. I was constantly looking over my shoulder wondering who was following me. I could feel the presence of people watching me."

. . .

SAM RETURNED TO NEW YORK to see his son. Now that Sam was no longer trading at all, he needed to come up with a different way of deceiving Bayou's employees and members. Pretending that he was trading from his desk in the chapel of the Trump house provided one scrim for the fraud. But how could he keep creating investor reports when all the staff knew he was in London? A Bayou employee was responsible for creating the net asset value reports—NAVs for short. His job consisted of taking the numbers from Sam, along with a summary of his commentary, and then plugging the returns into the document forwarded to Bayou's investors. The man Israel had picked for the job was a former school teacher, a gentle soul whose passivity was a major reason Sam had recruited him in the first place. Sam needed to convince him to send out NAVs he knew to be false.

"I called him to come see me at my house," Sam recalled. "I took him over to the chapel, to the loft where I'd installed a set of drums. I asked him to pick out any CD on the shelf and I would play along. So he picked out Black Sabbath, an old one called *Master of Reality.* I started to drum along with the band. He couldn't believe it. I was really playing. He was amazed. He knew I'd been a beginner only a few months ago.

"So I turned off the stereo and sat down to talk to him. I told him that things change in life—sometimes really quickly. I told him about Bob and the trading I was doing in London. I told him that our lives were all going to change for the better. I said that I'd signed a contract that would put me in prison for thirty years if I revealed the nature of the trades I was making. I said that I trusted him and cared for him— and I knew he felt the same way.

"I said we'd have to make up the commentary every week. The returns were real but we couldn't reveal where they were derived. I asked if he had a problem with that. He would have to work with Dan because I wouldn't be around a lot. He said that if Dan agreed not to yell at him and bully him he would do it for as long as we needed. I didn't tell him about the Problem, of course. I just said we were going to make a lot of money but he couldn't reveal where it was coming from. It was sort of a white lie. I believed in the trades, so I wasn't lying to him about that."

In mid-May Postbank gave notice that it was ready to receive $138 million to commence Katcharian's trading program. The account was in the name of ISL—with no mention of Bayou or Sam Israel. "I shall hereby confirm that we are a reputable bank that values the service of our clients and who respects their instructions and acts promptly and accordingly," the Postbank officer wrote to Israel. Sam refused to send the money into ISL's account. This time Sam was proceeding with caution, or at least his version of it.

"Maybe I was stupid, but I wasn't crazy," Israel recalled. "The money was supposed to only be for my signature. But it was going to be Katcharian's company's name? I was assured that Postbank wouldn't release funds without my approval."

Not wiring the money caused problems, Sam was told. He returned to London and met with Katcharian and Nichols. It wasn't clear what was going on with Postbank, Katcharian said. Katcharian lowered his voice and said he had confidential information to share. The Dane said that he believed there were problems inside the German bank—perhaps even fraud. The German banker was trying to scam Sam. This was a devastating turn of events: Nichols had warned Sam of the frauds and wannabes that populated the shadow market.

But Katcharian had good news. He had another way to trade—an easier and faster way to get into the program. He had a Fed trader in the Netherlands who could get Israel into the market immediately. The return on the secret medium-term notes that were available in this trade would be 100 percent in one week. Israel's cut would be 45 percent. Once Israel was able to regularly trade MTNs, through Katcharian's contact, he would be able to double his money every two weeks. Katcharian's solution sounded brilliant. In this new deal there were no up-front fees or broker charges. Tedious formalities would be replaced by a nimble deal that could be repeated rapidly.

Sam flew home to share the good news. Back in New York, Sam was euphoric. Debra Ryan immediately noticed the change in his spirits. "He was ecstatic," Ryan recalled. "Not because of the money he said he was going to make. Sam told me he was going to be a billionaire. He said he was being groomed to be the next George Soros. He said he was trading government money—CIA money. It was dangerous because there was a whole secret world of money. He told me about Bob and Ellen. He said they needed his intelligence and his trading skills. I didn't know what he was talking about. Who knows? Sam was the brilliant trader. I'm a painter. What do I know?

"But what really excited him was the charitable work he was going to do. He was going to set up foundations all around the world to help people. He said that even doing good was dangerous. Like curing cancer or AIDS. A lot of people make money from treating cancer and AIDS. The evil forces will kill to protect their fortunes. I didn't know what to make of what Sam was saying. It sounded scary. I was terrified for him."

Nichols called from London and said the deal had been postponed temporarily. Rival factions were trying to stop them, Nichols said. He told Sam to be on high alert. He was being watched. Sam hired a security firm to do a radio frequency spectrum analysis of the Trump house and Bayou's offices. Hedge funds were notoriously secretive, and it wasn't unusual for traders to hire security companies to protect their proprietary programs. But Sam wasn't trying to thwart a rival fund; he was trying to outwit the secret world government.

"Sam was convinced there were agents trying to keep him out of the trade," Dan Marino recalled. "He said it was why the trade was being delayed. He was positive that the boathouse was filled with bugs and taps on the phone lines. They were hearing what we were saying and developing plans to shut Bayou down."

In Sam's absence, Dan Marino had been forced to keep Bayou afloat by himself. Since the fraud at Bayou began, Marino had tried to deal with his anxieties through food. As a result, he'd gained more than fifty pounds, weight that transformed him from stout to corpulent and then to grossly overweight. Marino had also started to use Bayou's money to slake other thirsts. He purchased an eight-thousand-square-foot mansion on lush and lovely Bayberry Lane in Westport, Connecticut, for $2.9 million in cash. Set on two acres with a swimming pool, the house matched Marino's vision of wealth and elegance. Wandering the mansion and marveling at the designer touches—the wine cellar, the soaring ceilings, the massive master bedroom—he dreamed up plans to build a giant model railroad in the attic.

Lacking confidence around women, Marino had pounced on an opportunity to invest in a fashion company. A young designer named Holly Kristen had developed a line of dresses. Marino thought Kristen was attractive and talented, though he had no knowledge of the fashion industry. But Kristen's assistant was the prettiest girl he'd ever seen. Marino was in. Starting with $1 million, Marino funded

Kristen's first big show in Manhattan and harbored the fantasy of asking Kristen's assistant out on a date. As Kristen's financial backer, Marino was invited to go backstage at the fashion show, to roam through rooms teeming with half-naked models.

"I had no life," Marino said. "I had material possessions but they didn't satisfy the soul. I never had a good night's sleep because of the way the Problem weighed on me constantly. I would go to bed at ten and get up at three in the morning. A lot of times I'd close the door to my office in the middle of the day and pass out at my desk. I had 150 balls in the air all the time. I wasn't the greatest manager maybe, but I was a magician working with what was available to me at Bayou."

Over the months, John Ellis and his colleagues had come to Marino with more than a dozen investment opportunities. Adam Air was a company created by a former Goldman Sachs partner that was going to build very light jet airplanes for the private market. Marino was told it would be difficult to be permitted to invest, as it was exclusive to those lucky few who were socially connected. Marino imagined that Bayou could buy a dozen or more of the small planes and start an air taxi business for high–net worth individuals—a preposterous diversion from the fund's stated business model. But the company lacked direction and financing and ended up in bankruptcy—losing virtually all of Bayou's money.

So it went for Marino. Vectrix was a company with an electric scooter capable of zooming along at sixty miles an hour. FCV was a French cable television start-up. To John Ellis, Marino came across as a sad figure, socially awkward, hard of hearing, exuding an air of disappointment. By contrast, Ellis and his colleagues were graduates of Ivy League schools, world travelers, confident athletes. Sam worried that Marino was out of his league and too impressed by his new associates—a group Sam called the "*Mayflower* people." But there was nothing he could do to stop Marino from making investments in projects that Sam thought were foolish. Israel and Marino were at each other's mercy, each able to indulge their deepest desires as they attempted to solve the Problem by increasingly unlikely means.

BACK IN LONDON, following his own path toward salvation, Sam tried to solve the mystery of the shadow market with the shadowy Robert Booth Nichols. Keeping Sam's attention proved to be a full-time occupation for his handler. Ducking in and out of taxis, Nichols showed Sam how to check the reflection in his sunglasses to see if he was being followed. The paranoia Nichols engendered in Sam created a sense of adventure—but also dependence. Nichols was Sam's bodyguard. He was also inside Sam's head, monitoring his every hope and fear. Mind control was part of the lore of the cold war. It was also a tool of the trade for a confidence man. The long con essentially consisted of taking possession of the senses of the Babbitt for as long as was needed to make him part with his fortune.

Thus Sam immediately agreed when Nichols announced that they had to travel to Switzerland to resolve the difficulties with the trade. Sam decided to invite Debra Ryan along. He'd grown much closer with her in recent months. It was her birthday and it would be a romantic holiday.

As they checked into the five-star Hotel zum Storchen on the River Limmat in late May, it was evident to Ryan that Sam had fallen completely under the spell of Nichols. The power Nichols exercised over Sam scared her. So did everything about the supremely creepy couple.

"It was like a movie," Ryan recalled. "Bob was in their room sitting by an open window smoking a cigarette. He was tall, with dark hair, looking like John Wayne. He was a smooth talker, with a raspy voice. Old Hollywood was how he looked to me. Sam had told me how movies had been written about Bob—how the character in *The Bourne Identity* was based on Bob's life. I didn't know what was true or not. Bob was like God to Sam. When he was around Bob, Sam would suddenly find energy. He would overcome his back pain."

Sam had told Ryan that Ellen Nichols was expert at handling weapons and that she was Bob's partner in their life of intrigue. But Mrs. Nichols was nothing like the Angelina Jolie–esque operative Ryan had imagined. Ellen was in her fifties, with long blond hair and a pretty face. Dressed in jeans and a sweater, she had a high-pitched voice, cooing obediently to her husband, and she appeared to be like any middle-aged, middle-class American woman somehow swept up in an international thriller. But if Nichols was drinking too much, or talking too much, it was Ellen who kept him in line, in the manner of an ultraefficient executive secretary.

"Ellen was sitting at the desk typing on her computer," Ryan said. "She was a cold fish. Focused but cold. They all started talking about the secret deal. I hate smoke and Bob was chain-smoking, so I was about to leave. Then all of sudden Ellen's computer crashed. She got very upset."

"Someone has penetrated our system," Ellen cried in alarm. "They've shut us down. We've been infiltrated."

"Sam, what did you discuss in the cab on the way here?" Nichols asked Israel.

"Nothing," Israel said. "I swear we didn't talk about the business."

"All the cab drivers in Switzerland work for the CIA," Nichols said. "They're all informants."

"We didn't talk about anything," Israel said.

"Try to remember everything that you said," Nichols said.

Ryan looked on, bewildered. Israel and the Nicholses worked on the computer trying to get the Internet connection back. Ryan excused herself and went to their suite, terrified.

"That was when Bob told me it was time for me to start carrying a gun," Sam recalled. "He asked if I knew how to use a weapon. I didn't want to look like a pussy, so I said yes. It had been a long time since I'd held a gun. We had guns when I was a kid in New Orleans, but I hadn't touched one since then. Bob gave me a 9 mm Beretta with a silencer. He showed me how to carry it in the small of my back. He said the cardinal rule was to have the gun in a place where it was easy to reach. It had to be ready to fire—otherwise it was like having an empty canteen when you're dying of thirst in the desert."

The next morning was Debra's birthday. She and Sam woke and made love—passionate, frantic, intense love. But as soon as they joined up with the Nicholses the atmosphere turned claustrophobic once again. Debra wanted time alone with Sam. But the Nicholses wouldn't leave them be for even a moment. Left with no choice, the two couples went for a stroll through the historic section of Zurich. As they walked the cobblestone streets, Sam stopped at an electronics store to buy a new cell phone. The electronic signal of SIM cards in mobile phones was one way that rival factions tracked his location, Nichols had told him, so Sam was vigilant about changing cells whenever he traveled. But wandering the old city was pleasant and exciting for Ryan.

"I was starting to have a nice time," Ryan recalled. "Sam always wanted to spend money on me but I wouldn't let him. But this time he took me to a nice clothing store and bought me a bunch of new clothes. He was a great shopper—he could pick out clothes from the rack and they'd fit me perfectly. As we walked in one store, Sam turned me around and grabbed my face and kissed me with so much passion. We started to make out in the store, on the spur of the moment. I had never done that before, and I have never done it since. It was the best kiss ever. I told him that."

But the whirlwind romance was quickly replaced by Sam's default position under the sway of Bob Nichols: paranoia. Sam didn't tell Debra about the weapon he had hidden in the small of his back; the gun fueled Sam's fears, even as it gave him a secret sense of power. Nichols stoked Sam's anxieties relentlessly. The most mundane tasks—going for a walk, checking into a hotel, buying batteries for a camera—were infused with a sense of imminent peril. While Sam loved the drama, the stress wore on Ryan's nerves. Food could be poisoned, Sam told her. Assassins could stab him with umbrella tips filled with lethal doses of drugs. Every word was being listened to. Ryan began to wonder if people were following her. Were the bad guys coming to kill her? There were hundreds of operatives protecting Nichols at all times, Sam told Ryan. They were enveloped in a cordon of security befitting the president of the United States—or so Nichols had convinced Sam.

"Don't worry," Sam said to her. "Bob's guys are always watching him."

"So where are they then?" Ryan asked. "I don't see anyone."

"That's the point," said Sam. "You can't see them. You're not supposed to be able to see them. They're covert. They're blending in."

"Then why is Bob always standing by a window smoking a cigarette?" Ryan asked. "Any sniper could hit him."

Sam had an explanation for that too—he had an explanation for everything related to Bob. "Because he's protected," Sam said. "Because he's surrounded."

Ryan was unimpressed, but deeply concerned for Sam's safety—not because Nichols was necessarily telling the truth but because there were just too many warning signs, all of which Sam was ignoring.

"I told Sam he was either going to wind up dead or in prison if he continued dealing with the Nicholses," Ryan said. "I had an intuition about them. Dead or in prison—it was that simple."

DEBRA RYAN FLEW HOME, while Sam went off with the Nicholses for a luxury weekend on the Côte d'Azur. When Sam returned to New York he was followed a few days later by the Nicholses. Sam told Ryan that they were going to stay at his house for an unspecified period of time. Ryan wasn't happy with the presence of the interlopers. Nor were they pleased to have her around, especially with her dislike of cigarette smoke.

Once again Nichols wasn't going to let his Babbitt out of his sight—not until Sam had wired Bayou's money back to Europe. But it turned out that he had another motive for coming to New York. Nichols confessed that he had an eye condition that was causing his sight to fail. Nichols wept as he told Sam about his affliction. He was in desperate trouble, he said. His life would be in danger if his enemies discovered that his eyesight was going. Any sign of weakness would be fatal.

Ever eager to please his handler, Sam had Nichols put on Bayou's staff in order to provide him medical insurance. The pair traveled to New Orleans, where Sam arranged for Nichols to have an operation. But the doctor said that Nichols didn't need surgery; a course of medicine was all that was necessary. Yet Nichols remained terrified—at least, that was what he told Sam. It didn't occur to Sam that such a needy person might not be all that he claimed to be. Sam wanted to believe, so he *did* believe. It was as if he had found a new religion, and he'd taken up the faith with the fervor of a convert. The Problem was going to be solved and Sam would be absolved of his sins, if only he chased nagging doubts from his heart and helped the CIA asset mend his eyes.

In fact, religion was an explicit part of Bob Nichols's appeal to Sam. Ethnically Jewish but raised in a nonobservant family, Sam had attended Episcopal schools, and Christianity was the only religion he'd experienced. It was the faith he had carried into his adult life, to the extent that he had religious beliefs. But Sam discovered that Nichols practiced a very specific and extreme form of evangelical Christianity. It was part of the worldview of the Upperworld. There was an invisible war between good and evil raging all over the planet, Nichols told Sam. Nichols said he had been forced to do terrible things in the service of God and the United States. He broke down sobbing as he talked about his own faith and the importance of being born again.

"Bob was the single most knowledgeable person about religion I ever met," Israel said. "He had studied religion after he got out of the CIA's MK Ultra mind control program. He'd been so depressed he didn't leave his couch for three years. Bob said he was suicidal and searching for the true meaning of life. He had found it in 'teleo,' the word of Christ meaning 'It is over.' He told me he believed I had been sent to him by God. I was from the tribe of Benjamin and I was meant to be with him. Most people would sound crazy or like a zealot saying that, but Bob was completely sincere."

For weeks on end, the Nicholses dominated Sam's every act and thought. There were constant calls to London and Switzerland and the Netherlands. E-mails flew back and forth. Bob managed Sam's expectations, always at the ready with an explanation of why they were still delayed. As long as the $150 million remained in Bayou's account at Citibank, Nichols stayed at Sam's side in his role as the inside man, reminding him of what was at stake—financially, personally, religiously. All the while, Ellen Nichols fawned over Israel, calling him "my Sam" and laughing at his jokes and gazing in wonder at his powers as a trader.

"Most of the time, Sam and Bob were like two little boys playing together," Debra Ryan said. "They were always joking, being silly, doing stupid shit. Bob was a drinker, and Ellen didn't like it when he was drinking because he would start talking too much. She would get upset because she was so strict about not letting their secrets out. But Bob would get drunk and tell stories.

"Like the one he told us about a team of assassins that had come to kill him when he was doing business in a castle in the South of France. He said he heard the killers come into the castle, and instead of going towards the sound he stayed still to wait them out. He said he sat perfectly still for two days until the killers gave up and left. We were in the kitchen eating Chinese takeout at the time, supposedly having a normal conversation. But not Bob. He said to me, 'Debra, never go where the sound is when someone comes to kill you.' Like I was supposed to be getting ready for a team of assassins. I'm a painter, not a spy. He told me, 'They want you to go to the sound. That is how they will kill you. Stay still. Never move.'"

To pass time while the high-yield trade was being prepared, Sam had started to trade in the "real" market again. The volumes weren't large, as the bulk of Bayou's money was sitting in an account in Citibank. But even with small sums, Sam went on a tear.

"Bob watched me trade," Israel said. "He saw my daily profit-and-loss statements and he couldn't believe how well I was doing. One time I overheard him talking to a buddy of mine, a former Wall Street broker. I was up in the band room, which was on the balcony of the chapel. They didn't know I could hear. Bob told him that he thought I was a wizard who could make money out of nothing. Like a magic trick. My friend said I was right up there with the best traders on Wall Street. Bob thought I was a guru."

At the close of trading each day, Nichols tutored Sam in martial arts.

"Do you have any kill moves?" Nichols asked.

"In theory, not practice, obviously," Sam said.

"What good is theory going to do in a life-and-death situation?" Nichols asked. "Now that you're in the big time, you better prepare yourself."

"So Bob showed me how to rip a man's throat out with my bare hands," Sam recalled. "He showed me how to gouge out eyes. How to push the nose bone into the brain. How to break a man's neck from different angles. We practiced for an hour every day. He taught me how to use a rolled-up magazine to choke a man. I learned how to use a pen in the eye or the ear. Bob treated martial arts like a tool. For a guy in his sixties he was lightning fast."

Over time the Nicholses staked out space on the second-floor landing of the Trump house, an area with a couple of stuffed chairs, a television set, a desk, and an ashtray. It was where Sam kept a computer—where he'd first read *The Last Circle*. One evening, Sam offered to show Nichols around on the Internet. Always eager to impress his older mentor, Sam proudly began the tutorial by googling Nichols's name. At the top of the search results was the link to *The Last Circle*. Nichols began to read the unpublished manuscript. He claimed never to have seen it before, a ridiculous-seeming claim. Nichols feigned being unnerved by his online infamy.

"Bob never sought notoriety," Israel recalls. "The opposite. He talked a lot about how to make yourself vanish. He taught me how to create a new identity. You go to a cemetery and find someone around your age who is dead and both parents dead, too. Then you pick up his identity from the time he died. He showed me how to forge Social Security cards perfectly. He showed me how to forge a passport. He showed me how to fake all kinds of things."

"Can you make it look like I'm dead?" Nichols asked Sam, looking up from *The Last Circle*.

"What do you mean?" Israel asked.

"Can you trick up an article on the Internet to say that I've died?" Nichols said.

"I can try," Israel said.

ON JUNE 7, 2004, the broker from the Netherlands e-mailed to say the day for the trading to commence had finally arrived. But the next day the broker suddenly announced he wouldn't be able to complete the deal. He didn't explain why. Nichols said it was because he was afraid. He hadn't been seized by fear of getting caught committing a fraud, though that was the obvious answer. Nichols said the broker was terrified of rival factions and getting murdered for assisting with their trade. Violence was endemic in the shadow market. Homicides were routinely carried out by the Octopus and the bodies secretly disposed of to ensure there was no investigation. Such was the price of admission to the shadow market—a price the broker was too terrified to risk, according to Nichols.

Sam was outraged at the cowardice of the broker. The pair needed to partner with people who were not so easily spooked. Nichols agreed. To calm Sam down, he contacted his mentor, a former Reagan White House Treasury official named Phil Severt. Headquartered in Miami, Severt was able to act as a conduit to the shadow market, Nichols explained. Sam wasn't allowed to talk to Severt himself; Sam didn't have the national security clearances to move that high in the hierarchy. Only Nichols could talk to Severt.

Nichols reported that Severt had a solution at the ready. He told Nichols that the final settlement for the trade would be handled by a trader called Charles Jones. According to Severt, Jones was attached to the NSA. For the purposes of due diligence and money-laundering laws, Jones faxed Sam an electricity bill from his house and a copy of his driver's license—not the kind of documentation usually associated with transactions involving more than $100 million. There was one tiny detail left. Jones had to be authorized as a signatory on the Citibank account in order for the trade to go through. Sam agreed to the change. It was just a formality, Nichols assured him. Nothing important. A perfect stranger was about to be made signatory for an account with $138 million of Bayou's investors' money. The long con was nearing its climax; in the language of the trade, it was time to "take off the touch."

"All is set to go," Jones wrote to Sam. "We're going to be doing big things together. Roll up your sleeves."

CHAPTER THIRTEEN

As Real as Rain

T he fact that Israel had ceased trading had yet to be discovered by Bayou's investors. But Bayou's clearinghouse SLK was acutely aware of the situation. When Bayou pulled all of its money from its account months earlier, SLK's senior management had become concerned. SLK was a division of Goldman Sachs, and the investment bank had made $1 million from Bayou in the first quarter of 2004 alone. It was virtually risk-free high-margin money, the kind of profit that had prompted Goldman to buy SLK. Since then upper management had been in steady contact with Bayou, trying to find out when Sam would get his trading groove back.

"I told them Sam was doing some trades in Europe," Dan Marino recalled. "I said we were also possibly considering a merger or a buyout with a European organization. I didn't tell them the name of the firm, as that was confidential. Nor did I give them any details. I was very, very vague. I told them we would be back to our normal volume in the next four months. Then, if all went well, our volumes would increase quickly. I figured that Sam was going to get the money from London so we'd have a lot more money to trade. After that conversation, the calls from Goldman died down."

The story the employees were given was more involved. Sam was trading through a European company, they were told. There was a chance of a merger with another fund, but they shouldn't worry, as they would keep their jobs. The ploy worked. The staff was well paid, and asking questions would result only in their being berated by Marino—and likely losing the best-paid job they'd ever had.

On the rare occasions when Sam came to the boathouse, he told the staff that he'd been invited by various European governments to consult on how to make the hedge fund industry there as dynamic as it was in the United States—a self-aggrandizing claim that made Marino cringe.

"There was really no coordinated effort to fool the people in the office," Marino said. "The problem was going to be solved, Sam and I hoped. All of our troubles were going to go away. Nobody asked for details about what Sam was trading."

Bayou's performance had remained outstanding—on paper. The fund's biggest single investor was a fund of funds called Silver Creek. The head of Silver Creek wrote Sam to congratulate him on the continuing success and to up the ante on the $38 million they had in Bayou. "First of all thank you for the excellent stewardship of our money," he wrote. "Your risk adjusted return is off the charts. Two questions: How much money are you managing these days? And can we give you some more money?"

IN A SURPRISING WAY, this was a lighthearted time for Sam, after years of unendurable pressure. He was falling in love with Debra Ryan. He was going to be rich beyond his wildest dreams. Feeling lucky, he bought a handful of tickets for the Big Mega Million lottery, which had a cash jackpot of $120 million. He worked diligently on the charity that was going to be a beneficiary of the shadow market. He called the organization the American Academy of Excellence. It would be dedicated to educating disadvantaged children. "Students who are lacking essential educational resources and who are gravely economically disadvantaged and greatly underachieving academically will be the 'target population' graciously designated for tremendous assistance," the mission statement said.

One afternoon, he took the Nicholses to look at Chateau Lion du Lac, or "Lion of the Lake," the Westchester mansion he was going to buy for $10 million. The twelve-bedroom, seventeen-thousand-square-foot house had a ten-acre lawn sweeping down to the Titicus Reservoir. There were both indoor and outdoor swimming pools. The interior was decorated with extravagance that would have pleased the Sun King, Louis XIV.

"Why do you need this much house?" Debra asked, in amazement, when Sam showed her the prospectus for the estate. "It's ridiculous to have two people living here. It's pretentious."

"When you get to a certain status running a hedge fund, you can't have a tiny little house," Sam told Debra. "If you're going to have dignitaries and heads of state over for dinner you've got to show them what you're worth."

But Sam's anticipation was tempered by underlying anxiety. As the trade neared, Nichols told Sam to speak in whispers around the house, convincing him that "they" were listening to him—without specifying who "they" were. If "they" could damage Sam or Bayou in any way, "they" would. Sam followed instructions, whispering to Ryan even when they were in bed. He mouthed sentences and directed movement through hand motions. It was as if he were acting in a real-world thriller. Sam saw the sinister explanation in everyday occurrences—an idling black town car, a telephone repair crew working the lines down the street, a stranger's glance on the street.

As in London, Sam amassed an array of electronic surveillance gadgets, like the Spion Orbitor Listening Device, a handheld instrument with a "patented super mini-microphone" encased in a parabolic sound dish. "The Orbitor's 'ears' and 'eyes' are powerful enough to hear from one end of the football field to the other," it was claimed. Nichols sniffed at Sam's efforts.

"It doesn't matter what you have, Sam," Nichols said. "They're going to listen to your conversations without you knowing about it. They have devices that can hear you from a mile away. They've got satellites that can look through your house. They've got technology you don't even know about."

FOLLOWING THE INSTRUCTIONS of George Katcharian, Sam instructed Marino to contact Citibank and arrange to transfer $138 million to Postbank in Germany. But Citibank had questions—and concerns. What was a long/short, buy/sell hedge fund like Bayou doing wiring that much money to an account in Germany? What kind of trade was Bayou proposing to make? Who was behind Katcharian's company ISL? If Citibank permitted the transfer in such dubious circumstances, and Bayou was the victim of a scam, the bank could be held liable for failing to heed the telltale signs of fraud.

After years of reckless indifference on the part of regulators and banks, it was a long-overdue development. Israel, Nichols, and Marino went to see two Citibank executives at their local branch. Although he had been sworn to secrecy—upon pain of thirty years in prison— Sam patiently explained the shadow market to the regional managers. The Fed bonds, the thirteen families, the massive discounts—Sam and Bob laid it all out. Billions would soon be pouring into Bayou's coffers, Bob said. The Citibank officials looked at them as if they had taken leave of their senses. They had never heard of a secret bond market. Sam said he wasn't surprised. Their lack of knowledge fit with what Nichols had told him: Only the uppermost bank officials were aware of the market.

Israel asked to borrow a conference room to call a high-ranking Citibank executive in Manhattan. The man was second in command, acting as the right-hand man to chairman Sandy Weill—who in turn was an old friend of the Israel family. Sam knew the executive through his father. After Sam told the Citibank official about the shadow market, the man said he had never heard of it either. Sam was now genuinely shocked. How could it be? How high did a banker have to be to be initiated into the shadow market? Despite the man's denials, Sam insisted the high-yield trades were real. Back and forth, the two men debated the subject for twenty minutes. When Sam hung up the phone he was shaken.

"The Citibank people acted like Sam was from Mars," Marino recalled. "We left quickly. In the parking lot Sam freaked out. He told me he had made a big mistake coming to Citibank. He said he shouldn't have talked about the shadow market. He had exposed his hand."

That evening, Nichols and Sam decided they had to be more discreet. Talking about the shadow market was breaching the confidentiality clause of their agreements. Talking also risked alerting other factions that they were so close to realizing their dream. Nichols said the reason the senior Citibank executive had pretended not to know about the shadow market was obvious: Saying the market didn't exist was proof of its existence. Citibank was obviously trying to block their efforts and steal their trade.

WHILE ISRAEL CONTINUED TO TRY to convince Citibank to release Bayou's funds, Nichols regaled him with tales. An alien really had been captured in Roswell, New Mexico, in 1947, Nichols said. The creature had died of an overdose of strawberry ice cream, according to Nichols. The annual flu season was a method for the Octopus to cull the human population, Nichols claimed. So it went, as Nichols downed whiskey in the evening and instructed Sam and visitors who happened by the house in alternate world history.

But there was one story Nichols reserved for Sam and Sam alone. It was a tale so incredibly preposterous it could only be true. Or so Sam reasoned. It was a legend that had circulated in Special Forces circles for decades. The story was long and convoluted, and Nichols didn't possess the historical expertise to explain the context. But Sam sat rapt as Nichols narrated a story that ranked with the greatest mysteries of all time. The tale of Yamashita's gold was steeped in revisionist history and rife with the kinds of leaps in imagination common to conspiracy theories.

Perhaps the most bizarre aspect of Nichols's tale was this: It was true. At least in part. In essence. Maybe. The story began in the years before World War II. In the early 1930s the Roosevelt administration had been alarmed by the rise of fascism. American popular opinion was against "foreign entanglements," so FDR had resorted to covert diplomacy to assist its allies. The British were secretly funded and armed by the United States long before they fought against Germany. The same thing was true for China, at least according to leading economic historians. Much of what had happened is missing from the historical record. But it is true that Chiang Kai-shek, the leader of China, had been fighting the Japanese in Manchuria, as well as the Communist rebels of Mao Zedong. Legend has it that FDR had secretly provided billions of dollars' worth of Federal Reserve bonds to Chiang Kai-shek in 1934. The Fed bonds had been issued to enable the Chinese to purchase arms.

The Chinese had lost the war to the Japanese, and the nation's then-capital had been overrun and plundered, an event known to history as the Rape of Nanking. Precious metals, jewels, artwork from antiquity, billions in bullion—the sovereign wealth of China had been stolen as the spoils of war. The Japanese had then secretly shipped the loot to the Philippines, which they had also conquered. By the time the Americans were threatening to retake the Philippines in 1944 it was no longer safe to transport the treasure back to Japan. The Japanese government had thus ordered a general named Yamashita to create a network of caves high in the jungle on the island of Mindanao to hide the loot. After the work had been completed, legend said, Yamashita gathered all the Japanese engineers and soldiers who had worked on the project into a tunnel to celebrate. The men drank sake and sang patriotic songs about "banzai" (long life), surrounded by stacks of gold bars. In one corner was a "motherbox" that held twenty-five boxes containing billions in the secretly issued American Federal Reserve bonds. At midnight, Yamashita quietly excused himself. As he departed, the entrance to the caves was dynamited, burying hundreds of men alive—ensuring that the location of the treasure would remain secret.

The hunt for Yamashita's gold had been going on ever since. For decades, soldiers of fortune had traveled to the island of Mindanao in search of the treasure, just as men had gone looking for El Dorado. Major General John Singlaub, a founder of the CIA and the officer who headed intelligence operations in China during the war in Manchuria, had led one such expedition. According to Nichols, many men had been murdered trying to retrieve Yamashita's gold. But the descendants of Chiang Kai-shek were in possession of one of the boxes containing the Fed bonds. Nichols said he could broker the return of the bonds to the United States in return for a percentage of the face value. As long as they remained unaccounted for, the bonds represented a dire strategic threat to America. The southern Philippines was largely Muslim, and it had become a base of operations for Al Qaeda.

"Bob showed me photographs of the boxes containing the Federal Reserve certificates," Sam recalled. "There was a picture of a rusty old briefcase with the seal of the Fed on the front. It was one of twenty-five boxes that all fit together into the motherbox. There were photographs of Oriental men standing around a table—the emissaries of the family of Chiang Kai-shek. There was a picture of a canister that contained a deadly nerve gas. If the boxes weren't opened at a forty-five-degree angle, the canisters would explode and kill whoever tried to get at the Fed bonds.

"Those were the real boxes. But Bob said there were many counterfeits in circulation. He showed me photographs of the fakes, which were in Samsonite suitcases. He explained how to tell the difference between the real ones and the phony ones. Bob said he thought we could put a deal together to bring all of the bonds back to the United States. He could lead a mission to retrieve Yamashita's gold."

More than $700 billion in bonds had been issued. Nichols said that if the Fed paid even a fraction of the true value of the bonds it would amount to tens of millions. Nichols told Sam he'd flown to Singapore to meet with a man who represented the family of Chiang Kai-shek. But there was ill will on their side. Past attempts to have the Fed bonds honored hadn't succeeded, despite the existence of "heritage documents" detailing the provenance of the securities and ensuring their authenticity.

"The Federal Reserve denies the legitimacy of the bonds," Nichols told Sam. "They say the bonds are counterfeit. They say the Fed never issued the bonds. They mythify them to create plausible deniability. The Fed knows it doesn't have enough money to pay for the bonds, so it pretends that the bonds were never issued. The only way to repatriate the bonds is to have contacts at the absolute highest level of the United States government. That means the White House. That means the Bush family. They're at the level to know about the Fed obligations."

"The first cousin of President Bush is one of my best friends," Sam said. "His name is John Ellis. He's tight with the president. I can arrange for you to meet John."

"I need to know that Ellis has relationships at the correct level, or else it's in no one's interests to pursue this," Nichols said. "Not for you, not for the Chinese, not for me."

A meeting was arranged. Ellis was indeed as Sam advertised. A graduate of Yale and Harvard, Ellis belonged to the tiny ultraelite Bush clan, and he looked the part: tall, with a strong jaw, light brown hair, and the sturdy build of a former hockey player. Ellis was close with major figures in the White House. To convey a measure of Ellis's power, Sam told Nichols that Ellis had been a political analyst for Fox the night of the 2000 election. When the result in Florida seemed too close to call, Ellis had been the first commentator to say that his cousin George W. Bush had won. Viewers weren't informed that Ellis was Bush's first cousin and close personal friend. Ellis's call had created a tide of momentum that had never been reversed. Sam grinned as he claimed that Ellis had personally delivered the presidency to Bush. How was that for pull inside the White House?

When Ellis arrived at Sam's house, he was surprised to greet Nichols, who he found was an overweight, puffy-faced chain-smoker with no evident energy or enthusiasm. Beforehand, Sam had boasted about Nichols's swashbuckling adventures for the CIA. But Nichols looked depressed and physically unwell, not a real-life James Bond as Sam had intimated. As they were introduced, Bob and Ellen Nichols told Ellis they were born-again Christians—not simply religious but deeply faithful evangelicals. Evidently they believed their faith would impress Ellis—and make him trust their word.

Chinese food was ordered. Like his presidential cousin, Ellis was a teetotaler. He drank Diet Coke, while Nichols began his nightly ritual of downing massive amounts of scotch. The conversation was led by Nichols. Sam hung on Nichols's every word. It was evident to

Ellis that Sam was extremely enamored of Nichols—infatuated even. Ellis listened silently, warily, as Nichols described the shadow market and the incredible returns that could be made trading the secret Fed bonds. Nichols explained the classified nature of the "business with no name." It seemed highly improbable to Ellis that Sam and his dissipated companion had somehow managed to outwit the likes of Goldman Sachs and Salomon Brothers.

Nichols then handed Ellis a three-page memorandum titled "The Pakistan Problem." Evil forces were conspiring against President Bush, Nichols said. Radical Islamists were plotting to ensure that Bush would not be reelected. But Nichols said he knew how to change the political landscape and ensure that Ellis's cousin triumphed in the 2004 election. Nichols could win the presidency and save America all at once. Capturing Osama bin Laden was the key. Nichols lowered his voice and said that he knew how to find bin Laden.

As Nichols lit a cigarette, Ellis wondered if this was a prank. Was there a hidden camera somewhere? Sam had the eager look of a teenage boy. The notion that a half-drunk man sitting in a mansion in Westchester sipping a Jameson's on the rocks could locate the world's most wanted man—Ellis didn't know where to begin.

Nichols explained the details. The Pakistani government was run by a small group of generals known as the Corps Command. There were twelve generals in this group. Nine could be bribed. The other three were very anti-American but could be controlled, for the right price. Nichols said a Swiss trust fund he ran could be used to secretly funnel money from the U.S. government to the Pakistani generals. The money would be used to build a water purification plant on the outskirts of Karachi. The plant would be run for the benefit of the generals—but also the Pakistani people. In return, the Corps

Commanders would reveal the whereabouts of bin Laden. The Al Qaeda leader wasn't hiding in the mountains of Waziristan, as many suspected. He lived in comfort under the care and protection of the Pakistani military. Nichols didn't know his exact location yet. But once the covert cash was transferred to Nichols's Swiss account and then onward to the generals, bin Laden could be hit by a drone missile attack, or a Special Forces raid on his hideout. Nichols was claiming he could change world history and kill the most wanted outlaw of all time. It all seemed ludicrous to Ellis.

An hour had passed. It seemed that things couldn't possibly get stranger—until Nichols handed Ellis a sheaf of photographs. These were the images of the Federal Reserve bonds Nichols had shown Sam—the Federal Reserve boxes, the Oriental men gathered around a table, the canister of nerve gas booby-trapping the bonds. Ellis flicked through the pictures. "Despite repeated attempts by the US and other governments to 'mythify' the People's Republic of China assets in the form of Federal Reserve obligations, they do exist," Nichols's memo stated. "The parties I am associated with have a direct personal relationship with the sole duly authorized signatory of approximately $700 billion Federal Reserve obligations, and they are willing to cooperate over time in overseeing the return of these assets to the American government."

Nichols said that the Fed had undertaken a campaign to "mythify" the bonds. Nichols assured Ellis he was going to get the "real" Fed bonds. The Fed bonds were being held in a "security zone" on the island of Mindanao in the Philippines. Nichols was going to form a group to retrieve the bonds—a kind of real-life A-Team. Before they could depart, however, Nichols needed assurances from the president that he'd be supported. Nichols wanted Ellis to act as a back channel to the president. The president would understand the significance, Nichols was sure. Nichols's memorandum specified two requirements:

1. "COMPLETE ANONYMITY AT ALL TIMES."
2. "Irrevocable nonexpiring FULL AND COMPLETE diplomatic immunity by Executive Order, which shall be issued in duplicate and in perpetuity."

Nichols said the immunity had to be accompanied by a "black" passport, which could be created only by presidential decree. The passport wasn't diplomatic, in the ordinary sense. It was far more powerful. Nichols and the others would be free to cross all national boundaries without being stopped, searched, or asked any questions.

Ellis was flabbergasted. Was Nichols really expecting the president to endorse a harebrained caper involving treasure hidden in caves in the Philippines? Nichols was poker-faced, toking on another cigarette. Ellis was crucial to saving the presidency of George W. Bush, Nichols said. The solvency of the United States was at stake, as was the fate of the War on Terror.

Over the years, Ellis had dealt with many eccentric hedge fund traders. A shockingly large number were given to wild mood swings and nutty investment theories. But Nichols's plan and Sam's belief in it were totally irrational. Israel was obviously under Nichols's spell—so completely and utterly convinced that he appeared to have lost his mind. If Nichols was a con man—as appeared extremely likely—word of Sam's dealings with him would mean the ruination of Bayou. Inevitably, Sam's reputation would be destroyed. Ellis was concerned for his friend. He needed to figure a way to get Nichols away from Sam. How on earth was he going to get Sam interested in venture capital deals—*real* deals—with the freakish death figure of Robert Booth Nichols around?

Sam walked Ellis to the front door. Alone with Israel for the first time, Ellis expressed his concerns. Did Sam know what he was getting himself into? What the hell was going on? They stepped outside. A thunderstorm was rolling across Westchester, bringing howling wind and sheets of rain.

"Are you serious?" Ellis implored his friend.

"I know how it looks," Sam said. "But I'm telling you, this stuff is 100 percent real. Bob Nichols is real—as real as rain."

ELLIS DECIDED TO MAKE his own inquiries about Nichols. Through family connections, Ellis had been appointed a fellow in the Counter Terrorism Center at West Point, studying biological warfare. He'd come to know a number of senior military officers who could tell him about Nichols's alleged special ops history. It turned out Nichols was known to some of the soldiers as a kind of mythical figure in the world of black ops. "All hat and no cattle" was one reply. "Crazy," said another. Brigadier General Russ Howard, former head of the Special Forces "A-Team" (the real one), told Ellis that he had heard the legend of the Fed bonds in the Philippines. But actually going after them sounded like a wild goose chase.

Ellis contacted Fred Fielding, White House counsel for both Presidents Reagan and George W. Bush. Fielding was one of the premier Republican attorneys and deal makers in Washington. Fielding agreed to ask around. Within days, he reported that the word he'd received on Nichols was simple: Stay away—far, far away. The projects Nichols was discussing might be illegal, Fielding said. He told Ellis not to discuss them with anyone and not to get involved in any way. It was the response Ellis expected, though inflected with a degree of intrigue he hadn't anticipated. Nichols apparently did have special ops experience and connections inside the White House. But the nature of his relationships wasn't clear. Nichols appeared to be two things at the same time: a former intelligence operative of some kind and a scammer peddling financial frauds. He was a spy and a con artist. Or he was a spook who'd become a confidence man. During the cold war, the lines between real intelligence operatives and frauds had blurred badly. The U.S. government had hired countless "contractors" to carry out its dirty work. Nichols had apparently been one of those men.

But it didn't really matter. Sam was entranced. Ellis was stuck. There was no chance Ellis was going to talk to the president about Yamashita's gold. Nor could he turn his back on Sam. Ellis sat down to write Sam a letter on June 23. "As I told you on the phone I cannot help you on the project we discussed," Ellis wrote. "Legal counsel has informed me that the project may violate federal law and thus I am duty bound not to discuss it with my cousin or anyone in his employ. I am very concerned that by your association with Robert Booth Nichols you are putting yourself and your family in significant risk. I urge you, as a friend and someone who cares about you and your family, to break off your relationship with Mr. Nichols and return to your normal business activities."

Sam ignored Ellis. By the end of June, the attempts to trade in the shadow market had come to a standstill. Citibank refused to wire Bayou's money to Germany.

Then Citibank demanded that Bayou immediately transfer its funds to another American bank. The order applied to Sam's personal accounts as well. It appeared the bank wanted nothing more to do with Israel and his schemes. Marino gladly arranged for Bayou's millions to be transferred to another American bank. So the money had finally been sprung. The game was back on. But Nichols could see that Sam needed to be persuaded to transfer the funds to Germany. Sam needed the "convincer," as it was known in the long con—the act that would move him to actually wire the money to Europe. It was time to raise the stakes.

CHAPTER FOURTEEN

Exploding Heads

A t the instruction of Bob Nichols, on July 7, 2004, Sam flew Lufthansa to Germany. Nichols would follow the next day. Nichols and Israel were now going to cut out the middlemen and go directly to Postbank, a real entity, not another joker broker. Postbank had a real office in Hamburg. The Postbank official organizing the trade had real business cards with the title of Gebietsdirektor. His name was Golo Barthe. He was going to provide the "paper," enabling Sam's entrée to the elite market. At long last, Sam would be interacting with a legitimate businessman. Or at least that was what he was going to determine for himself, before he wired 100 million euros to Germany.

Nichols had told Sam to go to the airport Marriott when he

arrived in Hamburg. Sam had been directed to contact Nichols's arms dealer connection—the cousin of President Musharraf who worked in the Pakistani embassy in London. Kumar was his name. Sam had met Kumar once in the Royal Club at the Grosvenor Hotel in London. It was easy to recognize Kumar in the lobby of the Marriott, though he had the uncanny ability to blend into his environment. Kumar was small, thin, dressed in drab business attire. As they greeted each other in the lobby, it seemed to Sam that Kumar carried himself in the manner of a spy: He was watchful, graceful, like a passing shadow. Kumar had a small shoulder bag for Sam, which he silently handed over. Sam asked Kumar if he wanted to have a drink, but he politely declined and departed.

Sam went to the center of the city and checked into the Intercontinental, taking a suite with a view of Alster Lake. Alone in his room, Sam opened the shoulder bag. There was a heavy package wrapped in plain brown paper. Inside, a towel was wrapped around two 9 mm Beretta handguns. Each weapon was equipped with a silencer. Sam inspected the pistols lovingly—the polymer handle, the chrome barrel, the satisfying feel in the hand. In the weeks since Nichols insisted he be armed, Sam had developed a fascination with guns. Nichols had supplied Sam with a variety of pistols, always accompanied by a silencer for the close urban combat he anticipated.

Nichols arrived the next morning. The CIA operative was in full operational mode: Comprehensive surveillance countermeasures had to be taken at all times. Conversations had to be whispered or conducted in code language. Hundreds of enemy intelligence operatives had descended on Hamburg to try to stop them from making the trade, Nichols told Sam; the city was teeming with killers from rival factions. Sam had to be hypervigilant. Nichols inspected the weapons Sam had collected from Kumar. Nichols had brought ammunition. He loaded the Berettas and attached the silencers. He told Sam to place the gun in the small of his back. They were now armed and ready for their encounter with Golo Barthe of Postbank.

"Bob was one bad dude," Israel recalled. "He was so cool. He said we were finally in the right place at Postbank. He was going to tell Barthe about the Federal Reserve bonds in the Philippines. He said we would cut him in on that deal, too, once the trading programs were rolling. Everything was ready for the trades to begin. It was all set."

The meeting was scheduled for Saturday morning. Barthe's office was located on Valentinskamp, a short walk from the hotel. As Sam and Nichols cautiously made their way to the meeting, the streets of Hamburg's central business district were eerily empty. Turning into a back alley, as they'd been directed by Barthe, Israel and Nichols greeted the German banker at the rear entrance to a nondescript brown brick building. Barthe was dressed crisply, in a dark suit. He was in his early thirties, tall, handsome, the epitome of a young Euro sophisticate fluent in English.

Barthe ushered Israel and Nichols through the back door and into the lobby, which was completely deserted. As they walked to the elevator, Barthe told them that he didn't trust George Katcharian anymore. It was Katcharian who'd cut out Barthe and Postbank earlier when he directed Sam down another dead end. Barthe said that Postbank was a highly reputable institution that only conducted business with high-integrity traders, particularly in the high-yield market with its many impostors and frauds. Sam nodded in silent agreement.

Barthe had a modest office, the kind a midlevel functionary would occupy. Two cleaners were vacuuming in the hall, but otherwise the Postbank premises were deserted. Barthe explained that the transaction involved $2 billion in medium-term note prime bank debenture instruments. The instruments were "seasoned," meaning they'd been traded already. There was a stack of documents on Barthe's desk, ready to be executed by Israel.

To perform a final step of due diligence, Nichols borrowed Barthe's phone to call Phil Severt, the former Reagan official. Severt was in Florida. He was responsible for the charitable component of the trade. Part of the proceeds would be used to build the water treatment facility outside Karachi in Pakistan that Severt was promoting. For months, Sam had asked Nichols to let him meet the mysterious Severt. Nichols had told Sam it was impossible. Severt didn't take personal meetings. Not even a future Wall Street titan like Sam Israel ranked high enough. But Sam had been permitted to speak to the all-powerful Severt once before the Hamburg trip. The conversation had made a strong impression on Sam—in particular one strange phrase Severt had used.

"When we spoke, Severt repeatedly told me he had what he called a stupid face," Sam recalled. "It was weird. I asked him what it meant. He said he had the kind of face that was instantly forgettable. He could vanish into crowds. Severt said no one noticed him when he was in public because he was so bland looking. He said he was invisible because his face was so average—so stupid."

On the call from Postbank's office, Severt assured Barthe that the correct protocols had been followed for the Karachi initiative. As Sam filled in the documents to open a "nondepletion account," Nichols told Barthe that the initial trades were only part of a much bigger plan.

Nichols represented the covert financing of American intelligence agencies in a variety of ways. Everything was set. Once Sam wired the money the trades would commence. Sam was careful to maintain a serious demeanor given the gravity of what they were doing. He said he'd transfer enough American dollars to equal 100 million euros on Monday morning—at the current exchange rate it would be just over $138 million.

"After the meeting I left the building ahead of Bob," Sam said. "He was going to follow a minute behind me as a security precaution. I walked out the back door and into the alley. Then I took a right and started walking along the street. The area was like a ghost town. Across the street there was a man standing next to a telephone pole. He was short, maybe five-five, wearing a turban. He appeared to be Pakistani. Maybe Middle Eastern. One of his eyes drooped down. He had this weird expression on his face—like he was staring at me. Then he started to walk towards me. As I got near him, he passed by and he said—I swear to God—he said, 'You have a really smart face.' I stopped dead. I knew it was Severt telling me he'd sent people to watch us in Hamburg. Severt was tailing us—and he was letting us know it. So I threw the guy against the wall and asked what the fuck was going on. He wouldn't talk to me, not in English. All of a sudden he could only speak Urdu. He kept saying the same thing—'No sahib, no sahib.'

"I let him go. I walked a couple more steps, and then I turned around to see if Bob was behind me. As I turned, I saw the guy reach into his jacket and pull out a gun. Now Bob was coming out of the building. The guy was taking aim to shoot Bob. So I pulled my Beretta out and I shot at the guy. I hit him in the left hip. Everything was moving in slow motion. It was terrible—it was terrifying. By that time Bob had pulled out his gun, and he plugged the guy in the right shoulder. The guy dropped the gun and fell to the ground. I was furious. I felt like my life was in danger. So I walked over and stood over him and shot him in the head. Point blank. Killing him. His head exploded all over the sidewalk. Blood and brains were everywhere.

"There were no cars. No witnesses. Nobody was there. The silencers worked, so the shots didn't make any sound. No one had seen what happened. Bob grabbed me. He took the gun from my hand and we ran for our lives. When we got back to the hotel, I didn't know what to do. We went to Bob's room. I was crying. I was devastated. I threw up. Bob said I was the craziest person he'd ever met. But I'd saved his life. He told me he'd take care of it. Bob started to make calls. He got rid of the body. He had cleaners to take care of that kind of thing—to make a body disappear before the police were alerted. He got rid of the guns, too. He made it so there were no traces of the crime. It was clear that Severt had sent people after us. The question was why. Clearly Bob wasn't telling me everything. But this incident pulled us together. Bob and I were developing a symbiotic relationship. We needed each other."

HAD SAM REALLY KILLED a man? Had Sam invented the scene for this book as a perverse form of self-aggrandizement? Or had Robert Booth Nichols staged the encounter? As the inside man, Nichols had the responsibility to get the Babbitt's bankroll back in play. Sam's money was still sitting in an account in New York. Nichols had apparently concluded that he needed to eliminate any lingering doubts Israel might have and demonstrate beyond doubt that there were evil factions trying to keep them from trading. Sam needed to see that the shadow market was real. So was the Octopus. Terrifyingly real.

Staging a murder was one of the oldest ruses of the grift. It was the ploy that had provided the finale for *The Sting*—a movie inspired by the book *The Big Con*. Blood, guts, guns, the frisson of extreme danger, and the need to flee before the police arrived—the elements were eternal. *Cackle-bladder* was the term of art for the bladder filled with chicken blood concealed in the performer's mouth in the traditional fake homicide. By biting on the cackle-bladder when he was "shot," the "victim" made it appear that his own blood was running out of his mouth.

Had Nichols taken the classic structure of the long con and improvised ingeniously? Was the entire scene part of a remarkable piece of theater directed by Nichols? Instead of placing the cackle-bladder in the faux victim's mouth, he could've rigged the man's turban. Brains had indeed exploded on the sidewalks of Hamburg. Only they were animal brains. If Sam was indeed telling the truth about the murder, it seemed likely that Nichols had staged the stunt with incredible cunning. Kumar had supplied Sam with the weapon, at Nichols's direction. Nichols had arrived with the ammunition and loaded the Beretta with blanks. The silencer had worked perfectly, muffling the gunshot. The turban had been triggered to the split second. Turbans had been used by suicide bombers in Afghanistan. But the notion of using the same ruse to deceive Sam was inventiveness on a scale Sam couldn't imagine—literally. Sam was completely convinced he'd killed a man. As a teenager Sam had once walked into a deli in Manhattan immediately after an armed robbery, and he'd witnessed the shop owner lying on the floor after being shot in the head. The scene in Hamburg was just as real—and just as vivid.

As far as Sam was concerned, he was past the point of no return. He was now a murderer—like Nichols. Staging the murder made it impossible for Sam to leave the shadow market. He believed he could go to prison for the rest of his life if he was caught. He'd also saved Nichols's life, proving himself in the eyes of the CIA hit man. Now Sam truly belonged in the Upperworld.

When confronted years later with the possibility that Nichols had conned him, Sam vehemently disagreed. Of course there was no murder in Hamburg on the day in question—Nichols had cleansed the crime scene. Of course there was no German police investigation—the Octopus knew how to spray a jet of ink and disappear. Sam was convinced that Nichols had possessed the power to make all evidence of the homicide vanish into thin air.

"Bob controlled me from the first day we met," Sam said. "But not in this way. There was no chance he faked it on me. It wasn't a Hollywood setup. The guy's left hip was bleeding profusely. His brains were sprayed all over on the pavement. This was the real thing. I had nightmares about the scene for months. I would wake up in the middle of the night screaming. Bob told me to never mention it again—to not tell a soul. I haven't—until now."*

---

* During three years of reporting, Israel repeatedly said he was holding back one part of his story. His reluctance to reveal this final element of his tale came from fear of being further prosecuted, he said. When I related Israel's account of the murder to the FBI, it was met with extreme doubt. There was no body, no investigation, nothing to confirm Sam's claim to be a killer—thus no way to charge Israel with murder.

. . .

ON JULY 9, Sam wired $120,000,000 to Postbank—the most Bayou could afford to part with. Barthe converted the money into euros. Sam now had 96,864,000 euros. In the process of changing currencies, Bayou was shorted $60,000, the kind of thievery Sam feared—but failed to notice.

Before leaving Germany to evade retaliation from Severt's faction or arrest by the Hamburg *polizei*, Sam and Bob went to meet the man who'd make the trades on behalf of Postbank. Derek Mirsky was waiting for them in the first-class lounge at the airport. Mirsky was six-four, with dark hair and a thin, angular face. Like Barthe, Mirsky was in his thirties, urbane, and spoke fluent English. Mirsky wore a trench coat draped over his shoulder on top of his suit, an affectation that seemed torn from the pages of a spy thriller.

Sitting in the Lufthansa lounge, Nichols said he was concerned they were being followed—by another faction, the police, he couldn't tell. Nichols suggested they take a walk. The trio drove to a nearby castle. As they strolled the grounds to avoid their conversation being listened to, Mirsky explained that Sam's money would be "segregated." The account would be in Israel's name and that of Polaris Inc., the company Mirsky controlled. Trading would be on a joint basis, with 90 percent of the proceeds going to Sam and 10 percent to Mirsky. While decisions would be made together, Sam insisted that he have final say—at least on paper. The program would start the following week.

The homicide had altered the dynamic between Nichols and Israel. Sam had been the leading voice when it came to trading—at least that was what he thought. Nichols had taken charge of security.

But Nichols said Israel's skill and fearlessness were exactly the kinds of qualities "the boys" were looking for in an asset. For months, Nichols had been telling Sam that he was being groomed to become the next George Soros. Now Nichols suggested that Sam could become the next Robert Booth Nichols. Nichols conceded that he was getting older. He was exhausted by all the travel and need for vigilance. Nichols couldn't keep up the pace of being a real-life James Bond forever. He needed to find a successor, and it appeared that Sam had what it took—especially as a mythomaniac.

But when the pair returned to London, Nichols was agitated and impatient. Three months had gone by, and he hadn't made a dollar from the trades. What if the trade didn't happen again? What if Sam wired the money back to New York again? What if Sam decided not to trade at all?

Early on the morning of July 12, Nichols turned up at Sam's door at Claridge's in an anxious frame of mind. He knocked loudly. Sam found Nichols pacing in the hallway. Still half asleep, dressed in shorts and a T-shirt, he let Nichols in.

"I've got to talk to you," Nichols said.

"What's going on?" Israel asked.

"Look, you know I've got a bunch of deals going on," Nichols said.

"Yeah," Israel said.

"The condo I rent in Hawaii, I've known the owners for years," Nichols said. "It's going on the market. Prices are skyrocketing. Real estate is taking off there. The owner says I can get an inside deal on the place. I'll clean up."

Israel sat on his bed, still groggy.

"Then there are the gemstones we looked at," Nichols said. "From the guy with the motorcycle."

Israel nodded.

"But I'm strapped at the moment," Nichols said. "I've only got a couple of hundred grand in cash."

"What do you need?" Israel asked.

Nichols held Sam's gaze.

"Ten million dollars," Nichols said. "In cash. Right now."

"You know I love you," Israel sighed. "I'll give you anything I have. I have no problem lending you ten million. But there are two problems. Number one, the money in Postbank isn't all my money. A lot of it belongs to my investors. Number two, what if I can't get into the market? What if the Postbank deal doesn't happen, like last time? I needed that tranche from the last deal for my fund."

Nichols desisted—for the moment. The day was spent tending to last-minute arrangements with Barthe and Mirsky. That evening, Sam met Bob and Ellen for dinner. They ate in a pub in Mayfair, one of the ordinary places catering to tourists. Pints of beer and hamburgers were ordered. Israel had discovered that the dark and milky stout made by Guinness mixed well with his opiate painkillers. Five or six sips of stout and his back stopped hurting and he entered a kind of blissed-out oblivion.

"There's something about me I really didn't want to bring up," Nichols said. "I have a solution to the ten million. But it involves a very secret side of me. You have to swear to never tell a soul about it."

Nichols took a breath.

"You can trust me," Sam said reassuringly.

"There is something I have in my possession that is very dangerous,"

Nichols said. "It can be collateral for the ten million. You're going to take possession of it. But you can't tell anyone about it. You can't talk about it at all. Not to anyone. It can get you major fucking dead real quick. I want you to hold it until I give you the ten million back."

"I don't need collateral from you," Israel said. "If you tell me you're going to give the money back, I know you'll give me the money back."

"No, I can't do it any other way," Nichols said.

"Okay," Israel said. "So what is the collateral worth?"

"A hundred million."

"You're going to give me ten-to-one security?"

"If things go really bad, then it will only be worth fifty million," Nichols said. "But you'll still have five-to-one."

Nichols wouldn't say what the collateral was. But Nichols was drinking, and when he drank he was indiscreet—or at least that was the impression he wanted to create. Nichols said he hadn't told Sam everything about the Federal Reserve bonds he planned to retrieve from Yamashita's hidden caves in the Philippines. Pausing to make sure no one in the pub was listening, Nichols said he already had one of the boxes. It was stored in a vault in London. The box had belonged to the family of Chiang Kai-shek, but Nichols had been trusted to take possession of it. The box contained $100 million in Fed bonds. Sam would take possession of the box as security for the $10 million advance against the fees Nichols was about to earn from the trades.

Sam had a demand before he agreed to the deal. There was something he wanted from Nichols in return—something that he'd been nagging Nichols about since they first met.

"I'll give you the ten million on one condition," Sam said. "You have to show me the film."

"What film?"

"You know what fucking film I'm talking about."

"Five hundred people have been murdered because of that film," Nichols said.

Sam was not to be denied: no JFK assassination film, no $10 million. It was Nichols's turn to concede.

A screening was arranged in Sam's suite at Claridge's. A video player was brought to Sam's room by housekeeping and hooked up to the flat-screen television. To see the film properly and in perfect detail, Sam created a miniature darkroom by draping the heavy night curtain over the television.

"Bob was standing next to me, helping me by pulling the curtain more taut so I could see better," Sam said. "Bob was always giving me fatherly advice like that. He wanted us to go somewhere better to screen the videotape, but I didn't want to wait. If I was going to watch it in my room, he thought I should at least do it properly."

Nichols played the twenty-seven-second clip for Sam, not once but over and over again. It was just as Nichols had said. The "real" Zapruder film included seven frames showing Secret Service driver William Greer slowing the car and turning and shooting President Kennedy at point-blank range. Sam thought he could make out ten or twelve distinctive gunshots peppering the presidential motorcade, forever disproving the single-bullet theory of the Warren Commission. The grainy and grim footage was familiar—the car speeding up and slowing down, the movement of the Secret Service agents, the jerking of the president's head when he was shot in the throat, how Jackie Kennedy tried to leap out of the car. The First Lady had seen it all, Nichols explained, but she had been told that if she ever talked her children would be killed. The film was terrifying in its implications. Sam had seen the truth: Lee Harvey Oswald had not killed JFK. The Mafia and the CIA had collaborated. The assassination had been a coup.*

"The story was never covered because the press is controlled by the government," Sam recalled. "The networks, the wire services, the *New York Times*—they're all under the direction of the CIA. They all agree to keep certain covert material hidden from the people. But the film was absolutely authentic. I could see it for myself. In super–slow motion you see that there was something in the driver's hand and then it went back into his jacket. That was the altered film."

"Why can't we bring this out?" Sam asked Nichols.

"They'll just say it was doctored," Nichols said. "Then they'll kill whoever is involved."

THE NEXT MORNING, Israel and Nichols took a taxi to Rector Street near Piccadilly Circus. They entered a nondescript building, passing a security guard. This was the home of the London Safe Deposit Company, known as the "Queen's Vault" because British royalty stored their most precious jewels there. Israel and Nichols got in the elevator. To Sam's surprise it went down, not up, lurching to a halt in a bunkerlike sub-basement. At the far end of a long corridor was a door with a camera with a retina scanner attached. Nichols put his chin on the rest under the camera, and his eyeball was digitally scanned. Nichols pushed a button and the door opened. Down another flight

---

* The tale about Greer has circulated for decades, despite the obvious fact that none of the hundreds of witnesses saw him draw his weapon and shoot. Common sense raises the question of why an assassin would take the risk of firing from the front seat of the car in the motorcade in plain sight. Even among ardent conspiracy theorists, the Greer explanation is widely seen as baseless.

of stairs was a thick slab of bulletproof glass, behind which sat a friendly elderly Englishman with a Cockney accent. The clerk cheerfully signed Nichols and Israel in. Nichols said that Israel wanted to rent a safe deposit box as well. The clerk found that the box next to Nichols's happened to be available. The price was five hundred pounds for one year. Sam paid for two years in advance—for the rest of 2004 as well as 2005.

The clerk led Israel and Nichols down another hallway to a large silver Chubb walk-in safe—the kind of safe Sam's ancestors had once used to store the Israel family fortune in New Orleans. Nichols's safe deposit box was taken out, as was Sam's empty box. Nichols waited while the clerk left to provide them with privacy. Once he was gone, Nichols opened his safe deposit box and removed a blue shoulder bag. Inside the bag was a laundry bag from the Shangri-La Hotel, a chain of Asian luxury hotels. Nichols then pulled an antique brown leather and metal box from the laundry bag. The box resembled a briefcase in dimensions. It was crusted with rust. The seal said, "Federal Reserve of the United States" in the same font as the American dollar. It looked just like the briefcases Sam had seen in the photographs, back when Nichols had first told him about Yamashita's gold.

"This is incredible—" Sam said before Nichols hushed him.

"We'll talk later," Nichols said.

Israel polished the seal with his hand. There were numbers on the case:

M. BOX NO. 000120
S.C. NO. 1224-22
P.D. NO 11-22
A.C. NO 103-12-179992

Sam gingerly lifted the case and found it was surprisingly heavy, as if it were lined with cement. The rust made it look antique, as if it had been exposed to the elements for many years. The lock was vintage 1930s.

After placing the case in Sam's safe deposit box, Nichols summoned the clerk, who opened another smaller safe deposit box and then exited again. In this box was a videocassette recorder with a protective cover on top. Inside the VCR was a copy of the Zapruder film—the "real" one. Following Nichols's instructions, Sam placed the VCR in his safe deposit box and they left.

Outside, the two men walked through the streets of London without speaking. Both were careful to see that they weren't being followed. As they crossed through Piccadilly Circus, Nichols told Sam how he'd obtained the briefcase. A Swiss lawyer he'd contacted was an intelligence operative retained by the Chinese government to deal with the sale of an entire vault filled with Federal Reserve notes— billions upon billions upon billions of dollars' worth of bonds. Not the actual Chinese government but the "quasi" government of Chiang Kai-shek's exiled ancestors, the Mai Wahs.

"You can never open this box," Nichols said. "If you do, you're opening Pandora's box. It is rigged with explosives. If it isn't opened at exactly the right angle, in exactly the right way, it will blow up and you'll be dead."

"What happens to the box after you repay me?" Sam asked.

"You keep that box," Nichols said. "I expect to be getting more of them soon. But you can never tell anyone about it. If something happens to me—if I get killed—someone will eventually contact you and tell you what to do."

"What about the Zapruder film?" Sam asked.

"That's for your own protection," Nichols said. "Now you're in all the way up to your ass. There's no looking back."

ON JULY 13, $10 million was transferred from Sam's account in Postbank to an account in the name of Robert Booth Nichols. In sealed testimony years later, Nichols would describe what he did with the money Israel gave him, even as he claimed it had been a perfectly legitimate transaction, not a confidence game. First, the money had been quickly wired to a series of accounts in Singapore, London, and Liechtenstein, before the German authorities could attempt to stop the transfer. Flush with his windfall, Nichols had then diced up the $10 million among his associates. Many were people Sam had never met. An Asian man who had acted as an intermediary in getting the Federal Reserve bonds received $200,000. The attorney Nichols had used to authenticate the MTN agreements was paid $50,000. So it went as Nichols gave cuts to the bit players he'd used along the way.

In all, Nichols doled out $1.4 million. This covered his expenses—hotels, airfares, meals, drinks. There was also the overhead of establishing the big stores, like paying off security guards at Barclays in London. Then there were payments for Kumar and the stunt con man who'd faked his own death in Hamburg—the man with the exploding turban. No checks were issued or records kept. In Nichols's world everything was done in cash.

Even after taking care of his comrades, Nichols had done extremely well. As he'd told Sam, he'd purchased a luxury condo on Kahala Beach. But he didn't limit his real estate purchases to Hawaii. Until then, Nichols's only assets had been twenty acres of crocodile-infested rainforest in Australia. Now Bayou's investors' money allowed him to purchase a beautiful piece of land in Prescott, Arizona, for $1.5 million and begin making plans to build a million-dollar home on the property. As a cash reserve, he kept $2 million in a bank in Singapore and $1 million in his HSBC account in London. It was more than enough money to keep himself in the manner to which he was rapidly growing accustomed.

Nichols's income for the year 2004 was exactly $10,000,008. The extra eight dollars came from residuals for his role in the movie *Under Siege*. Naturally Nichols paid no income tax—since he'd been instructed by alleged CIA operatives to never pay tax because of national security. Only now there was a more quotidian explanation: How would the American government ever find out about the $10 million?

In the end the big con had gone perfectly: telling the tale, playing the big store, using the turban as the cackle-bladder for the convincer. The final step in the long con was called the blow-off. It was a critical moment. A method had to be devised for Nichols to depart the stage without causing suspicion in Sam. Ending a con without the Babbitt's notifying the law—or even realizing that he was the victim of a confidence game—was exquisitely difficult. "In the most sophisticated cons, the doe may ever after remain unaware that he has been bilked, merely registering the affair as a gambit that failed," Luc Sante wrote in an introduction to a reprint of *The Big Con*. "The Cheshire-cat aspect of the long con merits attention. Humor is never far from the heart of the con. The con which hoists the victim by his own petard combines formal elegance, careful imitation of legitimate enterprise, and rough justice into what can only be called parody."

Such was the case with Sam. The secret market was real, Sam believed. So were the Federal Reserve bonds Nichols had given him as collateral for the $10 million. Returning to the Queen's Vault the day after he had taken possession of the Fed box, Sam removed the briefcase and inspected it more closely, taking photographs with his digital camera. He didn't dare try to open it, fearful that it was booby-trapped and would explode. He was giddy with excitement at the world he now belonged to. The con was complete. All that remained was for Nichols to come up with an excuse to quietly leave London and disappear into a comfortable retirement dividing his time between Hawaii and Arizona. "Exit Robert Booth Nichols" would be the stage direction as the curtain came down on his bravura performance.

But then something very strange happened—or didn't happen. Nichols didn't vanish. Sam wasn't given the slip. There was no blow-off. Nichols remained Sam's constant companion and handler in London. He appeared to anticipate the trades in Germany just as much as Sam. It seemed that Nichols wasn't content with a score of $10 million—not with more than $100 million still on the table. No self-respecting inside man could exit the stage with the Babbitt holding on to such a sum.

The two men completed each other. It was as if they were each convincing the other that their fraud was real. In Nichols's eyes, Sam really was the wizard of Wall Street. Likewise, under the gaze of Sam Israel, Nichols was a covert operator who'd been the inspiration for *The Bourne Identity*. In their twisted way they'd become true friends. Both were fakes who found authenticity in the other. Both were playing a game of make-believe that best resembled a Russian Matryoshka doll, with each delusion containing another delusion inside the next delusion.

CHAPTER FIFTEEN

Deliverance

T he mechanics of the secret bond market had never been entirely clear to Sam—or to Nichols. The obvious reason was that the entire market was a concoction. But the fraud was enabled by the mysterious nature of postmodern capitalism. New financial instruments were being created all the time on Wall Street, "structured products" that were traded by banks in "private placements." One of Bayou's major investors, Deutsche Bank, was involved in a bet that exemplified how wispy and abstract trading could get. To Sam's delight, the bank had invested $32 million in Bayou purely as a hedge against an insanely arcane investment it had made in a security created to enable bets on a basket of hedge funds—one of which was Bayou. The Deutsche position in the basket of hedge funds didn't involve putting money into any actual funds. The security was "synthetic," in the language of Wall Street, like collateral debt obligations and other derivatives that had become a multi-trillion-dollar market. It was a bet on a bet, which the bank had decided to hedge by actually investing in Bayou.

The mind-bending complexity of Wall Street enabled flimflam artists in the shadow market to talk mumbo jumbo and appear to be making sense. Perversely, it was the correlative of what Sam did with Forward Propagation at Bayou. Sam's trading program didn't actually work—at least in the way Sam claimed. But he could talk about it as if it did. The same logic applied to Postbank. Thus Golo Barthe could call Sam and say that an $18 billion letter of credit had been issued by a bank in the Netherlands. The transaction was secured by Israel's 100 million euros. Barthe told Sam to contact Postbank's bond traders in Liechtenstein—the tranches had been traded there. Sam immediately phoned the principality. The conversation was conducted in broken English and slightly confusing, but it was clear that the man was saying that the trade had indeed gone through. Two tranches. The profit was $300 million—and that was only the start. It was happening, at long last. Sam and Bob Nichols began to plan to celebrate that evening. But Sam didn't let his excitement go too far, not this time, not after his earlier disappointments. He wanted to confirm the trades and get the money in hand first.

"I called Postbank to arrange to get the money wired to my account," Israel said. "But they denied the trade had ever happened. Postbank said the trade had never taken place. They said that the guy in Liechtenstein had never told me that he made the trade. They said he didn't speak English well enough. They pretended that they didn't even know what kind of trade I was talking about. I went apeshit. It was all a lie. They'd made the trade and they had made a lot of money and they were trying to keep it.

"I flew from London to Hamburg that day. I met with two of the top dogs at Postbank. Bob and Ellen came with me. Things had gone up way higher than Golo by that point. I insisted on a translator and stenographer being present. They told us that Golo Barthe was just a regional retail sales guy for Postbank—which was obviously not true. I told them that I was going to go to *Der Spiegel* with the story. I said I had a tape recording of my conversation with the trader in Liechtenstein and I would release it to the press. Postbank had just gone public and now it was cheating me out of $100 million? A German bank was defrauding a trader named Israel? How was that going to look? I said that I knew they were trying to boost their balance sheet. They tried to bully me—to get me to back down. But I put on a masterful performance."

Postbank said it would consider how to deal with the situation. As the trio left the meeting, Bob Nichols embraced Sam with delight. "Your professionalism was incredible," he said.

"You're the most dangerous man we've ever met," Ellen Nichols added. "With the possible exception of 'Double Deuce'—the great English spy."

Sam was floating on air. That night they all went out to dinner with Barthe. The deceptions of the senior executives were deplored. Treachery in the shadow market was rampant, Bob said. Derek Mirsky, the young rakish trader, was going to trade MTNs the following day in Frankfurt, Barthe reported. Nichols gave Barthe a grim warning to pass along to Mirsky: If he screwed around he'd be in deep, deep trouble. Ordering rounds of scotch on the rocks—Sam stuck to wine—Barthe and Nichols both got wildly drunk. Outside in the parking lot, Barthe smashed his car into another car and they all ran into the night laughing. Life was a lark again. Sam was on his way back to the top.

The next morning Sam went to Postbank to withdraw a few thousand euros from Bayou's account for walking-around money. The bank clerk entered Bayou's name in the computer and found the account— but no money in it. One hundred million euros were gone; all of it had been withdrawn. The clerk panicked. Bayou Funds LLC's "non-depletion" account was depleted in the extreme. Sam's signature was supposed to be required for any withdrawal. But he had also signed a power-of-attorney agreement giving Mirsky power to give "irrevocable" instructions to Postbank. The power of attorney had evidently fooled a clerk.

Ten horrifying minutes later, the money was found in the account of Polaris Inc.—the company Mirsky controlled. It was very nearly a bank heist of staggering proportions. John Dillinger could only dream about scoring more than $100 million. By pure fluke Sam had stumbled into the plot before Mirsky had made good his getaway. Postbank immediately froze the Polaris account and the German police were notified. By then, Mirsky had vanished.

When Sam was called in for an "interview" with the German police, he decided to bring a lawyer. A thick file with George Katcharian's name on it was placed on the table by two German detectives and a government bank regulator. Katcharian was the London specialist in the shadow market whom Nichols had introduced to Sam. Katcharian had led Sam to a daisy chain of joker brokers, each more crooked than the last. But Sam did not reach the obvious conclusion.

"I told the German police the truth to a degree," Sam said. "I said I was there to do some bond trading. But I didn't specify the programs.

I was trying to be helpful without revealing that I'd signed secrecy agreements not to tell. They said Katcharian was a very dubious character. The same for Mirsky. Those two were definitely people of interest to the German police."

The possibility of trading had been stopped cold by Mirsky's attempted theft. Despite repeated pleas from Sam and his German lawyers, Postbank kept the money in Bayou's account frozen. To the Germans Sam wasn't a potential victim—he was a suspect. Money laundering was one of the most complex crimes to recognize. Legitimate and illegitimate businesses commingled in ways designed to bewilder banks. Postbank could be liable if it allowed the money to be transferred when Israel was surrounded by such dubious figures. Until the suspicions of fraud were fully resolved, Bayou's money was trapped.

Sam called Marino in Connecticut to explain what had happened. He told Marino that he was going to "take care" of Mirsky. Since the staged homicide in Hamburg, Israel had begun to imagine himself as a killer—as both a matter of remorse and a source of pride. Sam told Marino that Nichols had made "arrangements." Sam said Mirsky had been jumped and beaten up and left for dead. It wasn't true. But Sam wanted Marino to think he had taken action. He also wanted Marino to know what happened to people who double-crossed him.

"For all I know he's dead in the gutter, that motherfucker," said Sam.

Marino was duly intimidated—and frightened. The longer Sam was with Nichols, the more it seemed to Marino that Israel was capable of real violence. "After that call I was expecting the FBI to come knocking on Bayou's door any day," Marino recalled. "But they never came to Bayou. They never asked to talk to the chief financial officer—me. It makes you wonder."

. . .

SAM HAD TO GET BACK to New York. He had to keep Marino in line. He also had to keep up appearances for Bayou's employees. He left his German lawyer in charge of efforts to get the money in Post-bank unfrozen and flew home. One of Bayou's largest investors had demanded a meeting. Consulting Services Group of Memphis had more than $30 million in the fund. Years earlier, Sam had hired the son of a CSG executive to work on the trading floor, believing it was part of a quid pro quo for getting more of CSG's money. The unspoken arrangement had worked, as far as Sam was concerned. But the son had suddenly resigned. Marino suspected the son had witnessed something that tipped him off about the fraud. Marino's dread was seemingly confirmed when Lee Giovanetti of CSG called and said he wanted to inspect Bayou's records; he had doubts about how the fund was being run.

Sam had no choice but to agree to the sit-down. But Marino made sure Sam wasn't in the office when Giovanetti and his team actually arrived. Left on his own, Marino showed Giovanetti into the conference room. When Giovanetti demanded to see Bayou's internal financial statements, Marino said no. The records were confidential. He could look at the audit, Marino said, like any other investor. Tempers flared when Giovanetti cast doubts on Bayou's "operational procedures." Then the subject of Richmond-Fairfield was raised. This was too much for Marino. Leaping to his feet in fury, Marino screamed that he was outraged, *outraged*, by the slander implied in the question.

The CSG team departed. A sternly worded letter from Giovanetti arrived the next day, declaring that CSG was redeeming its entire investment. Sam's reply affected indignation. "The meeting was a scripted, farcical attempt to get us to jump through onerous hoops in order to justify taking your client's money out of Bayou," Sam wrote. Sam said he resented the personal criticism from an erstwhile friend. "I have been taken advantage of by many 'friends' because of my trading abilities," Sam wrote. "Our motto is very simple: 'If you don't believe, you're free to leave.'"

DAYS LATER, Sam was dressed in a pair of sweatpants and a T-shirt when he answered a knock on his front door. FBI Special Agent Carl Catauro and Financial Investigator Kevin Walsh introduced themselves and explained that they were concerned that Bayou had been the target of an attempted fraud in Germany. Sam invited the agents in. He assured them that transactions involving Postbank had been the result of an unfortunate misunderstanding. It was being sorted out by lawyers in Germany.

To the FBI agents, Israel appeared composed, but also slightly manic. Then Sam started to tell a story that stopped the agents in their tracks. He said that he was trading in a secret bond market in Europe. The money in Postbank was in a "nondepletion account" that enabled the money to collateralize trades in securities in the secret market. Other funds would "ping" off the Postbank money. There was no risk. The returns were amazing, Sam grinned—billions and billions. The FBI officials looked interested—then concerned. Sam assured them it wasn't a fraud.

Catauro and Walsh exchanged glances. Sam offered the FBI agents a tour of the house and the chapel, proudly showing them his collection of reptiles. He took them up to the music studio in the chapel's loft and bragged that it was where he jammed with the Allman Brothers.

He said he was going to throw a party the next time the band was in New York. Lying down on the couch in the chapel, wincing from back pain, Sam assured the two FBI officials that they'd be invited.

The agents didn't pretend to be experts on international commerce—certainly not compared to a big-time hedge fund trader like Israel. But the tale about the shadow market didn't add up. They said they were concerned he was being duped. Sam confidently replied that he knew what he was doing. He told them about Robert Booth Nichols and how the bond market financed CIA covert activities. Sam said that part of the proceeds was used for charitable purposes. He told them about the American Academy for Excellence and all the good works he was going to do. He was so convinced he began to convince the FBI investigators. Was it possible that such a market existed? Was Sam trying to abscond with Bayou's money? If it was real—if Israel knew more than they did—why had they never heard of the trading programs before?

"Only the upper levels of people in the government know about the existence of the market," Sam said. "Regular FBI agents don't know about the programs because you aren't high enough."

Sam lit a cigarette—a habit that had grown since he had fallen under the sway of the chain-smoking Nichols. "All of this has to be off the record," Sam said. "If word of the market got out it could destabilize the American economy. It would rock the financial world."

Catauro and Walsh left the Trump mansion in a daze. "What the fuck was that?" Catauro said as they walked across the circular driveway in the shadow of the Eros fountain. "Can this thing exist?"

"I have no idea," Walsh said, shaking his head.

In the following weeks, Catauro and Walsh visited Sam a number of times. Walsh began to take a special interest in the case and

Sam's tales. He looked up Nichols and *The Last Circle* online. Was there really such a thing as the Octopus? Had Danny Casolaro been murdered? Had Sam really glimpsed an alternative reality? Like everyone who came into contact with Sam, the two investigators were disarmed by Sam's sense of humor and self-deprecating friendliness.

But their boss, Special Agent in Charge Steven Garfinkel, wasn't satisfied that Israel had been sufficiently warned. In fact, Garfinkel was absolutely certain that Israel was either caught up in a fraud or perpetrating one. A confidential FBI background report described Robert Booth Nichols as an "international con man." It was evident that Sam didn't know the nature of the person he was dealing with. Garfinkel decided to accompany Catauro and Walsh on their next visit. Like his colleagues, Garfinkel was amazed by the opulence of Sam's house. The three FBI agents found Sam upstairs in the master bedroom. As usual, Sam was happy to see them. He suggested they step outside on the patio off the bedroom so he could smoke a cigarette. To Garfinkel it seemed that Sam was displaying no anxiety or uncertainty when he should have been extremely concerned. Garfinkel got straight to the point.

"Sam, you're getting ripped off," Garfinkel said. "I don't know exactly how or by who, but it's guaranteed you're being defrauded."

"You're not ranked high enough to know what's going on," Sam said.

"If there is a shadow market, diagram it for me," Garfinkel said. He handed Sam a pad of paper. "Show me how it works."

Sam took up a pen and started to draw squares placing the Federal Reserve and the "prime banks" who traded in the shadow market on a grid. The explanation for how the American government funded the black ops of the CIA sounded absurd to Garfinkel. But the language

Sam used to describe the transaction was familiar. *Nondisclosure, high-yield, ready, willing, and able*—Garfinkel recognized it as the language of fraud. He looked Sam in the eye and said as directly as he could that he was absolutely positive someone was trying to steal from him. Sam would have none of it. He told them that he was going back to Germany in a few days to get his money unfrozen. The FBI could come with him. They would see that the shadow market was real.

Garfinkel was exasperated. Robert Booth Nichols was a con man, Garfinkel stated, as if it were a matter of fact. Sam had told them about the $10 million he'd "lent" Nichols. But when Garfinkel asked if it was a consulting fee, or protection money, Sam was evasive. As the conversation progressed, Sam became less vehement in his certainty. It seemed to Garfinkel that Israel was contemplating the possibility that the lead FBI agent might be right. Israel said that Nichols had become a close personal friend. He was like a member of Sam's family—he was "Uncle Bob" to his son. Garfinkel thought Sam's expression betrayed the dawning fear that the FBI was telling him the truth.

"Nichols is full of shit," Garfinkel said. "He's no assassin. You've been reading too many books."

Sam's shoulders slumped. He lit another cigarette.

"Sam was trying to come off as a big-time financier," Garfinkel recalled. "But he couldn't pull it off. He couldn't explain how the deal worked. His diagram was nonsense. But it was also true that 99 percent of the people on Wall Street couldn't explain how derivatives worked, and that was a trillion-dollar industry. I thought he was a moron. Kevin and Carl were nice to him. I wasn't. I told him he was a fucking idiot."

"Either you're a victim or we're going to lock you up," Garfinkel said.

. . .

ISRAEL WASN'T WILLING to confront the possibility that he was being defrauded. Sam preferred magical thinking and the euphoria of believing deliverance was at hand. He preferred to inhabit a world populated by rival factions and secret bonds, all of it in the grasp of the tentacles of the Octopus. Looking for affirmation, he started to become more promiscuous in sharing news about the billions he had coming. Sam didn't talk directly about the shadow market with Bayou's employees and investors. He hinted, alluded, teased. Bayou was going to have a billion under management by the end of the year, he said. The staff got excited. More money meant bigger bonuses.

"During this time, Sam was very active, very optimistic," Dan Marino recalled. "He was running around like a chicken with its head cut off trying to get the trades done for us—that was how he put it. It was 'us.' For the most part, he avoided coming to the office. He said he was too busy. I would go to his house to see him and give him an update on Bayou. But there would be a thousand phone calls and constant interruptions. I had reservations about the shadow market. But he would insist that he was getting closer. He said I had to trust him."

For sharper investors the notion that Bayou would more than double in size in a matter of months was problematic. Growing too quickly was one of the perils of running money. There was a qualitative difference between the skills it took to operate a successful $300 million fund as opposed to a $1 billion fund. *Style drift* was the industry term for the phenomenon that frequently occurred when a trader suddenly traded much larger amounts.

"Comments started to filter back from investors that they were concerned and considering withdrawing," Marino said. "They felt that Sam couldn't handle a billion dollars. Then some investors started to withdraw money. Sam's reaction was indifference. He was sure we were going to get the billion. He said, 'Who cares? Who needs their money?'"

By October redemptions totaled $20 million—in addition to the money CSG had pulled out of Bayou. Marino was able to meet the calls with the money still in Bayou's coffers. But the trend was disturbing. Bayou's sterling reputation was under assault. Then a background report by a financial research company called Back Track fell into the hands of one of Bayou's largest investors, Silver Creek. The report contained evidence of Bayou's regulatory encounters as well as incendiary allegations about the fund by a former employee. Marked "Confidential, Subject to Protective Order," the thirteen-page report noted that Sam hadn't graduated from Tulane—a minor piece of résumé padding but it didn't inspire trust. A lawsuit for $12,000 in back rent brought by his landlord in the early nineties was unearthed. Sam's drunk-driving conviction in 2000 was noted, along with his possession of cocaine.

The report wasn't conclusive, but it unnerved Silver Creek. Confronted with the report, Israel had to think quickly. There was enough money in Bayou's accounts to redeem Silver Creek. But the whole scheme was teetering on collapse if Sam wasn't able to turn around the run of redemptions. On a call with Silver Creek's Eric Dillon, Sam said the drunk driving was a single mistake—the kind of thing that could happen to anyone. And the NASD regulatory finding was about small technical matters. Sam waved away the complaints of the former employee, saying he was disgruntled. Silver Creek was convinced by Israel—but it was a close call. Too close for comfort.

Israel had been back in New York for weeks on end, and there still had been no movement in Europe. Bayou's millions were still jammed up in Germany. It looked like the shadow market was just that—a shadowlike specter. Sam tried to keep a brave face, but the stress was killing him. He wasn't physically able to carry on because of pain radiating out from his lumbar spine to his right leg. In October, he underwent a dorsal column simulator trial, followed by the implantation of a device that transmitted high-frequency signals to his spine. Laid up in bed for the following week, Sam discovered that the device made only a small difference. The extra-strength fentanyl patches he'd been prescribed were little comfort. Life had become a misery again. With the money frozen in Postbank he was trapped. If only he could get the money released. Then he could make a trade. Everything would be better.

While Sam convalesced, Nichols called to say he'd found a deal in London through a small brokerage firm called ODL. Nichols sent a detailed memorandum outlining the trade. Nichols told Sam he'd visited the floor of ODL and found that it was a real brokerage. The floor was so chaotic and packed with traders that Nichols had nicknamed it the "snake pit."

Everything was contingent on getting the money out of Postbank. Sam had hired a posse of German lawyers and "financial consultants" to help him convince the bank to let the money go. But the German bankers were adamant: They had to be completely convinced there was no taint of fraud associated with the transfer before they'd release Bayou's euros. It was logically impossible. The German police and bankers knew that Sam had associated with George Katcharian and Derek Mirsky—both frauds. Sam pleaded, begged, wheedled. But he was incapacitated, physically and financially: stuck in bed, he was unable to make a move in the shadow market.

Then a miracle happened. For no apparent reason, on October 25, the sum of 90,585,928.54 euros was wired from Postbank to an account in HypoVereinsbank. At the exchange rate of the day, it amounted to $114,943,578.86. Sam rejoiced. Incredibly, Postbank had wired $10 million more than it should have. The accounting error was inexplicable—if indeed it was an error. Sam believed the mysterious millions amounted to hush money to keep him quiet about the way the bank had cheated him on the Liechtenstein trade weeks earlier. There was no other way to explain the discrepancy.

Now that the money had been released, Bob Nichols said the trading firm ODL was ready to go. But if Sam didn't come to London immediately he was going to take the ODL opportunity to another client of his. Scared of missing out, Sam decided to brave British Airways' first-class service to Heathrow. He was ready to roll the dice again.

CHAPTER SIXTEEN

The Snake Pit

D uring the nineteenth century, harpooned whales were brought to the wharves of Nantucket and Cape Cod, where they were set upon by sharks. So it was upon Sam's return to London. On his previous trips, he'd met Nichols's intelligence asset colleagues. Now he was introduced to a new circle of shadow marketers Nichols had discovered. It was a society populated by a peculiar mix of the devious, the dangerous, and the deluded—all promising access to a magical land of billions and trillions. One key player was Philip Winsler-Stuart, the head of the Royal Knights of Malta. Aristocratic in bearing, Winsler-Stuart was in his late fifties, thin, tanned, always impeccably dressed in Savile Row suits. A simple computer search would have revealed the many layers of deception surrounding the bogus versions of the real Knights of Malta that had been concocted. These groups were tied to the Freemasons, the Rothschilds, and the pope in Rome, at least according to the more fervid online conspiracy theories.

Another remarkable individual was the Prince Alessandro di Stromboli, who presented himself as a member of Italian nobility and wore gaudy medals and ribbons on his chest to prove it. His wife, the Principessa Stromboli, was a vision of faux gentility: Overweight, overindulged, overly made up, she was draped in exotic silks and chiffon and talked often about her castle in Italy. Like Nichols's CIA pedigree, the prince's claim to such a grand heritage was not proved, but neither was it disproved. The prince and the princess let it be known they were deeply involved in charity work—conveniently exactly the kinds of good causes favored by the Octopus.

James Fairweather was a moneyed gentleman from Zimbabwe who possessed the manners and affect of a graduate of one of the best British private schools. Fairweather was accompanied by an attractive American woman named Katherine Carnegie, a member of one of the billionaire families that ran the secret market. Carnegie was tall and willowy, with flowing brown hair and a flirtatious smile. Sam and Carnegie got along famously, trading stories about their illustrious ancestors as Sam hit on her in his goofball manner. Sam fancied she might be interested in him, since she laughed at his jokes and fawned over his tales of derring-do.

Sam was now supposedly inside the innermost sanctum of high society. But for people involved in transactions that netted profits of billions upon billions, they all had one curious characteristic in common: They were apparently broke. The Knights, the prince, the princess, even Ms. Carnegie—they all needed Sam's ten-figure bank account to get into the market. Each was able to facilitate one or another aspect of the transaction, from providing the approved charitable cause to claiming to have contacts who could obtain "freshly cut" or "seasoned" paper. But Sam was the sine qua non: But for his $120 million there would be no deal.

Barely noticed among Sam's flamboyant fast friends was a nondescript man named Barry McNeil. The ordinary-looking McNeil didn't claim any grand lineage or membership in a prestigious organization. He wasn't a spy or killer. McNeil held himself out as a humble financial engineer in the field of structured alternative investment strategies. He was the ex-boyfriend of Katherine Carnegie. A South African investment advisor from the city of Pretoria, McNeil spoke Afrikaner-inflected English. Five-ten, burly, in his late forties, he had sandy hair, a soft chin, and ruddy cheeks—the kind of man who loved rugby and beer. He wore cheap crepe-soled business shoes, and his suits were purchased off the rack. He looked like a country club bore, not an international finance savant.

Sam and Nichols convened with McNeil in the lobby of Claridge's to discuss the multi-billion-dollar high-yield bonds he proposed to trade. Sitting next to McNeil during the pitch was James Fairweather and a man named Tim Conlan. The trio passed over their business cards. All represented themselves to be "introductory brokers" for ODL. In London, it was a term of art—and artifice. Introductory brokers were salespeople who brought new business to financial firms. But there were subtleties that weren't explained to Sam. The only actual employee of ODL was Conlan. Barry McNeil and James Fairweather were not legally associated with ODL in any way. They were freelance operators with the patina of legitimacy that came from possessing a business card. Their relationship with ODL was strictly transactional. If McNeil and Fairweather landed a new client for ODL, like Sam

Israel, they'd be paid a commission based on the trading volume generated for the firm.

"Bob told me McNeil was part of a group inside this small brokerage company called ODL," Sam recalled. "I asked why McNeil would trade through a little brokerage instead of one of the big players like Goldman Sachs. Bob said that different groups moved around and used lower-profile firms to trade to avoid attention. They made the trades, paid the firm, and then moved on. It seemed reasonable to me. Bob wanted me to vet McNeil as far as trading went. Bob didn't understand the ins and outs of trading like I did. I could see that Barry had trading knowledge. He knew his stuff."

For all his sad sack anonymity, when McNeil talked about the shadow market he was articulate, persuasive, ingenious. McNeil said that the alternative bond market was unregulated, so he wasn't able to undertake the transactions directly, even though there were eager buyers and sellers looking to fulfill the contracts. That was why McNeil had turned to ODL. As a trading company, ODL was regulated by the Bank of England and the Financial Services Authority. As a broker, McNeil "arranged" the transactions, but ODL made the actual trades through Euroclear, the well-known and highly reputable Belgium-based settlement agency that completed trillions of dollars' worth of trades in bonds, equities, and derivatives. In America, the kind of deal McNeil was promoting was known as a "pink sheet" trade—an over-the-counter deal not registered with the SEC. Sam knew about the over-the-counter market for unregulated securities in the United States. So many trades were made in the OTC market— swaps, options, derivatives—that it dwarfed the stock exchange. Few people knew this fundamental fact of Wall Street: Private side bets were much bigger business than the "market" covered by the cable business channels.

If Sam acted quickly, McNeil said, he could be the first to actually invest in the paper. McNeil said there was no risk to Sam's capital. The first trade would be with Société Générale, a French prime bank. There was to be a "contract's worth" of $50 billion of bonds, priced at forty-five cents on the dollar. Each $100 million tranche would sell for $45 million. Because the paper was discounted so aggressively, it wouldn't be difficult to find American pension funds and regional banks in Europe to invest.

Despite Sam's impression to the contrary, it was Conlan who'd brought McNeil and his colleagues to ODL in the first place. Conlan put a legitimate face on the deal, even if it was an unlikely one. He was in his early forties, with a crooked nose bent by years in the boxing ring. Unlike the poseurs with claims to knighthoods and royalty, Conlan spoke with a Cockney accent. For years he'd been a knockabout broker in London struggling to make a living, with little hope of getting ahead financially

Then, in the fall of 2004, McNeil had turned up in London promising to make Conlan rich—filthy stinking rich. Conlan had met McNeil years earlier, in South Africa. In Conlan's experience, South African financial people were a dubious lot, given to lying and cheating. But when McNeil came calling, Conlan had been unemployed and desperate. Hearing McNeil's tale of massive profits, Conlan decided to take the project to people he knew at ODL. He told ODL that commissions alone would run to millions of pounds. The proposition sounded dubious—but what if it were true? The risk for ODL was minimal; the reward potentially fantastic. Thus had Conlan been hired and business cards furnished to McNeil and his string of brokers.

"Barry was very impressive as a financial engineer," Tim Conlan recalled. "Maybe not all that plausible, but he made it sound true. According to Barry, the kind of people in this market didn't trade bonds in the normal market. It wasn't like normal bond trading, where there are lots of trades all the time. Goldman Sachs and Bear Stearns didn't trade these bonds. It was a different world. There were barriers to entry. The amount of money was one. It had to be one hundred million dollars to get in. But the biggest barrier was who you knew. To invest, you had to be approved and become part of it.

"Barry said there were 'exits' in place for the first issuance—that was the term for buyers for the bonds. ODL was going to provide the platform to settle, clear, and execute the trades. That was what I brought to the table. Barry was going to trade one hundred million two or three times a day until the fifty-billion-dollar facility was drawn down. Even a small fraction of the commission would be a big amount of money. I had a number in my head. I was going to make millions."

The psychiatric term for a shared psychosis is *folie à deux* (a madness shared by two). In the case of Sam and Bob, it appeared to take the form of a *folie imposée*, in that the belief in the myth of the shadow market had been imposed on Sam by the dominant Nichols. But in the shadow-market circles of London it seemed to be a *folie à trois*, *à quatre*, *à plusieurs* ("the madness of three, four, many"). The isolation and self-reinforcing culture of the shadow market acted like a hothouse. The men involved had all reached middle age with the disappointments of failure—Israel as a hedge fund trader, Nichols as a spy, McNeil as a financial wizard, Conlan as a broker.

"I was extremely excited," Tim Conlan recalled. "Everyone was.

Including everyone at ODL. Sam was a big hedge fund guy from New York. It was the dream ticket. He was an experienced trader with a big fund. Sam had one hundred million in cash. I genuinely thought it was going to work. I believed that Barry believed it was going to happen. Barry was a great theorist. He told Sam it was very difficult to find people with one hundred million who were willing to invest.

"Nichols didn't say much. He just watched. He was a big guy, tacky, in a scruffy suit, with dandruff. I saw that he was carrying a handgun. I didn't know what he was supposed to be doing—Sam's security, I guessed. I had the strong impression that Nichols was connected to some American intelligence agency. You don't carry a revolver around London if you don't have the proper authority. He carried the weapon on the airplane, I was told. So how do you do that if you're not with the government?

"It seemed to me like Nichols wanted to be in on everything that Sam did. He was all ears. Sam was his little thing. He didn't want anyone else getting his attention. He was jealous, protective. If you wanted to deal with Sam, you definitely had to go through Nichols. But it was clear that Sam didn't need a lot of pitching from Barry. Sam believed it to start with."

Nichols had good reason to be jealous of Sam's attention. As news of Israel's reappearance in London spread, rivals attempted to seduce Israel away from the CIA asset. A self-styled operative from the Israeli intelligence agency, Mossad, promised Sam he'd make billions trading letters of credit. The terms were preposterously complex, involving brokers from Peru, Brazil, and Malta, as well as an "underwriter" from Texas who supposedly pledged $5.8 billion—without a scintilla of proof of the existence of the money.

Nichols called this pretender "the hat," a reference to the yarmulke he wore. Nichols said the hat was a fraud, but Sam didn't listen. He flew to Amsterdam and Barcelona to try to make the trades. A distinctive pattern emerged, though. Each time Sam left Nichols's protection, he was attacked or assaulted; his suite in Claridge's was broken into in the middle of the night, prompting Sam to shoot his Browning 9 mm (with a silencer) at the fleeing figure. The assault appeared to have been orchestrated by Nichols.

Israel went into what he called "full James Bond mode." Nichols convinced Sam that the only way to ensure his safety was to move to the Grosvenor Hotel. It was neutral territory, Nichols said. He also convinced Sam to go to the offices of ODL and see for himself that it was real. ODL was located in Salisbury House, an imposing nineteenth-century building on the north side of London Wall. Despite the large marble entrance on the ground floor, ODL's trading room on the sixth floor was small, cramped, shabby. Barry McNeil and Tim Conlan led Sam and Nichols into a conference room to meet with one of the principals of ODL, Garrett "Graham" Wellesley, Viscount Dangan, the only son of the seventh Earl Cowley and a great-grandnephew of the Duke of Wellington. Unlike the various poseurs Sam had met in recent days, the viscount was the genuine article. In his early forties, tall, correct in his manners, Wellesley had an uncanny resemblance to the Duke of Edinburgh, husband of Queen Elizabeth II. At a glance it was obvious Wellesley was an actual aristocrat, though he was far from pretentious.

"Do you know who the Israels are?" Sam asked as they were introduced.

"Yes, I do," replied the viscount.

A friend of Wellesley's had worked for Sam's uncle's business before it had been purchased by Goldman Sachs. Wellesley knew the

Israel family was one of the truly elite clans in the business. The viscount's history reached back to the Napoleonic Wars, but it paled in comparison to Sam's when it came to trading—which made Sam's behavior all the more puzzling.

"Sam put his feet up on the table of our conference room," Graham Wellesley recalled. "He was wearing rubber boots—the kind you go duck hunting in. He was big-shotting it large. He portrayed himself as someone who came from a world few people even know about—the Rothschilds and the others. He told me his mother was a Rothschild. He was extremely cocky."

Barry McNeil had already pitched the secret bond market to Wellesley. The viscount had been dubious about the existence of the shadow market. He'd never heard of bonds being so radically underpriced. But ODL was small and entrepreneurial, and Wellesley and his partner had only recently obtained control of the company, so he was reluctant to turn his nose up at any business. As a brokerage, ODL didn't take responsibility for what was being traded, after all. Provided the parties were matched—there was a willing buyer and a willing seller—why refuse to trade the securities? Provided certain requirements were met, of course, like full disclosure, and the assurance that no laws were being broken.

"So much money was being talked about that even my broker was going to make an absolute fortune," Wellesley recalled. "I thought we'd make the trades, subject to this, that, and the other thing. I was interested to see if Barry could find the bonds. There are mispriced things in the world. Everyone in the market spends their life looking for arbitrage.

"If one hundred million was leveraged to three—which was a very conservative estimate—Sam would be able to buy three hundred million in bonds at forty and sell it for eighty. So now he could buy six hundred million and then $1.2 billion and $2.4 billion and so on. It was astonishing. For ODL the commissions would have been astronomical. It geometrically increased in size. If we got 1 percent for brokering the deals, it would add up to a hell of a lot of money.

"I didn't believe it entirely, but it wasn't my place to care. It wasn't up to me to question a hedge fund manager like Sam Israel who was running hundreds of millions of dollars. This was real, that was for sure. Who was I to doubt the trades? I was just an executing broker. I was the equivalent of a bank teller questioning a depositor why they are withdrawing money."

On December 7, 2004, Sam wired 90 million euros to an account in ODL. At the exchange rate of the day, it amounted to $120,879,000. Now that the trading was about to commence, McNeil invited Sam and Bob Nichols to a signing ceremony. The event was held at the Rothschild House in Berkeley Square, a neighborhood that had long been home to London's beau monde; Winston Churchill had grown up there, and it was the home of P. G. Wodehouse's fictional upper-class twit Bertie Wooster, as well as the swashbuckling Victorian character Harry Flashman. The house was going to be the headquarters of ODL, McNeil told Sam as he greeted him at the entrance. Once the trading started, ODL would move from its run-down trading floor to the luxury and elegance befitting a multi-billion-dollar trading entity.

"It was a beautiful mansion," Sam recalled. "It was worth at least fifty million. There was an anteroom. There was a grand staircase with a gorgeous chandelier. The house was obviously hundreds of years old. We were led up the stairs to the second floor and through a labyrinth of rooms. We got to the dining room and there were papers laid out for signing. We were going to do a couple of really big deals with the Rothschilds themselves. There were ten of us in the room, including me, Bob and Ellen, and Paul Rothschild.* It was funny because Rothschild and I were trying to figure out if we were related in some way. My mother was born a Rothschild, so we probably were at some point. We signed the documents, and bottles of Cristal champagne were brought out. We made a toast to the deals and what we were doing together."

"To our mutual profit," the celebrants said, chinking glasses. "To the profit of the world."

But the house was not the future home of ODL. Nor was it the place of business for the Rothschilds, or the Carnegies, or the Knights of Malta. The house was for sale. Barry McNeil had told the realtor he was going to buy it—affecting indifference to the multi-million-pound asking price. Drawn by the promise of a huge commission, the real estate agent had agreed to let McNeil use the house for the night. The deception was pure genius. Sam and Bob sipped their stems of Cristal and soaked up the atmosphere. It was as if an entire age of excess had been brought to life under one roof—the frauds within frauds within frauds within frauds turned into an epic delusion.

"I wasn't fooled by it all," Wellesley said. "Real aristocrats would never drink Cristal champagne. It was nouveau riche. Gauche. I didn't rate Sam intellectually. I thought his behavior was bizarre for a big-shot hedge fund trader. He came from a highly accomplished family, which can magnify any sense of insecurity or lack of self-worth. Nor did Nichols appear to be the sharpest knife in the drawer. But Barry was extremely clever. He had someone inside a Swiss bank working

---

* Probably an impostor.

for him. He disguised the deal in layers of international companies and legal documents. I could see it would be impossible to attach any responsibility to him."

WITH ISRAEL SIGNED ON, McNeil was able to use the participation of a major New York hedge fund trader as a marketing tool to bring in other high–net worth individuals. If a trader of Sam's lineage and accomplishment was investing such a massive sum, prospective investors should feel lucky to be in on such a rare and lucrative deal. For weeks, ODL teemed with wealthy people coming to learn more about the magical new bonds. Investors from Italy, South America, the United States, and Switzerland came to ODL. McNeil had hundreds of prospects on the hook, many of them tax-evading expatriates living in London. He had created his own string of introductory brokers, self-styled financial consultants chumming the waters with promises of extraordinary returns. They didn't just target the rich, they went after their lawyers and accountants—people who were very often just as unsophisticated as their clients, and just as easily seduced by the promise of easy money.

Holding meetings in a conference room at ODL, McNeil was very matter-of-fact as he explained the mechanics of the trade. He had a clipboard and a flowchart on a blackboard showing how the trading worked. Investors would double their money in a matter of weeks. Because $100 million was too rich for all but the super-rich, McNeil thoughtfully agreed to lower the entry-level investment to $10 million. It was an affordable way to access the kinds of returns titans like Sam Israel received, McNeil said. McNeil could turn $10 million into $20 million in a matter of weeks. All at no risk!

As the owner of the brokerage, Wellesley stopped in to say hello to new investors. It was a goodwill ambassador gesture. It was also a way to track the commotion. Wellesley watched with curiosity as McNeil and Conlan conducted tours of ODL's premises. It was very odd to give a tour of a brokerage to a prospect. There was nothing to see, apart from rough-edged men sitting behind computer screens cursing and slowly building up plaque on their arteries. The traders weren't swapping mythical secret bonds; real securities were flitting across their screens. But that wasn't the impression evoked for the more impressionable. McNeil was insistent that his new clients see how real ODL was—proof that the shadow market really existed.

The money began to pour into ODL's coffers. However unlikely the investment strategy McNeil proposed, there was no denying the substance of his clients. Like the former owner of Manchester United, who had recently sold his shares in the soccer team, netting nearly $200 million in cash, and was looking for ways to invest the money. Then the chairman of one of the world's largest food service companies arrived at ODL. He was followed by a man who represented himself to be a director of the bank Credit Suisse and said he was going to introduce his Swiss clients to ODL. It all seemed preposterous to Wellesley—but there it was before his eyes. The black comedy reached a new height when ODL was visited by a priest dressed in a flowing red robe who claimed to be a cardinal from Rome representing the Vatican; no less than an agent of God's representative on earth wanted to hear McNeil's pitch.

"I felt like I was living inside a comic book," the viscount recalled. "The Italian prince was talking about the powerful interests he represented. The head of the Knights of St. John was in our offices. I was getting scared. I'd been in business for years and I'd never made easy money fast. It was always hard work. The more money involved, the harder the work gets. This was just too easy. It was too good to be true.

"Then Barry started to talk about investing in ODL. One day he said to me, 'My conglomerate would like to purchase shares in ODL.' Barry knew that ODL was a small company—forty million pounds in revenue, earnings of around ten million pounds. So I started to tell him about our operations—the number of clients, how the business worked. We were sitting in my office. Barry didn't seem particularly interested in the value of the business or how it functioned. It was unusual. He didn't ask about earnings or multiples of earnings. It was like he was saying, 'Don't worry about the price. We're going to make so much money it won't matter.'

"What he did say, explicitly, was that he wasn't valuing ODL on its current income. The money that was going to be made from his trading would be factored into the price. He wasn't trying to talk down the value, or find a way not to have to pay up front. The opposite. Barry was trying to hit the greed button in my head—like he was with everyone else. It looked to me like he feasted on people who thought they could change their lives with ten million—or in Sam's case billions."

EAGERLY AWAITING DELIVERANCE, Israel and Nichols were in the Royal Club one evening when Sam said he had a confession to make. An event had been nagging his conscience for weeks. Sam decided to come clean. Lowering his voice, Sam said that he'd talked to the FBI in New York. Nichols reared back in alarm, his eyes flashing with anger and fear. Only a couple of times, Sam said. He had no choice—he couldn't refuse to talk to the FBI. They had come to him after the money was frozen in Germany. There was nothing Sam could do but answer their questions. Sam conceded that he'd told them about Bob's CIA history and the shadow market. He'd also told them about the $10 million loan. Trying to calm Nichols, Sam said he'd deftly dealt with the FBI and there would be no further problems. It was taken care of, Sam said; it wasn't a problem.

Nichols freaked out. He knew from previous bitter experience that once the FBI was involved in your affairs it was virtually impossible to get them to go away. Sam's talking to law enforcement had put Nichols in direct legal jeopardy, though he didn't tell Sam the nature or extent of any criminal charges he feared. Nichols said he needed legal protection—retroactive protection, showing that the money Sam had "loaned" Bob was a real transaction. Nichols needed to show that Sam hadn't exchanged $10 million for a briefcase filled with Federal Reserve bonds that might be worthless. Sam was eager to placate his insistent partner. Together they wrote a Financial and Security Consultancy Agreement that recited Sam's desire to enter "certain buy/sell relationships in Europe" to "maximize profits for himself." The agreement said that in return for $10 million Nichols would act as a security consultant for Israel for five years.

The document was backdated to July 11, 2004—the day before Sam had transferred the funds to Nichols's accounts. Then Nichols had Sam execute an "Acknowledgment" that required him to agree to discuss the "tangible articles" issued by the Federal Reserve that he had stashed in a safe in the Queen's Vault with only "credentialed authorities of the U.S. Treasury, the U.S. Federal Reserve, or authorized officials of top tier banking institutions." The contract was ludicrous: How was the con man going to enforce its terms? But Sam signed, attesting, "I fully understand and acknowledge the sensitivity, confidentiality and risks associated with this matter."

BY THE END OF THE YEAR, Sam had no choice but to return to New York to deal with the legal formalities of his divorce. On New Year's Eve, Tim Conlan called from London. He was ecstatic. The Soc-Gen paper had arrived. McNeil had done it. Only a limited amount of paper was issued at the end of the year, to enable banks to settle their capital accounts. But McNeil had managed to find a tranche.

"Barry made everyone believe they were on the cusp of making a killing," Graham Wellesley recalled. "There were faxed confirmations from banks. There were signed documents. People were coming and going. It was just about to happen. Everyone thought they were going to be on Easy Street—clients, brokers. Everyone was wound up on greed extraordinaire.

"I told Conlan that I wanted a list of every aspect of the bonds McNeil was going to trade. Then I called my compliance officer. I told him to physically walk over to the Soc-Gen office in London and meet with them personally. I wanted everything confirmed—the yield, the maturity date, the bond number. Something smelled off. So when my compliance officer checked, the numbers of the bond didn't match. There were discrepancies. I wasn't going to let the trade go through. My firm would be liable if the wrong bonds were purchased and Sam lost his money. That night, Sam called ODL. He was furious. There was only a kid from the back office working that late. Sam tore the kid a new asshole. He was screaming at the kid, saying, 'You fucking idiot, you do what I say.' The next day I went to Barry and told him that I had refused to do the transaction."

"There were a lot of disappointed people," Conlan recalled. "Expectations were high. Mine included. I expected the trade to work. So did Sam. It was hard to know what was really going on. It was a murky world. Whether it was true or not, I didn't know. But the paper wasn't delivered. Barry was supposed to deliver the bonds. There was always an excuse. The exit wasn't ready, he said. They were still 'cutting' the paper. We obviously didn't have the correct people to deliver the paper."

SAM BROKE THE BAD NEWS to Marino at the Trump house: They were still trapped. Their fates were tied together. Each had the ability to destroy the other. It was an idea that was starting to crowd Marino's thoughts. "I was angry with him," Marino said. "He kept saying it would work, but I started to lose hope. I didn't have any belief in him anymore. I wanted to stop the fraud, but I was scared of Sam. I thought he would hurt me physically. I didn't know what was real and what wasn't. If I went to the FBI and the bond market was real—then I'd ruined our lives because I wouldn't believe him. At the same time I had so many questions and concerns and I couldn't get a straight answer out of him. I thought he'd go ballistic if I didn't do what he asked."

Marino thought Sam had become like the lead character in "The Secret Life of Walter Mitty," the James Thurber short story about a mild-mannered man who fantasizes about his grand adventures—like being an assassin on a suicide mission, or a fighter pilot on a dangerous raid deep in enemy territory. "Sam always exaggerated the stories he told people, even in front of me when he knew that I knew they weren't true," said Marino. "I would know the precise facts, which differed from his story, but he'd still go on and on. It was what supposedly made him a character. He was the hero of each and every story he told. The difference between Walter Mitty and Sam was that Mitty only daydreamed about his exciting life. Sam went out and actually lived his adventures. Only things didn't happen the way Sam described them. He couldn't help himself. I spent a lot of time trying to catch him in a bona fide lie that I could document. But I wasn't able to do it."

CHAPTER SEVENTEEN

Yamashita's Gold

In January of 2005, Sam received an invitation to the inauguration of George W. Bush. The invite was a token of the political IOUs Sam had accumulated by donating hundreds of thousands of dollars to Bush. Sam wasn't particularly political. He considered the contributions to Bush to be a form of life insurance. The president was the only person in the country with the power to commute federal prison sentences. Sam wanted to know he could reach Bush through his cousin John Ellis if the day came when he needed a favor.

Sam didn't bother to attend the inauguration or the balls he was also invited to. It was freezing in Washington and his back was killing him. Besides, there was the weight of the depressing news about

Bayou. The Problem was more than $150 million, if the fake performance for the previous year was included.

Bob Nichols remained in London trying to get Barry McNeil's trade completed. Then came word that 22 million euros had been transferred out of Bayou's account at ODL. There was no explanation for the bizarre transaction. Who had made the withdrawal? Nichols? McNeil? ODL said it was an administrative error. Because it was noticed quickly, ODL had been able to get the money back to Bayou's account within two days. But it was another bad sign: The sharks of London were gnawing on Bayou's money, only to be gaffed away at the last moment. It seemed that it was just a matter of time before someone succeeded in stealing all of it.

The failure of the Soc-Gen trade had been a severe blow to Sam's morale. Calling from London, Barry McNeil offered a variety of reasons for the ongoing failure to find the "paper." There was no paper being issued because it was too early in the year. Trading occurred only intermittently. Sam had to be patient. But Sam didn't want to hear excuses. He wanted action. Bob Nichols had remained in London to ensure that the trades were done. But there was no movement, no sign of progress—at least not that Sam was told about.

Bayou appeared doomed, but it emerged that the fund still possessed some measure of luck—even if it was dumb luck. When Sam's trading partner Jimmy Marquez had left Bayou years earlier, the fund had purchased 1 million shares in a clean coal company called KFX. For years, Marquez's final trade had appeared to be just another woebegone reminder of his failure. Then fortune smiled on Israel and Marino.

"We were at the bottom of the barrel cashwise," Dan Marino said. "We didn't have enough money to operate the business and handle the withdrawals. There was the money in London, but Sam insisted that he needed it to make the trade in the secret market. Pretty much the only liquid asset we had was the KFX position. Sam used to ridicule the position because it was Marquez's trade. But at the beginning of 2005 the stock went way, way up. We sold it all. That day we made fifteen million. It was the largest amount of money Bayou ever made on a trade."

The windfall didn't give Sam hope. It bought some time—maybe six months. But he needed to make ten times that amount to save Bayou—and himself.

"I knew I didn't have much time left," Sam said. "If I wired the money back to New York and gave up, I figured I could probably stay in business for another year or two just by cheating. But I was getting tired of people fucking with me. I was really on edge. I was never sleeping. I was threatening people. Brutally. I was screaming at everybody. No one was helping. No one was performing."

EVENTS IN EUROPE were taking yet another unlikely turn. Alone together in the bars and casinos of London, Bob Nichols and Barry McNeil began to develop their own relationship. Passing the evenings in his usual haunts, Nichols drank heavily and regaled the South African with tales of his career as a covert operator. Along the way, Nichols told McNeil about Yamashita's gold and the cache of Federal Reserve bonds hidden in caves in the Philippines.* It was the tallest of his tales, normally met with skepticism if not outright disbelief. But

---

* That this exchange took place is based on Nichols's subsequent testimony, which remained under seal until it was leaked to the author by a confidential source.

McNeil had an astonishing reply. He told Nichols that he knew all about the hidden caves where the Japanese army had stashed the looted riches of China at the end of the Second World War. More than that: McNeil had been inside the caves. He'd seen Yamashita's gold with his own eyes! This was incredible news. Some of the fiercest Special Forces soldiers ever had gone to the island of Mindanao to hunt for the gold. All to no avail. And yet the pudgy and unprepossessing McNeil had ventured into the mountains and found the treasure? He'd staged an assault on the fortified redoubt deep in terrorist-protected jungle? The thought beggared belief. The deed was the ultimate measure of derring-do—the kind of thing Bob Nichols did, or claimed to do.

But wait: There was even more. McNeil told Nichols not only that he had confirmed the existence of the treasure with his own eyes but that he was now raising money to launch a mission to reclaim the fabled Fed bonds. McNeil and his team of mercenaries were going to return to the Philippines. This time McNeil was going to stage a raid. He was going to transport the gold bars by charter plane to Lugano, Switzerland. He had an interest in a gold-refining facility there where the ingots could be recast and sold for billions. Nichols knew Lugano well. The small mountain city had more banks per capita than any other place on earth; it was a venue of choice for money launderers and tax evaders. McNeil told Nichols that he could invest in the venture—but only if he acted quickly.

"Barry told me he'd been in the caves as well," ODL's Tim Conlan recalled. "He was a conspiracy theorist. Barry believed that thirteen families ran the world. That was the reason the bonds were structured the way they were. He said there really were Federal Reserve bonds hidden in the Philippines. He was going to get them."

McNeil seemed to have conjured a level of surreality that outdid string theory. Nichols had used the tale of Yamashita's gold to scam $10 million from Sam. Now McNeil was going to use the exact same yarn on Nichols? What if Nichols actually believed in Yamashita's gold? What if he believed the tale of the Rape of Nanking and the network of caves filled with Chinese treasure? What if Nichols was a fraud who was convinced that he'd stumbled onto the real thing? Then there was this possibility: What if the legend was true? What if Yamashita's gold really did exist? What if there *was* treasure stored in caves in the jungles of Mindanao?

Nichols put $1 million into the venture. He didn't tell Sam of his investment. The delays were straining relations between Israel and Nichols in any event. But the fact that Nichols put a million dollars into Yamashita's gold appeared to be confirmation of what Sam had believed all along. Whatever the truth about Nichols was—whether he was a con man, hit man, madman, or all of those things—he evidently believed in the Federal Reserve boxes.

McNeil wasn't done with his string of incredible news. He called Sam from London and said he'd found paper to trade—once again, at long last. This time it was a zero bond issued by the French banks Paribas and BNP. The trade was going to be done through ODL. In a zero bond, repayment comes in one lump sum at the end of the term, so it is a structure normally used for extremely safe investments like U.S. Treasury bills and savings bonds. It is also perfect for fraud: Because there are no payments for years, if a fake zero bond was issued it takes a long time for victims to know they've been had.

Sam flew to London, once again bringing Debra Ryan as his companion. Nichols had warned Sam that the city was teeming with operatives out to thwart them once again. When they arrived, it was immediately obvious to Ryan that Sam was still brainwashed by Nichols and his paranoid worldview.

London was damp, overcast. Ryan went shopping for a winter coat for Israel. The sales clerk at Harrods looked exactly like Sam: husky, balding, pasty-faced. Ryan told the clerk that he resembled her boyfriend and they shared a laugh. He tried on coats for her. When she returned to the hotel and told Sam about the clerk, he was furious. Sam said that someone had come to reception pretending to be her and trying to get into the room. Was the clerk a doppelgänger deployed by one of the rival factions? Sam told Debra that the sales clerk at Harrods could be "part of it."

"I asked Sam, 'Part of what?'" Ryan recalled. "What was 'it'? It gave me a headache just thinking about it. Was he in harm's way? Was I in harm's way? I didn't want to be in the middle of it—whatever it was."

On Saturday night the participants in the Paribas/BNP deal met at London's Ritz casino for dinner. Entering the grand room, Ryan was amazed by the casino's opulence. She was wearing a new designer dress Sam had picked out for her—a metallic silver skirt with matching blouse. Sam was wearing a suit and tie, as were all the other men—Bob Nichols, Barry McNeil, and Graham Wellesley from ODL.

"Ellen tried to sit next to Sam, but I insisted on sitting beside him," Ryan recalled. "She was still trying to put a wedge between Sam and me. I didn't know the others. I was trying to figure the people out—who was manipulative, who had the money, who was in control. Across from me was Katherine Carnegie. Sam was having a great time. He talked about putting on a benefit concert in China. He was going to get the Allman Brothers and their rock star friends to play. I'm not a big drinker so I was bored. The room was gorgeous—

rich jewel tones, gold leafing, dark wood. Looking around, I realized that some of the wood in the casino was faux finished. It was painted so perfectly and magnificently. The mahogany wasn't real but it looked amazing. I was blown away. It was fake—but really expensive fake."

"It was a fantastically extravagant dinner," Graham Wellesley recalled. "There was champagne, caviar, like in a James Bond movie. Sam was sucking back lobster. Drinks were free. That was how the casino operated. They only gave you that kind of treatment if you were a big loser, or they were trying to get you to gamble there. Normally, a professional hedge fund manager would be a highly quantitative, serious man. The last way he would portray himself would be as a whale in a casino, with lots of booze and money flying around. A serious hedge fund trader would never go to a place where they get comped. The global hedge fund business is very small and very gossipy.

"Sam was the impresario. He dominated the conversation. That irked me a little. But he had $120 million in an account at ODL. There was no denying that. But even that was strange. The money had been sitting dormant for more than a month. It was in a money market account, which was basically like a checking account. Usually with that amount of money you try to make it work all the time. Sam didn't seem to care. I said to them all that I didn't believe the bonds really existed. They told stories about how they would generate funds for the CIA. They said the CIA used the drug trade to finance its operations. I listened in disbelief. I kept asking them to show me a real deal—to describe even one transaction that had actually occurred.

"They couldn't give me a straight answer. They talked about trying to source bonds. It was about the Mai Wah family or the Philippines or some similar nonsense. There were all these schemes. I told them all that I was going to check out every aspect of any instrument they wanted me to buy. Because if I buy something for a client of ODL and it was wrong, I could be liable."

THE BILL FOR DINNER was $8,000. Sam insisted on picking up the tab. The next day, Wellesley decided that passively watching McNeil operate wasn't enough. The viscount needed to take positive steps to be sure ODL's clients weren't ripped off. When McNeil brought a potential investor to ODL, Wellesley now went to the conference room to warn them. He sat down with the prospects and explained in detail the perils of believing the conspiracy theories involved in the so-called shadow market. Wellesley told them that he'd never, not once, seen such a trade actually happen. He explained that McNeil wasn't employed by ODL. He didn't directly say that McNeil was a fraud. He had no actual proof, only strong suspicions. But the stern warning given by the senior figure at ODL had the expected impact. Even the most gullible or reckless couldn't ignore the viscount.

"Why are you scaring off clients?" Conlan complained.

"I'm just telling them that they should have written reassurances," Wellesley said. "They can't rely on what you say. They need it in writing."

Conlan's shoulders slumped. There was nothing to say: Wellesley was the boss. "Okay," Conlan said, sighing.

When he was told about Wellesley's warnings, McNeil was enraged. How dare Wellesley sabotage the trading when they were so close to the end? McNeil had spent months building the business. Between Israel and the other investors, McNeil had $160 million on deposit in ODL. But it was useless: Wellesley was adamant. Clearly no new money would be put into the shadow market. The flow of clients turned to a trickle and then stopped altogether. The jig was up. McNeil ceased coming to ODL.

Sam had no idea what was happening inside ODL. Wellesley had not shared his suspicions with him. Sam had been swept up by a more immediate concern—one that could crush Bayou. He discovered that financial disclosure documents sent to investors had contained accounting mistakes. The documents were entirely fraudulent, of course. But even in inventing numbers Dan Marino had made an error. It was an idiotic situation, but that was true of so many things related to the Problem. Bayou's largest investor was Sterling Stamos, a prominent and powerful fund that ran money for the Wilpon family, owner of the New York Mets. Sterling Stamos had initially invested in Bayou to draw down its exposure to Bernard Madoff's hedge fund. The change in strategy had proved effective: Bayou had matched Madoff's performance, a truly incredible feat that could be explained only by the fact that both were frauds. But CEO Peter Stamos was now worried about Marino and Bayou's back office operations. With $40 million invested in Bayou, Stamos was one investor Sam couldn't blow off. If they redeemed, the fund would be in danger of collapsing. Sam flew back to New York to try to talk to Stamos.

"Sam told me that it was just a regular annual meeting with the manager of the fund," Marino said. "He didn't want me there. He didn't say why. But I had the sense something was going on. Something felt wrong. So on the day of the meeting I drove to the city myself, without telling Sam, and I met him outside the building and told him that I was going to invite myself in. Sam stopped me from going with threats. He said that if I came in the whole relationship would be blown and I'd be the cause of Bayou's failure. He made me feel very bad about coming to the city."

Israel met with Stamos and his top staff. Sam said that he was about to raise $2 billion from European sources. He didn't specify who'd given the commitment, just that it was "European" money. Stamos wanted to know if Sam could scale up his strategy with that much more capital.

"I can do it," Sam said. "All the stocks I trade are very large, very liquid names. There's a tremendous amount of liquidity in the things I trade. I can get in and out of any position within a minute or two."

Stamos said he was concerned about Dan Marino and the operations of Bayou, especially given the sudden growth. It was clear that Marino had to be dumped if there was any chance of keeping their money in Bayou. This was a fork in the road for Sam. In truth, he would be more than happy to get rid of Marino. In Sam's view, the overweight and overbearing accountant had become a kind of monster. But Israel couldn't fire Marino—not without winding up in prison.

"I told them that I needed to be able to run the business the way I saw fit," Sam said. "I didn't say outright that I'd get rid of Dan. I told them I would take it under advisement."

Marino was pacing outside, desperate to know what had happened. Sam lied and told Marino that his name hadn't come up at the meeting. "Sam told me that they'd only talked about what to expect for the coming year," Marino said. "But I could hear the inconsistencies in what he was saying. I knew there was something wrong, but there was nothing I could do about it. It was starting to feel like it was too late to do anything."

Within days, Sterling Stamos sent a letter stating they were redeeming more than $40 million. Bayou didn't have the money—unless it came out of the $120 million sitting in ODL. Israel and Marino had an epic fight. The liquidity of the fund was in crisis, Marino said. No money was coming in. Worse, Sterling Stamos wasn't the only investor redeeming. The whispers about Sam's stability and Bayou's strange business practices had grown louder. New investment had slowed, in large part, because Sam was in London for weeks on end. Worst of all, Sam refused to meet with new investors.

"Once the trades are going we won't need those investors anymore," Sam told Marino. "I'm not wasting my time."

"If you just meet with them, we'll stay afloat until the trade happens," Marino replied.

Israel pointed to all the money Marino had drained from Bayou's coffers. The companies he'd invested in had multiplied: BMG Golf, Double Triangle, HRsmart, Windtalk, Bio Conversion Technologies. Marino had parted with more than $50 million—more than enough to cover the redemptions. While both Israel and Marino had indulged their fantasies—Sam as the great trader, Marino as the titan of venture capital—both had crippled the fund.

Ultimately, Bayou withdrew $20 million from ODL to cover the redemption payment to Sterling Stamos. Sam now had exactly $100 million to make his trade—or, to be precise, $800,000 less, due to an error in calculation. Until then, Marino had rarely been forced to "dip" into Bayou's funds to pay redeeming members. But they were in a new and dire situation.

"All through this, we had to keep the staff happy," Marino recalled. "Sam wanted to be generous with year-end bonuses, even though we didn't have the cash and they weren't doing any work or making any money for the fund. Sam's view was that he had to pay them well so they would stick around. If they left and started saying things like 'I didn't understand how Bayou made money'—well, that would not be good. It was a form of bribery. Sam was a very big proponent of that."

Israel and Marino ended virtually every conversation screaming at each other. Israel spent all his time holed up at the Trump house. For years the two men had lived with the threat of mutually assured destruction. Now they were both self-destructing at an alarming rate. Marino's overeating had made him obese. His health was in free fall because of the stress of running Bayou.

"I just wanted out," Marino said. "There were many, many times I debated with myself about simply giving up and walking into the FBI office. I figured I might get some consideration in my prison sentence if I did that. Once, after a horrible fight with Sam—in front of all the employees—I drove to Manhattan and sat in my car in front of the United States Attorney's office. I sat there for two hours staring at the building. I actually walked up to the front door, up to the metal detectors and security guards at the entrance. I was within five feet of going in when I turned around. In the end, I didn't want to go to jail. There was no incentive for me to stop the fraud. I wasn't confident that I'd get a favorable deal from the prosecutors. I thought I had a better chance of solving the Problem and still making money in the process. At least it gave me and Bayou a fighting chance."

IN FEBRUARY OF 2004, Sam checked into Beth Israel Hospital for yet another surgery, this time to repair a torn rotator cuff in his shoulder. After the operation, a sling and brace kept his arm at a forty-five-degree angle. He convalesced for a few days, but he had a family tradition to attend to. Every year he went to Mardi Gras no matter what. The Israel family had been prominent participants in the celebration for five generations; Sam's father had been Duke of the Rex, the most prestigious organization at the carnival. Sam chartered a Gulfstream private jet, sparking a confrontation with Marino about his spendthrift ways. Israel said he was going to take a dozen of Bayou's most important investors with him. Marino didn't want to go: He was petrified of being away from the office for even one day, lest one of Bayou's employees stumble on evidence revealing the scam.

"My family rented a floor of the Lafayette Hotel every year," Sam said. "It was always huge fun. But this year I spent the whole time I was there working the phones calling London. I had to get the ODL deal done. The horrendous nightmare would be over. I had Bob working in London. But he couldn't get ODL off their asses. Either they were scared or something was wrong. On the day of the parade, I was in a store in New Orleans buying beads and trinkets to throw into the crowd when I started to yell at Bob on the phone. I told him I was going to get the bonds myself. I knew the powerful families were in the Caribbean at the time—that was where they congregated during the winter. They owned a few of the best islands. I was screaming at Bob, saying, 'I don't fucking care who does the trades, I don't fucking care about a few percentage points.' I was trying not to scream too loudly because a bunch of my investors were with me.

"It was clear to me that Bob didn't know how to get it done. I kept asking where the paper was and he didn't have an answer. He said there was a dearth of bonds. The books were done for the year. There were only certain times when trades were available. The families only allowed a specific number of tranches so they could retain control. I told Bob I didn't care—I was going to kill McNeil and the ODL people. They put me in an awful position. My name was going to be bad in this market."

Then Barry McNeil called. The first tranche of $100 million was going to trade on Fat Tuesday. But nothing happened. Once again, Sam called McNeil.

"Why the fuck aren't you trading my money?" Sam yelled. "Do the fucking trades. Get it done."

"There's nothing to be done," McNeil said. "The markets are scarce."

"Fine," Sam shouted, hanging up. "I'll get the paper myself."

THE MYSTERY OF BARRY McNEIL'S constant failure to consummate a trade could be solved with two words: Graham Wellesley. The ODL executive in London knew that McNeil was up to no good—he just couldn't see what was behind all the commotion. The first time a trade had been about to happen, Wellesley had discovered differences in the bonds being sold and those described in the trading instructions. The variance seemed designed to create a smoke screen, leaving Wellesley to explain why ODL had enabled a fraudulent transaction.

"The exact same thing happened when Barry tried to trade the second time," Wellesley recalled. "There were discrepancies. Small ones but enough to stop the trade. I knew something was up. I didn't know what. But I wasn't going to agree to trade anything without knowing it was legitimate."

So Barry McNeil quietly departed the scene. Not in a dramatic fashion. There was no falling-out. There were no harsh words. McNeil had been defeated. He'd failed, it seemed. He hadn't made any trades. His attempt to defraud Israel and the others had come to nothing. No money had changed hands. Downcast, it seemed, McNeil flew back to South Africa with Katherine Carnegie; she was still his girlfriend, it turned out, despite her fake flirtations with Sam.

"There was never a time when Barry said the trade wasn't going to happen," Tim Conlan recalled. "There was no big crash. It was delay, delay, delay. I began to wonder about the bond market. Did it even exist? I didn't worry about there being something wrong—as in dishonest. But what was really going on?"

BAYOU'S AUDIT FOR 2004 was released at the end of March. Richmond-Fairfield reported that the fund had $410,626,200 under management. The real number was anyone's guess. The loss, in terms of actual money, was perhaps $75 million. If the accumulated performance was considered part of the "lost" money, then nearly $250 million was gone—money that had never existed in the first place. With $100 million in London and $50 million tied up in dubious VC investments, Bayou was essentially broke. But that didn't stop Marino from wiring $15 million to the Cayman Islands to keep his venture capital plays alive and provide getaway money.

As Israel and Marino drove to Manhattan to see another investor who was considering redeeming, Marino's cell phone rang. It was FBI Special Agent Carl Catauro looking for Sam; the office had given him Marino's number because Israel rarely answered his cell phone. Marino passed the phone to Sam. Marino listened as Sam discussed the FBI's investigation of Bob Nichols and the European trades. Marino was flabbergasted. Hanging up, Sam assured him that the FBI had no clue about the Bayou fraud, which was true, though amazing; the bureau knew that Sam was involved with Nichols and other scammers, but no serious investigative steps had been taken to see what was going on at Bayou. Marino didn't reply. He stared out the car window.

In the following weeks Sam frantically worked half a dozen cell phones trying to find a trade. Back and forth to London he flew. He was escorted to the airport by a local cop he'd befriended who lit up his cherry tops on the way to JFK so Sam could cut through traffic. At the security line Sam flashed a law enforcement badge he'd obtained. He'd created a persona for himself as a man like Bob Nichols—but it was all a concoction. The end was nigh, he knew. For the Easter holiday Sam flew to the Caribbean island of St. Barts with Debra Ryan. If Sam was going to go down, at least he'd have a tan. He told Ryan that the billions were going to start to roll in. He lolled naked on the deck outside his villa, as if he didn't have a care in the world.

But Sam's desperation was expressed in the increasingly improbable schemes he got involved in. Months earlier, he had met a South African broker who claimed to represent the De Beers, one of the Chosen families. Out of the blue sky, the broker said he'd found "paper" to trade. But the minimum investment in these bonds was $500 million. Told that Sam had "only" $100 million, the South African generously agreed to drop the entry level—but just this one time. As always, though, the deal wasn't completed.

Sam was now completely isolated from his old friends. He never returned calls or e-mails—personal or professional. Worried, one of his best friends came to the Trump house and confronted him about the people he was surrounding himself with—users, hangers-on, sycophants. Bayou's employees were constantly seeking favors from Sam. The same was true of the strangers Sam was now associating with. But Israel wouldn't listen to his friend, which led to an argument that quickly escalated to a shouting match. Sam shoved his friend against the wall and threatened to throw him off the balcony where they were standing. Both calmed down, but it was a shock to Sam's friend to see him so alone and so different from the gentle goofball he'd known so well. It was as if Sam was no longer able to see the obvious truth about other people—or himself.

To stave off the sense of claustrophobia closing in, Israel grew even more manic and unpredictable. Willing to try anything, he revived the idea of going after Yamashita's gold. He reasoned that he could get a reward of $75 million if the Federal Reserve paid even 3 percent of the face value of the $2.5 billion in bonds that was supposedly in the "motherbox." Sam didn't know about McNeil's planned mission or Nichols's investment in it. A retired Special Forces soldier named Jimmy Bates agreed to lead the mission. Sam flew to Baltimore in a private jet with John Ellis to meet Bates. The colonel seemed extremely paranoid as he talked about how the federal government used satellites to track people. Bates paced around the hotel room frantically. In return for $1 million up front, Bates said he'd form a team of Filipino Special Forces soldiers he knew to stage a raid. Mindanao was home to an extremist group with the unlikely name MILF, for Moro Islamic Liberation Front. What if the Fed bonds wound up in the hands of MILF and Osama bin Laden? Bates wondered. If Al Qaeda controlled billions it would be a cataclysm of biblical proportions.

As improbable as it sounded, Bates really was a Special Forces veteran with top-secret clearance from the Pentagon. Bates proposed that once the Fed bonds had been obtained they should be flown to Guam, where they could be appraised and quietly brokered to the government. Sam was ready to fund the venture once the trading began—if it ever did.

Down to his final days, Sam gave up on ODL. The whole interaction had been pointless and maddening—and it had consumed a huge amount of Sam's most precious commodity: time. As spring of 2005 arrived, it was only a matter of weeks (or even days) before Bayou's fraud was exposed, Sam was now certain. Sam contacted a man named Lew Malouf in California. Malouf supposedly owned the Sacramento Kings—but a simple computer search would have revealed that he spelled his last name differently from the real owner. He claimed he ran a secret Fed trading program for Pacific Rim countries. Malouf told Sam that he had "paper" ready to trade. He said that Sam's profit would be $695 million. As ever, all Sam needed to do was wire $100 million to Malouf's account. "Now for the surprise," Malouf e-mailed Sam on the eve of Sam's sending the money from ODL to the United States. "With the deployment of 12 cycles you will actually receive $1,597,750,000. But there is one small catch. We might have to use an alternative company name on the bank account. This will only be done if necessary and the bank says, 'It is time to change names.' But it will still be your profit."

"I had a sinking feeling about the deal," Sam said. "But believe it or not, I still believed it was going to happen. Malouf swore it was going to happen any day. We were going to get paid any minute. They said the programs were already trading, we just had to get in on the action."

When the equally hopeful and deluded Robert Booth Nichols heard of Sam's new venture, he was concerned he was going to miss out on the big payday. Nichols wanted to ensure that he received 10 percent of Sam's windfall, as they'd agreed, still more proof that the CIA asset believed in the shadow market. Sam assured him that there would be more than enough money to share. But Nichols wasn't satisfied. The trust the two men had for each other had been destroyed. Nichols dispatched his wife to California to introduce herself to Malouf and his brokers. He sent an introductory letter with her. But Malouf wasn't interested in honoring any side agreements.

Shut out of the deal, Nichols decided that he'd had enough. He'd scored $10 million from Israel. He was sixty-one, with failing eyesight and poor health. He needed to put some distance between himself and Israel. The bewildering swirl of events that had started in a taxi in London was about to come to an end. The mystery of Robert Booth Nichols wouldn't be resolved—at least not yet.

"We had a big blowup," Sam said. "It seemed contrived to me—like he was deliberately picking a fight. We'd written in our agreement that he was going to be the head of security for me for five years. That was supposed to be payment for the ten million. To make it look legit. But now Bob didn't want to perform the services. He said he'd given me the booby-trapped box in the Queen's Vault and that was worth ten times more than the ten million. All of a sudden he didn't want to be involved anymore. He didn't want to talk to me. It all came apart very quickly."

At the same moment, the Malouf deal seemed to come together. Sam sent wiring instructions to London for ODL to transfer $100 million to an account in Hong Kong that Malouf had established. But there was an obstacle in Sam's way: again Graham Wellesley, the great-grandnephew of the Duke of Wellington. Wellesley was now certain that Israel was involved in criminal activity of some kind. Under British law, ODL was not permitted to directly contact the American authorities; Wellesley had to work through regulators in London. He asked them to notify their counterparts in New York about Sam's highly suspect activity.

"So the regulators called me from New York," Wellesley said. "I told them what was going on. They said, 'Whatever you do, do not return the hundred million.' Sam didn't know anything about any of this. I couldn't tell anyone, not even my staff. It was strictly confidential. I told the Americans that I needed an injunction or something because it was Sam's money. The money was on call. I couldn't just refuse his request to get the money.

"When Sam tried to take the money out I delayed. I told my staff to wait until the banks in the United States had closed for the day. So that bought another day. The next day I had my operations guy send Sam an e-mail saying he had 'forgotten' to send the money. Sam freaked. You don't forget to send one hundred million. Sam called up from New York screaming and yelling, 'You fucking assholes. Pay my goddamn money back.' He had a hell of a temper. He said he was going to kill my operations guy. I don't think he meant it. But still."

Unaware that ODL hadn't actually wired the money, Malouf informed Sam that the funds had arrived in Hong Kong. The money was in the account of a company called Majestic Capital Management, which was controlled by one of Malouf's collaborators. But the buffoonish Malouf hadn't performed even the most simple steps to disguise his intentions. The money was supposedly at a brokerage account in a discount trading website connected to Wachovia Bank. The online balance was stated to be $100 million. But Marino was able to see that Malouf had created a fake account—a phantom.

"I tried to explain this to Sam but he wouldn't listen," Marino said. "You'd think that after committing a fraud for so many years he'd recognize a fraud. But he didn't."

For Israel, doing something, anything, was better than doing nothing. Sam repeated the demand that ODL release "his" money—this time to an account in the United States that Malouf's coconspirators controlled. Wellesley could hold out for only so long. Despite the viscount's express request for guidance from American regulators, they had done nothing; the negligence of the authorities seemed to know no bounds. On April 12, 2005, ODL wired $99,191,102.18 to a suburban branch of Wachovia Bank. The money was no longer in Bayou's name. Following Israel's instructions, the funds were sent to Majestic Capital. It was the usual modus operandi of the shadow-market con. Once the money was out of Sam's control, in a so-called nondepletion account, the only question was whether Malouf could convince Wachovia to release the funds before the law caught up to the scam—if the law ever took any action.

"I was truly desperate," Sam said. "I was appalled. I was like a guy at the casino who had lost everything. He's got enough left for one last bet. So I put it on the roulette table and let it spin. I figured I had one hundred million. I was still alive."

CHAPTER EIGHTEEN

Redemption

C ameron "Kip" Holmes worked in the Financial Remedies section
of the Arizona Attorney General's Office. It was a backwater in
the financial regulation world, a metaphorical million miles from New
York and London. But Holmes had made himself a leading expert on
the secret bond market. Holmes had participated in seminars that
had resulted in the publication of a book called *The Myth of Prime
Bank Investment Scams*. To those who'd studied the phenomenon,
the variety of fraud Sam Israel had fallen prey to was the "crime of
the century." There weren't just a few prime bank scammers in Europe. It was a global industry, the disfigured offspring of the secretive Federal Reserve system. Thousands upon thousands of "financial

advisors" around the world ran schemes to get their clients to invest in high-yield investments. Many likely believed in the existence of the market, though it is likely that many were also running Ponzi schemes.

By the time Sam met Robert Booth Nichols in 2004, more than $10 billion had been lost to high-yield fraud, according to the best estimates. Countless billions have been lost since, despite warnings from the SEC, the IMF, the World Bank, and the International Chamber of Commerce. There were endless variations to the scams, but the themes were common. All claimed securities were issued at steep discounts for the lucky few able to make the trades. MTNs, zero bonds, debentures—all the structures promised to double or triple the investor's money in a matter of weeks. The best marketing tool was the corrupt institutions propping up American capitalism: the bankruptcy of the Federal Reserve, the duplicity of Wall Street, the machinations of the federal government as it created a New World Order.

Over the years, Holmes had been extremely aggressive in using the jurisdictional powers from his obscure Arizona office to indict and prosecute fraudsters; if high finance was like the Wild West, then Holmes was the laconic sheriff with the quick draw newly arrived in Dodge City. It seemed obvious to Holmes that something was amiss when he received a Suspicious Activity Report regarding $100 million on deposit in a branch of Wachovia in suburban New Jersey. The branch manager had become alarmed when a man turned up and tried to transfer the money, saying only that it was for "Fed-rate bond deals" and refusing to reveal more lest the bank "steal" his "positions." A drive past the headquarters of the company called Majestic Capital by a bank employee revealed it was a small bungalow in a residential area. Holmes's basic research revealed that Malof didn't own the Kings. The real owner was named Maloof, Holmes discovered, noting the difference in spelling. The Suspicious Activity Report Holmes received stated that a Hollywood production company was also supposed to receive the funds, a dubious proposition considering that Pacific Media Entertainment's prior films included *Viva la Vulva* and *Self Loving: Portrait of a Woman's Sexuality*. Then there was the gold mine in Arizona.

"The mine was supposed to be worth $152 billion," Holmes recalled. "It was obviously a ridiculous amount of money. I was in Arizona, so I went out and looked at the location of the gold mine. It was flat desert scrub, creosote bush, palo verde trees, a few saguaro cactuses. It happened that my father was a geologist, so I knew that there was no chance gold was going to be found there. It was geologically impossible—the area was an alluvial plain."

Holmes didn't know precisely what was going on and it didn't much matter. The Arizona gold mine fraud was enough for him to exercise his jurisdiction. He had no idea who rightfully owned the money. He only knew that there wasn't $152 billion in gold hidden under the desert and that if he didn't act quickly someone somewhere was going to lose $100 million.

ON THE VERY SAME June morning that Kip Holmes issued a warrant freezing the money in Majestic's account, Lew Malouf called Sam in New York. Malouf said that the trading had commenced. The money in the account in New Jersey was "rolling." Bayou's $100 million had been "flipped" a couple of times. The big payoff was coming within hours. Sam didn't know how to take the news. Like a prizefighter on the losing side of a fifteen-round slugfest, he was battered, bruised, blinded. He was throwing haymakers, hoping to get lucky, hoping to land one big blow and save the day. Was this the miracle comeback? Was this salvation? Was Sam's entire insane voyage going to end with one of the greatest trades of all time?

Dan Marino was eating breakfast at a cafe in Connecticut when Bayou's office manager called. The office manager frantically urged Marino to contact Wachovia. Bayou's money had been frozen.

"I have bad news," the Wachovia official said when Marino called. "We have received a warrant instructing us to seize all the assets in the accounts of Majestic Capital."

He offered no further information. Nor could he legally. Holmes's warrant was issued under seal. Who had seized Bayou's money? Why? In a panic, Marino rushed for his car, calling Sam on his cell. Sam was stunned. It was impossible, Sam said over and over as if trying to convince himself. He called Wachovia and discovered it was true— the funds were frozen. What faction was behind the Arizona lawman? Sam wondered. Bob? The Russians? The CIA?

"Dude, the money is fucking frozen," Sam said when he got Malouf on the phone. "It can't be trading."

"That's not true," Malouf replied. "We're getting paid today."

Sam exhaled heavily. The money was frozen, Sam said. Malouf told Sam he would check and call him back. Sam's cell rang a minute later.

"We've been penetrated," Malouf said.

Malouf didn't specify who'd penetrated the transaction, or why. Sam wasn't listening anymore anyway. While Malouf faked fury, declaring that the government had acted illegally and he was going to sue, Sam knew he was talking nonsense.

"Lew Malouf—now *that* guy was a fraud," Sam said, sighing in recollection. "Part of me thought the program was going to work right up to the second I got the call saying the money had been frozen. When I found that out I knew I had a serious problem. I felt awful. I tried to focus on trying to get the money, but I was crushed, devastated, remorseful—and mostly disappointed in myself. I'd let down everyone who'd trusted me and loved me. I'd always been the underdog who exceeded expectations. At least that was how I thought of myself. I didn't want to fail."

IN NEARLY A DECADE, the charade of Bayou Funds had transformed from accounting trickery to true-crime thriller to tragedy to parody. Now Sam was confronted by the absolute certainty that the Problem was going to be revealed any day. Instead of crawling into a corner and waiting in dread for the knock on the door, Sam played for time. Using the only skill he had left, Sam went on the grift. He was no longer the whale with $100 million. Sam was a street-level con man, like the dozens he'd encountered on his magical mystery tour. The sophisticated fraud of Bayou was replaced with "419 scams"—so named because of the section of the Nigerian criminal code devoted to obtaining property through false pretenses. Sam's conduit this time was a lawyer in L.A. named Jan Heger who specialized in "alternative" investment strategies.

"I called Heger and told him I was in trouble," Sam recalled. "I needed to make one hundred million right away, plus another hundred million on top of that."

Heger said he happened to have billions of dollars' worth of deals sitting on his desk at that very moment—like $100 million in cash and $20 million in rubies that belonged to the president of Ghana and could be purchased for a small up-front "commission." Sam believed Heger. Initially. A little. At least he tried to. Heger seemed to know what he was talking about—in Sam's exhausted and conspiracy theory–addled mind.

To get going, Sam wired $300,000 to Heger. At the lawyer's direction, Sam went to the airport in New York to greet a flight from Ghana with the rubies aboard.

"The eagle has landed," Sam told Marino from the airport.

"Really?" Marino asked, incredulously.

"Come to my house tomorrow and we'll go over the details," Sam said.

"I went to bed hoping that it was a godsend," Marino recalled. "The next day I saw Sam at his house. He was upstairs in his bed, like always. No one else was around. He was extremely nervous even though he was trying to appear in control. He told me that the shipping manifest had been incorrect so customs wouldn't let the package into the country. He said the shipment had gone on to Montreal. I didn't care anymore. I don't know if Sam was simply lying or if he'd constructed a fantasy world in his head that was so disconnected from reality he couldn't tell the difference. By the end I figured he was trying to steal the hundred million for himself and leave me holding the bag."

But Marino was wrong about Israel. Sam never considered running away. Nor did he think about stealing Bayou's money. He could have disappeared many times, taking along as much of Bayou's money as he wanted. He had had more than enough opportunity to purloin a huge amount of money and vanish. The wonder was that he didn't do precisely that, at least as a contingency plan. As the noose had tightened around Sam's neck, it seemed as if the only sane response would have been to transfer a goodly sum—say $10 million—to a Swiss account. With a little planning, Sam would have had an excellent head start on the law. He could have settled down in a hacienda in Costa Rica. Or Phuket. Or Cape Town, a destination favored by high-end fugitives like Barry McNeil because of the pleasant climate and proximity to Mozambique, where a man on the lam could acquire a new identity and a passport on short notice.

Instead Sam kept up the fight, or what now passed for it. Heger's deal flow turned into a torrent. One day he offered Sam $40 million in gold for a mere $40,000 up front. Eighteen thousand dollars in "duties" would fetch Ghanian jewels with a value of $40 million. Two and a half billion dollars' worth of bonds held in boxes entitled "President 12" could be had for just over five grand. In a matter of weeks, Sam's $300,000 was gone. Heger e-mailed Sam to say he needed more money. "To spend $1 million to obtain $100 million is a small price to pay," Heger wrote. "I realize we do not have this kind of budget, but if we did I believe there would be no doubt that we could go to at least $2 billion."

THERE WAS NO LONGER enough money for Bayou to function. The folly of the shadow market had been complemented by Marino's venture capital misadventures. The result was not enough cash flow to run the business, let alone maintain the fraud. Sam e-mailed Bob Nichols to demand the return of the $10 million loan. Nichols ignored him. Lying naked in his bed in the Trump house watching *SpongeBob SquarePants*, Sam confided to one of Bayou's employees that he was going through a liquidity crisis. The divorce had depleted his funds, Sam said. The employee was friends with a highly regarded

Wall Street trader named Steven Starker. Sam knew Starker slightly from his son's Little League baseball teams.

Starker agreed to see Sam. He knew Sam's reputation as a trader and admired the way he had remained involved in his son's sports despite running a successful hedge fund. Sam told Starker he needed a short-term loan. Sam threw out the number of $3 million. Israel seemed calm, in control. Starker wired the money from his Goldman Sachs account the same day.

A few more weeks had been bought—but at the price of soul-sucking deceit. Marino stopped paying rent on the boathouse. Accounts payable went unpaid. The signs of a business on the verge of collapse were growing more obvious when Eric Dillon of Silver Creek Holdings called Sam to ask about Bayou's auditor and rumors circulating that Bayou might be "liquidated," the industry term for a hedge fund paying back its investors and going out of business. Sam told Dillon that there was no truth to the reports. Silver Creek had more than $50 million in Bayou. Trying to put Dillon at ease about Bayou's books, Sam said that Bayou would change auditors next year to a large and well-known firm. The ruse didn't work. On July 12, Dillon sent a letter giving fifteen days' notice for the withdrawal of all its money in Bayou. Sam called Dillon and flew into a rage. How dare he imply Bayou was anything less than 100 percent honest!

By the next day Sam had calmed down—and realized that he needed to buy time. He knew the power of reverse psychology. He called Dillon and apologized for his outburst. Instead of following the terms of Bayou's agreement, which gave Bayou thirty days, Sam said he'd accelerate the redemption schedule. Silver Creek could have its money back on August 1. It was a head fake. Dillon went for it—or so it seemed. But this time Sam was being played: Dillon hadn't been assuaged. He was planning on traveling to Bayou's headquarters to find out what was going on.

The choices confronting Israel and Marino had narrowed to three: disappear, turn themselves in, or announce that they were shutting the fund down. If they went out of business, under Bayou's partnership agreement they had another ninety days to undertake an orderly liquidation—time to try to find a way to avoid the seemingly inevitable discovery of the Ponzi scheme, time to pray for divine intervention.

"It is with great regret, but with an overwhelming sense of pride and accomplishment in a job done to the best of our abilities, that I announce the closing of the Bayou Family of Funds at the end of July 2005," Sam wrote to investors. "Upon completion of the final audit, all investors will receive a 100% payout on their investments."

The explicit reason for closing the fund was that Sam wanted to spend more time with his family. Sam spread the word informally that the divorce had taken a heavy toll on his personal life and he wanted to devote himself to his kids. The response from investors was uniformly supportive. The human price paid by traders like Sam was part of the lore of the business. It was refreshing to hear of a hedge fund trader who was willing to give up the big money. Sam's ploy was counterintuitive and brilliant.

Israel and Marino let the staff go. They didn't have the money to meet payroll. Employees were told that Sam was going to focus on his European trades and pursue charitable causes with his personal wealth. Marino was going to continue with his "investments." Bayou's employees didn't take the news well. More than $1 million in bonuses had been promised—money that would never be paid out.

The phones at Bayou rang constantly as bewildered investors tried to find out what was going on. There was no one there to answer. Israel's short-term loan from Starker came due. Sam ducked his calls. "I hope my credibility hasn't suffered too much," Israel e-mailed to Starker. "But you did me a major favor and I would NEVER screw you—nor anyone else for that matter." Sam then sent Starker a check for $3.15 million. The check had the character SpongeBob SquarePants on its face. It bounced.

In early August, Sam tried every last-ditch deal that came his way to stave off disaster. He attempted to acquire $9 billion in Japanese bonds from an Egyptian con man. Sam was going to "hypothecate" a gold mine for $230 billion—another telltale term for prime bank fraud. Through a string of brokers, Sam proposed using a "real" painting of David and Goliath by Caravaggio as collateral for an $80 million bond trade. When he was told about $13.5 billion in gold certificates issued by the Royal Pacific Reserve & Central Bank, he jumped on it. The securities were issued by the "prince" of the nation of Caledonia, a secessionist movement in Australia that had purportedly formed its own country—a scheme described by the authorities as "delusional."

"I am literally out of time now," Sam wrote to a shadow-market acquaintance as he trolled for more deals. "I am trying everything. Please let me know if any of these projects are valid. I will be available for the next twenty-four hours. Don't worry about what time you call. Anything you can do will literally save my life."

August 12, 2005, was a Friday. Marino cut a check to Silver Creek for $53,089,300. He explained that the check was postdated to Monday—knowing perfectly well there was no money left in the account. On Monday, Eric Dillon of Silver Creek came to Bayou's office. The check had been turned down because of insufficient funds. There was no one in the boathouse. The back door was unlocked. Dillon entered and made his way upstairs to Marino's office, where he found a draft of a suicide note Marino had written revealing the fraud. "I am sorry for the destruction I caused," Marino's note said. "I know God will have no mercy on my soul."

Dillon called the local police, who called the FBI. FBI Special Agent Catauro and his partner Kevin Walsh had been planning to pay a visit to Marino the following day to talk about his relationship with Bayou's auditor Richmond-Fairfield. The pair drove to Bayou's office on Signal Road. As they pulled into the parking lot they were passed by a blue Bentley. They tailed the vehicle, running the plates, and discovered it was Marino. After a few miles, Marino pulled over. Afraid that Marino might be armed and about to harm himself, Catauro leapt from the car.

"Are you following me?" Marino asked.

"We know what was going on," Catauro said. "Get out of the car and let's deal with it."

DAYS LATER, Sam sat at a conference table in the offices of the U.S. attorneys for the Southern District of New York. He was accompanied by his defense lawyers, a crack team paid for by his parents. Gathered around the long conference table were prosecutors and FBI agents. Sam had prepared a letter, which he read aloud.

"My name is Sam Israel and I am a criminal," he said. "I am a liar and a cheat. I would like to believe that is not what I am, but it is certainly what I have become. The whole time I wanted to make back the money I had lost. I spent a year chasing dreams to do so."

Israel and his lawyers told the authorities about the box stored in a safe deposit box in the Queen's Vault in London that contained Federal Reserve bonds worth $100 million. CIA asset Robert Booth Nichols had given it to Israel. He would have opened it long ago, Sam said, but the box was booby-trapped. If it wasn't opened at precisely a forty-five-degree angle it would explode. A lethal biological agent would be released. An uneasy silence descended. Was Sam insane? Was he joking? A nervous giggle traveled around the room.

"Don't you wonder if the Federal Reserve bonds are real?" one of Sam's attorneys asked the assembled officials. "Doesn't some part of you wonder if it could be true?"

The FBI in New York contacted its legation in London to retrieve the box. The London police wanted to explode the box and avoid the risk of injury or contamination. But the FBI insisted on gaining possession of the mysterious Fed bonds. So it came to pass that the streets around Piccadilly Circus were sealed by the police. Traffic came to a halt while the London bomb squad was deployed to defuse the box. Specialists dressed in explosive ordnance suits designed to withstand a chemical weapon attack reached the basement of the Queen's Vault. The men gingerly removed the contents of Sam's safe deposit box. Inside they found a blue shoulder bag. Inside that bag was a laundry bag from the Shangri-La chain of luxury hotels. A heavy box was removed from the laundry bag. The box appeared to be lined with cement. The hasps on the lock were rusted and crimped with age. There was a faded Federal Reserve mark on the front of the briefcase, just as it appeared in the photographs Sam had taken.

The vault was cleared and a bomb-defusing robot was sent in to open the briefcase. The robot pried open the ancient lock. Click. The seal opened. There was no explosion.

. . .

THE BRIEFCASE WAS REPATRIATED to the United States. The Federal Reserve was called in to inspect the bonds. The quality of the paper seemed authentic; the bonds were composed of the same material Crane & Co. had supplied the Federal Reserve for generations. The coupons for the bonds were payable over thirty years at 4 percent interest, not an unusual structure in 1934. The signature of Treasury secretary Henry Morgenthau was authentic. And it was true: Morgenthau was a close personal friend of FDR who'd been charged with conducting covert economic diplomacy for the United States before World War II. According to leading historians, it was entirely possible that the U.S. government *had* secretly funded the Chinese government of Chiang Kai-shek in ways that remained classified secrets. After the communists took over China in 1949, there was no sovereign to claim ownership of the bonds. On their face, the bonds appeared to be what Nichols maintained: valid obligations of the Federal Reserve. The debt had been swept away by the sands of history.

But there were oddities. There were grammatical errors, as if the words had been written in pidgin English. There were misspellings as well. The Federal Reserve claimed that they'd never issued bonds—they issued only *notes*. It was like saying the U.S. government had issued pounds or euros instead of dollars. The Fed said that the government seal on the box wasn't from the Fed; it was the State Department's version of the seal. There was a document inside the box offering "Global Immunity" to whoever discovered the box. But the terms of the protection were absurd. "This Global Immunity was issued to cover the finder of this bond from any criminal offense or liabilities, and to be duly covered by complete immunity documents for his/her safety."

Then there was the matter of denominations. Nichols had told Sam that the Fed notes inside the box were worth $100 million. But there were twenty-five notes in the box. Each of the bonds had a stated face value of $100 million. That meant the total value was $2.5 *billion*. Either Sam had pulled off one of the greatest trades in recorded human history, with a rate of return of 2,500 percent—or he had been conned.

FEDERAL PROSECUTORS immediately froze the accounts of Robert Booth Nichols that they could identify. When Nichols learned that the millions he'd deposited with HSBC in London had been seized, he called the Serious Fraud Office there. The call was taken by Detective Inspector Michael Manley, a savvy veteran. Nichols told Manley that the money he'd received from Sam Israel was the result of a legitimate contract. Nichols was happy to fax a copy of the agreement to London—the fake contract he and Israel had backdated. Nichols said he had been paid to be Israel's broker for high-yield prime bank bond trades. It was obvious to Detective Inspector Manley that Nichols believed in the existence of the secret shadow market.

"There was no question that Nichols had been conned as well," said Manley. "Fraudsters often believe in their own fantasy world. Nichols fit the profile of many of our victims—and so did Sam Israel. Greed was the motivation. Neither of them was using his own money in the first place. All they were thinking about was the huge returns. There was no reason to believe that Nichols was running the prime bank scam. From our telephone conversation I could tell he wasn't a complex man. He was not sophisticated about finances, no matter what he said."

Nichols said that he was willing to fly to London to prove to Manley that the shadow market existed.

"If you come to London I will arrest you," Manley told Nichols. "I will charge you with fraud and money laundering."

The U.S. Attorney's Office in New York sued Nichols for the return of the $10 million. Half was gone. As the lawsuit progressed, Nichols was summoned to Manhattan to swear a deposition. Nichols had aged badly in the three years since Sam's arrest. Now that he was in his midsixties, a lifelong chain-smoker and heavy drinker, his poor health was evident to the assembled attorneys. So was the faded Hollywood glamour. In front of a videographer, Nichols recounted his decades working as an asset for the CIA. By the terms of a previous agreement the proceeding was to remain under seal, for reasons that weren't explained. Nichols's name wouldn't be released to the press, nor would any evidence of his long and mysterious association with the intelligence apparatus of the U.S. government. Questions at the deposition would be asked only by federal attorneys, once again with no explanation offered.

Nichols's testimony must qualify as some of the strangest evidence ever offered in a federal proceeding. Nichols told his life story, from his days at Hollywood Professional School to his nights cruising the five-star bars of Honolulu for the CIA. He stated under oath that he'd been an underworld asset for the U.S. government for decades. He gave an example of the kind of work he did: secretly funneling funds to the Pakistani military's Corps Commanders as a bribe to let the United States stage covert attacks to kill members of Al Qaeda—exactly the kind of mission that would result in the death of Osama bin Laden three years later.

But when it came to Sam Israel, Nichols's testimony was transparent perjury. Nichols said it was Sam who'd approached him in London and proposed that they trade high-yield bonds in the shadow market. The story made no sense—but neither did a lot of what Nichols said. Prosecutors knew the sequence of events from Israel and the reams of documents he'd produced; all of the evidence made it clear Nichols had instigated the venture. But Nichols was an accomplished liar. He kept the basic story intact, changing only a few key facts to deflect blame, defying anyone to catch him.

Nichols also testified that Israel had also brought up the subject of Yamashita's gold and the Federal Reserve bonds. Sam had recruited Nichols to negotiate the return of the bonds, in return for the money Sam had paid under a valid contract. The CIA asset dared the government to prove otherwise.

"I would like to see someone else do the things I did for ten million dollars," Nichols sniffed.

The federal attorney was flummoxed, stammering, outwitted. Was it purely coincidence that Israel had asked after Federal Reserve boxes that Nichols just happened to have in his possession as an emissary of the Chinese government? the attorney asked.

"I don't really believe in coincidence," Nichols replied. "But it seems that it was strange—it was very strange to me that he brought up this particular, you know, topic, that I was familiar with."

"Why would the Chinese government call Robert Nichols if they wanted to contact the United States government?" U.S. Attorney Alberts asked.

"I don't know," Nichols said. "I don't know."

"Did it seem strange to you at all?"

"No," Nichols said. "Not at all. I have dealt with many foreign governments."

"What was the value of the contents of the box?"

"My personal opinion? Going on what it said on the face, one hundred million dollars."

"Was it one hundred million per certificate?"

"I don't know," Nichols said. "I wasn't there to see the box opened. I would have liked to have heard about the chain of custody. I would have liked to have had forensic people there when the box was opened. I would have liked to have had metallurgists and people who deal with the history of this kind of artifacts watching and checking. But you just pulled the box out of the safe in London and took it to the Federal Reserve and popped it open and said, 'Oh, it's all false.' It's like asking the Federal Reserve if it is a legitimate box. If they say yes, the federal government owes a trillion dollars. If they say no, they owe nothing."

"Is that because you think the federal government might lie about whether or not there are legitimate financial certificates so it doesn't have to repay the money?"

"It's a possibility," Nichols replied.

SO ENDED THE STORY of the Octopus. Or so it seemed. The entire shadow-market episode seemed to have ended in a blind alley. The same was true for the mythified Fed bonds. None of the scores of confidence men Sam had encountered along the way had made any money, apart from the $10 million Nichols had scammed. No trades had been made. All the sound and fury of the secret bond market had come to naught.

But then curious things started to happen in London. One day Tim Conlan received a call from Barry McNeil's former landlord. During the months McNeil had attempted to trade on the shadow market, he'd rented a small flat in a working-class section of East London. The landlord said that McNeil had left without paying his last few months of rent. Departing in haste, he had left behind some of his personal effects. Among the items were reams of paper with ODL letterhead that McNeil had apparently purloined. There was also a digital printer, enabling him to send letters to prospects on ODL's stationery without anyone else's knowledge. But the main reason the landlord had contacted Conlan was the fact that there was a stack of business cards with his name on them. McNeil had been using Conlan's cards to pass himself off as an employee of ODL. But why?

Then ODL started to receive unusual faxes. People claiming to be investors with money on deposit with ODL (Bahamas) Inc. were demanding to know what had happened to their funds. Graham Wellesley received half a dozen faxes from high–net worth individuals requesting information regarding their investment. But there was no ODL (Bahamas) Inc.—at least not a legitimate company. ODL had never incorporated in the Bahamas. The investors said they had dealt with ODL's introductory broker Barry McNeil.

"Fictitious ODLs started to pop up all over the world," Graham Wellesley said. "People were claiming to be principals of the company. There were ODL accounts in Swiss banks. Investors sent money to ODLs that I didn't even know existed. They showed me correspondence on ODL letterhead, signed by a CEO who wasn't me. There was a very selective clientele for these transactions—wealthy individuals.

It was only when McNeil's investors started to complain that I learned about what had been going on. The whole thing was a scam."

When Wellesley traveled to China to meet with a potential client in an industrial city an hour north of Beijing, he was shocked when the wealthy industrialist told him that he'd had prior dealings with ODL. The man presented Wellesley with the ODL business card of Barry McNeil. The South African broker from ODL had told the Chinese investor about the shadow market and the secret Federal Reserve bonds. The Chinese investor had deposited $100 million in an account with ODL Securities (Switzerland) Inc. at Credit Suisse in Zurich to trade in the shadow market. It was an account controlled by McNeil. Although he'd been fooled by McNeil, the Chinese man had the sense to travel to Switzerland to personally supervise the transaction. He'd spent a month staying in a five-star hotel in Zurich waiting for the trades to occur.

Wellesley told the man that he had been extremely lucky. The shadow market was a con, Wellesley said. McNeil was a fraud. McNeil had succeeded in stealing money from many of his investors. Putting together the amounts from investors in ODL (Bahamas), Wellesley said that McNeil had taken upwards of $10 million—and perhaps much more.

"Most of the victims of the scam couldn't go to the police because they'd invested money from their Swiss bank accounts," Wellesley said. "It was money that had never been declared for income tax. The money was secret. If they went to the police, the first question would be about the origin of the money they'd lost. It was like robbing a drug dealer. Barry had committed the perfect fraud—and he'd gotten away with it."

·   ·   ·

THE SAGA OF BAYOU was over—even if Barry McNeil would never be prosecuted. The same was true for Bob Nichols and the legions of con men Sam had encountered.

On January 30, 2008, Dan Marino was sentenced by Judge Colleen McMahon. April 14 was Sam's turn. Both received twenty years. The sentences were among the most severe ever imposed on white-collar criminals. An FBI agent in the courtroom with Israel leaned over and whispered in Sam's ear that he had two words for him: Costa Rica. It was a joke, but the implication was clear: Sam should run in the face of such an unjust sentence.

One small measure of mercy was meted out to Israel. Normally a federal convict who pled guilty was taken into custody at the time of his sentencing. Israel's lawyers asked that he be allowed to remain out of prison for a few weeks to ensure that the protocol for continuing his various medications was in order. The judge agreed to permit Sam to turn himself in on the day his sentence began.

"Here's the deal," Judge McMahon said to Sam, staring at him sternly from the bench. "The only reason I am allowing you to do this is to make sure that the correct medications follow you wherever you go. You will turn up at two in the afternoon on the appointed day."

CHAPTER NINETEEN

The Afterlife

O n Monday, June 9, 2008, a disgraced Wall Street hedge fund trader named Samuel Israel III decided to end it all. Given the desperation of his circumstances, the only way out seemed to be suicide—or at least the appearance of it. Sam knew that if he turned himself in and went to prison, he was effectively ending any chance he had of ever being free again—which was itself a form of suicide. Years of heavy substance abuse, a dozen back operations, and open-heart surgery had left his body in ruins. Broke and broken, Sam reasoned that if he was gone at least his children could collect on his multi-million-dollar life insurance policy. Ending it all would allow him to retain a measure of dignity and autonomy. It would be a final act of atonement—and defiance.

On the day Israel was supposed to turn himself in, he drove his GMC Envoy toward Bear Mountain Bridge in upstate New York. It was a scorching hot day, with temperatures nearing 100 degrees. As he rounded the curve, the half-mile-long suspension bridge came into view. He tried to calm his racing thoughts as he parked the vehicle in the middle of the bridge, next to a cone placed there by a worker doing maintenance. Sam stepped over the railing onto the ledge and steeled himself. He stared down at the drop. One hundred and fifty-six feet. High enough to reach terminal velocity. The bridge seemed to sway in the haze. He told himself he wasn't afraid. He'd soon be forgotten, he figured. Another Wall Street scammer who got what he deserved. Body rain. He took a deep breath and leapt . . .

And landed. Two feet below the ledge, Sam lit on a platform that a construction crew had been using to repair the bridge. Or so he claimed. He waited a few seconds, his chest pounding. He peered back over the railing, looking for the Mexican kid from a local bar whom he'd paid a hundred bucks to pick him up, no questions asked. As the kid squealed to a halt, Sam jumped over the railing and dove into the backseat. They sped east, toward the Taconic Parkway.

The sirens started to wail on the bridge almost immediately. Crouched in the backseat, Sam was terrified. The Freelander camper he'd bought was parked in a rest area, near an exit ramp. When the kid dropped him off, Sam waited until he left before he made his way to the camper. He wanted to be sure the kid didn't see the vehicle in case the police questioned him. From here Sam was going to stay local for a few weeks until things calmed down—until he was declared dead, or they figured out that he'd faked his suicide and gone on the lam and the immediate frenzy of a manhunt died down. This was to be his last performance. His disappearing act. His final con.

. . .

THE PLAN HAD BEEN hatched in haste. After he'd been sentenced, Sam had asked John Ellis to appeal to his cousin President Bush for some kind of reduction in his punishment. Sam considered twenty years outrageously harsh: He'd lost money, he hadn't stolen it, nor had he killed anyone—at least that the law knew about.

"I wanted John to deliver a letter to the president asking for a reduction in my sentence," Sam said. "But Ellis said it wasn't going to happen. Once I realized that there was no way I was going to get clemency—that was when I panicked."

Sam's plan had been thrown together in a matter of weeks. He had no particular destination in mind. The Grateful Dead's song "Goin' Down the Road Feelin' Bad" played on the stereo. Sam indeed felt terrible. He dreaded not seeing his children and Debra Ryan. Sam had contemplated the best place to be a fugitive—perhaps a distant country with poor relations with the United States, like Zimbabwe or Venezuela. Then one night he'd had an inspiration. Sam was watching a movie called *RV*. The Robin Williams comedy was about an overworked and overstressed man who'd convinced his dysfunctional family to rent a mobile home and drive from California to the Rocky Mountains.

"I started to laugh," Sam recalled. "Then I suddenly got the idea to head out on the road to see the United States in a recreational vehicle. Just like in the movie. I'd be free."

To fund the journey, Sam started to trade under an Ameritrade account he created using an alias. He started with a small stake but quickly hit a winning streak buying and selling Goldman Sachs, IBM, Wal-Mart, Research in Motion. For years Sam had been tormented as a trader. He hadn't even looked at the market in months. But in his hour of need it seemed that he couldn't lose. "I had started to doubt if I still had the ability to trade," Sam said. "I'd had this horrible loss period. I'd lost my fund, my reputation, everything. I wasn't a rock star anymore. But then I was back trading and it felt great to be doing it again—and to be making money. I was really on a roll. In and out, in and out. Like old times. I followed my trading program and I didn't try to second-guess it, or get ahead of myself."

Sam bought the luxury twenty-six foot Freelander and installed a Tempur-Pedic mattress. Upgrading the sound system cost $4,000. Flat-screen televisions and upscale kitchenware and designer linens made the camper homey. Sam bought two cell phones, two digital voice recorders, a GPS, and an iPod he loaded with the Allman Brothers. The book *Getting Out: Your Guide to Leaving America* provided detailed planning information for living as an expat, including tips on the best beaches in Central America. In one packet, Sam kept 175 fast-acting morphine tablets, along with a stack of fentanyl patches. Sam thought of this collection as his "suicide pack," ready for use if he got cornered by the law.

Israel was confident that Nichols had trained him well for life on the lam. To create a new identity, Sam searched online for a deceased person who had been born at roughly the same time. He wanted a bland-sounding name. He decided on a white male named David Klapp who had died in Waterloo, Iowa, in 2001. Nichols had taught Sam how to obtain Klapp's Social Security number. Sam then bought a lamination kit and proceeded to make up a handful of identification cards for Klapp. Sam started with a Social Security card and a birth certificate. He then created an ID for Klapp as an ordained minister, in case he needed to don the disguise of a clergyman (Nichols had recommended it as a way to hide in plain sight). Sam had stayed up late into the night forging an array of cards—Special Forces, karate black belt, scuba diver license.

Sam had stuffed thousands of dollars into plastic shopping bags and hid the money under the driver's seat of the Freelander. His idea was to stay on the eastern seaboard of the United States for a time. After a month or so he'd head north into Canada. Israel would then drive across the continent staying in campgrounds, where identity checks were more lax than in hotels or motels. As time passed and the pursuit cooled, David Klapp would reenter the United States and make for Costa Rica to settle down in a hacienda on a quiet beach. After a year or two, he'd return to the States and build a new, quiet life.

"I didn't think I'd be public enemy number one," Israel says. "I thought everything would die down. Eventually I'd be able to come back and take up my life again. Not as Sam Israel, obviously. I would move to some town in Pennsylvania, near the New York border. I'd be able to see my son. I would see Debra. I figured no one would care about some white-collar criminal from years ago. The law had better things to do than chase me."

As June arrived and the day drew nigh, the hood of Sam's truck was covered with pollen from the oak trees in the driveway of the bungalow. Sam wrote the words "Suicide Is Painless" on the hood. It was a reference to a song in the movie MASH. He then bought a scooter to use for short trips and in case he needed to make himself scarce quickly. This was when his preparations became complicated.

The Saturday before Sam was supposed to turn himself in, he drove Debra Ryan to the auto-body shop where he'd parked the camper. Ryan freaked out, seeing that Sam was seriously planning to run. He asked her to help him lift the scooter onto the rack on the back of the camper. A huge fight ensued. Sam threatened to kill himself if she didn't help him. She didn't think it was an empty threat. He was out of his mind with pain and exhaustion, and the prospect of twenty years in prison was terrifying. Ryan had lost a close friend to suicide, so she knew the awful guilt suffered by the survivors.

"You know they're going to kill me in prison," Sam said. "They tried it once, they'll do it again."

Ryan knew Sam was talking about the CIA—and how he believed poison had caused his heart condition. As usual, Ryan didn't know what to believe. Sam had repeatedly told her how the Octopus disguised murders as illnesses, including his heart condition.

"I can't go to prison," Israel howled.

Ryan relented, hoisting the scooter onto the camper. On Israel's last night of freedom, he paced back and forth frantically in the bungalow the couple now rented. At midnight he left the house, saying he was going to buy cigarettes. Ryan went to bed, praying that he wouldn't run—and that he wouldn't kill himself. At three in the morning Sam appeared in the threshold to their bedroom, sweating, desperate, pleading for her help again. He said he needed her to follow him to the rest area where he was going to leave the camper. They had another screaming argument. Why was Sam getting her involved in his troubles? Ryan demanded. Sam had said that if she loved him she would help. Once again, she conceded.

Lying in bed waiting for the sun to rise, Sam choked up and told Ryan that he was sorry that they couldn't have the relationship they deserved. Ryan begged Sam to reconsider his plan. If he ran, the law would come after her, she said. She felt like her entire world was collapsing. She was terrified for his life, and for hers. But Sam wouldn't listen. Before dawn, he turned his back to her and left silently.

"Don't go, don't go," Ryan screamed.

Driving away shaking with fear and sorrow, Israel concentrated on the specificity of what lay ahead: the road, the bridge, the end.

POLICE DIVERS SEARCHED the Hudson River for Sam's body in the hours after his vehicle was found abandoned in the middle of Bear Mountain Bridge. Law enforcement rapidly reached the conclusion that Israel had faked his suicide. When notified, Judge McMahon was enraged. The U.S. Marshals were called in and told to make Israel a top priority. Far from drifting into obscurity, Sam had put himself on front pages all over the world. The audacity, the lack of remorse, and the sheer contempt he'd displayed seemed to capture Wall Street in the gilded age. The words "Suicide Is Painless" written on the hood of the Envoy seemed like a taunt.

Sam's whereabouts became a subject of intense speculation in the press and on Wall Street. Was he in Cape Town? Thailand? Timbuktu? "The Search for a Missing Trader Goes Global," the *New York Times* reported on June 14, 2008. The melodrama of a disgraced financier leaping to his death gave way to the mystery surrounding a Wall Street fraudster who'd gone on the lam. Sam was a tabloid star.

Once again, Sam had the world fooled. While the marshals scoured the planet, Sam had remained close to home. After picking up the camper, he'd made a short drive to a run-down campground in Tolland, Connecticut. Realizing that he hadn't planned thoroughly, Sam set about attending to the details of making his new identity more authentic. He swapped his license plates with those of another camper. He went to the local department of motor vehicles and got a driver's license application. After a couple of weeks, he relocated to a campsite in western Massachusetts, intending to return for his driving test in a few days.

"I didn't try to avoid people," Sam said. "I was friendly, open. I was like my old self again—the real Sam Israel. I grew a beard and let my hair go. When people asked what I did for a living, I said I was a consultant. If they asked what kind of consultant, I'd ask what kind of consulting they needed, as a kind of joke. It was going well. I had one close call when there was a roadblock with the police, and I got scared as shit. But overall I was fine. I was free and clear. The FBI and the marshals had no clue where I was. They had zip, nada, zilch."

The FBI continued to question Debra Ryan. She truthfully said she had no idea where Sam was. Then she wondered aloud if Sam had met up with the CIA asset Robert Booth Nichols. She wasn't serious. But the FBI took the suggestion deadly seriously. Confidential FBI files described Nichols as armed and dangerous. If Sam was with him, then he also had to be considered armed and dangerous. The change put Israel in an entirely new kind of peril.

"One night I was in the camper watching *America's Most Wanted* on TV and there was my face on television," Sam recalled. "I knew it was bad. There was a big storm that knocked out the signal and I was sitting in the dark. I couldn't believe that they'd put me on TV. There were murderers and rapists and terrorists on the run. They were going to put me on the FBI's Most Wanted list? It was terrible. But on the other hand, I wasn't too worried. The picture on TV didn't look that much like me.

"The next day I came across an article in the newspaper about Debra. She'd been arrested. I saw her face in the paper—the look in her eyes, how scared she was. That was when I knew I had do something. I couldn't possibly let her take the hit for me. I loved her. I couldn't hurt her. But that didn't mean I had to turn myself in. By then I was so twisted, I figured if I just killed myself—if I just ended it all—they'd let her go. My prognosis was awful anyway. I had my suicide pack—the morphine tablets and the fentanyl patches.

"I left a note in the camper and drove the scooter to a deserted area a few miles away from the campground. I found a cul-de-sac where there were no houses around. I walked into the woods. There was a covered footbridge leading over a small river. It was heavily forested so I got lost pretty quickly. After a while I found a small clearing overlooking the river just above a set of rapids. It was beautiful. I'd brought a couple of packs of cigarettes. I sat there smoking and thinking from noon until the sun started to set. It was misty at twilight, overcast. I knew it was time for me to go. But there was something about the act of putting pills in your mouth, knowing that you're going to die—if you believe in God, like I do, it means that you know you're not going to be with God. It was tough. But I was in an untenable situation. So I did it. I took the pills. I took my own life.

"At two in the morning I regained consciousness. Or I thought I did. I wasn't sure. It was pitch black—complete and total darkness. I looked around and wondered if this was it—if this was the afterlife. Then I heard the sound of the rapids and the river. I realized I wasn't dead. Or I thought I wasn't. I was freezing because I was only dressed in a T-shirt and shorts. I started to shake and chatter. I was hypothermic. I had to leave. But I couldn't see where I was going. I couldn't see my own hand in front of my face. I started to stumble through the woods. I was tripping and falling and getting cut by branches. It was terrifying."

By dawn, Sam had made it back to the trailer park. The camper was squalid, the floors littered with dirty clothes, overflowing ashtrays, scraps of food and paper strewn everywhere. When he lay down to rest he threw up the opiates he hadn't digested. He was now out of pain medication. He'd lost the means to end his life—as well as the means to make life bearable.

"I figured God didn't want me to die for some reason," Sam said. "So I had to deal with the situation. Like Hunter Thompson said, 'Buy the ticket, take the ride.' I had to see what was going to happen in my life. I didn't know if it was something good. Or something bad. I had to find out. I had to man up and turn myself in. I had to find what my purpose in life was now going to be."

Sam drove the scooter to the nearest village. The police station was closed. He drove on to the town of Southwick. It was still morning. He sat outside and smoked a final cigarette. Then he entered to find a clerk behind a glass window.

"My name is Sam Israel. I'm a federal fugitive—a wanted man."

The clerk looked up, skeptically. "You dangerous?" he asked.

"No, I'm white collar," Sam said.

"Let me get a couple of guys from downstairs to talk to you," the clerk said.

"Please do me one favor," Sam said. "Please don't call the press."

The clerk looked at Sam like he was bragging, or lying, or crazy.

When two police officers arrived at the desk, Sam repeated his name and the fact that he was a fugitive. They clearly thought Israel was a nut. One of the policemen typed "Sam Israel" into the computer.

"Holy shit!" he said. "Everyone wants you."

By the afternoon FBI Special Agent Carl Catauro and his partner Kevin Walsh were in Southwick to take Sam into custody.

"No matter what happens to me, every day is going to be better than living like this," Sam told them as they placed handcuffs on his wrists. "I don't have to lie anymore. My conscience is free. I'm free at last."

Epilogue

I n September of 2008, I met Sam Israel for the first time at Valhalla
State Prison outside New York City, where he was awaiting sentencing for absconding. As Sam was led into the visitors' room wearing
an orange inmate jumpsuit, it was evident how hard prison life had
been on him in the weeks since he'd turned himself in. He tried to
carry himself with an air of jailhouse bravado, but he appeared dazed
and confused. The day before, he'd broken his hand in a fight. Denied
painkillers for his back, he'd been given psychotropic medications that
badly slurred his speech and dulled his thoughts. Still, there remained
a glimmer of the prankster in his eye. On the wall there was a sign
saying, "Absolutely no gum or candy in this area." As we sat alone in
an interview room, Sam pulled a couple of FireBall candies from his
pocket and handed me one with a wink. The act was classic Sam, I'd
come to learn: devious, defiant, impossible not to like, a boy who'd
never really grown up.

I had come to discuss with Israel the idea of writing about his fraud
at Bayou—at the time one of the largest in the history of Wall Street.
But he told me there was another story—a story that would blow my
mind. Sam took my pen and wrote the words *"The Last Circle"* in my
notebook. He told me about Robert Booth Nichols, the CIA asset

who'd been his "handler" in Europe. Then he drew a diagram to illustrate how the shadow market worked. The Federal Reserve was bankrupt, Sam said. The American financial system was an elaborate Ponzi scheme. It was just a matter of time until the scale of the deception on Wall Street was revealed.

Three weeks later, the global financial crisis struck. Sam wasn't surprised by the catastrophic crash. Nor was he surprised by the collapse of Bernard Madoff's multi-billion-dollar hedge fund and the many mini-Madoffs that followed. Sam was sure that there were hundreds—if not thousands—of hedge funds that were Ponzi schemes but that few would ever get caught. Countless financial advisors were lying about the returns they were getting on their investors' money, Sam said, from small-time scammers in strip malls to hedge fund heroes in the skyscrapers of Manhattan.

At the time of Sam's arrest, Bayou had been described by prosecutors as a $450 million fraud. But the number had been grossly inflated, in much the same way the dollar value of drug busts are exaggerated to make law enforcement look good. The real loss was not much more than $75 million, if the exorbitant legal fees of $30 million for the bankruptcy attorneys were taken out. Putting money into Bayou, it turned out, really amounted to a bad investment. But such was the fate of many investments in the lost decade as people discovered the houses and shares they'd bought weren't worth nearly as much as they'd imagined. In fact, if investors had kept their money in Bayou until the crisis of October 2008—if Sam had been able to keep the fraud alive long enough—the fund would have outperformed the S&P.

In 2009, Sam received an extra two years for absconding. Debra

Ryan received three years' probation for abetting Sam's escape.* To serve his twenty-two-year sentence, Sam was sent to a federal prison in Butner, North Carolina, the same facility where Madoff serves his time. Still plagued by back problems and inadequate medical care, Sam has made the best of the situation. For pleasure, he plays in a few jam bands and follows the stock market—like many of his fellow inmates. "Everyone thinks they're a trader in prison," Sam told me. "They all think they have a program to trade foreign exchange, or the stock market. Everyone's got a system—some edge that's going to let them kill the market. They have no idea how hard it is to really be a trader."

Dan Marino is housed in a penitentiary in Kentucky. Marino's bitterness about his plight is heightened by his estrangement from his family and lack of connections to the outside world. As I completed this book, Marino e-mailed me to say he'd met another inmate who had access to the shadow market. "His company is building a pipeline in Russia," Marino wrote. "He says the bonds are very real. He uses many of the same terms Sam used. He says part of the profits have to be used for humanitarian purposes. He says the CIA uses the process to support black ops. He wants me to be the broker for the next trade, when he is released next month. I am not sure what to make of this."

I sent Marino a copy of *The Myth of Prime Bank Investments*. Still an obscure, rarely prosecuted crime, prime bank fraud continues to mutate into new forms and claim new victims, from high–net worth

---

* The judge specifically instructed Ryan to have no contact with Israel while she was on probation. A further state conviction for attempting to smuggle $300 to Sam in prison in a magazine (the money was for him to purchase a better mattress) resulted in another year of state probation.

Babbitts to get-rich-quick dreamers. As I discovered on my trips to Europe to report this book, the bond promoters Sam had encountered continued to deceive people who believe in the myth of high-yield investments. When I met the ODL broker Tim Conlan in London, he told me that he was working on transactions that involved "paper" that was going to fund projects in eastern Europe. Conlan had been trying for years to make a trade—and had never succeeded, to his continuing mystification. He said that Philip Winsler-Stuart—one of the brokers involved in the ODL initiatives—had succeeded in making a trade. "He's retired to the Caribbean," Conlan said with evident envy. "He actually did the transactions in the shadow market, so he has been able to move to the islands."

As further proof of the wretched lure of the shadow market, George Katcharian had earned a place on the Most Wanted list in the United Kingdom for investment fraud. One victim lost nearly $20 million. In April 2012, Katcharian was captured and returned to the United Kingdom to face charges in a case involving more than $30 million. The attorney Jan Heger has also finally been stopped. In 2008 Heger was charged with fraud for promoting investments in nonexistent gold mines in Ghana—a scheme much like the one he tried to get Sam to invest in. Heger had stolen nearly $1 million from his clients—a sum that didn't include the money he scammed from Sam. Heger ran from the law but was arrested in Bangkok and extradited to the United States.

In June of 2009, two Japanese nationals were stopped crossing from Italy into Switzerland carrying a false-bottomed suitcase containing $134.5 billion in Federal Reserve bonds. Law enforcement declared the bonds to be phony. The *New York Times* ran an article titled "Mystery of Fake U.S. Bonds Fuels Web Theories." But Sam believed that the bonds were real. It was how the world economy actually functioned as nations transferred sovereign wealth hidden in Swiss vaults. He told me that he had been offered the same bonds. They were authentic, Sam said, but the Fed claimed they were frauds because it wasn't willing to honor obligations undertaken decades earlier and now lost in the pages of history. The Japanese men were never charged with a crime and the Italian authorities refused to identify them, or reveal what came of the bonds—only underscoring the mystery of Yamashita's gold.

Which led to the final mystery of the Octopus. Under an agreement negotiated with the government Robert Booth Nichols was supposed to surrender $5 million in cash in February of 2009. That month Nichols was in Switzerland, accompanied by an old friend of Sam's from Wall Street who had fallen under his spell and handed over $1 million to the con man for a dubious investment in a water purification plant in Alabama. The purpose of their trip can only be guessed at. But not the outcome. According to the official report, Nichols died from a heart attack in his five-star Swiss hotel room. It appeared that decades of smoking and drinking had finally caught up with the sixty-four-year-old man. But the timing was suspicious, as were the circumstances. There was also a blow to Nichols's head, for example. And Sam's stockbroker friend had arranged for Nichols's remains to be immediately cremated in Switzerland—an act that triggered still more conspiracy theories. The FBI obtained a death certificate from the Swiss authorities, legally putting the matter to rest. But did the spy really die? When I contacted Sam's friend to ask about Nichols's sudden demise, the man's voice trembled with fear. He begged me to not include his name in this book. Nichols had terrified him. The Octopus had terrified him. Nichols "died" as he lived: shrouded in mystery.

"Some people who were close to him contend that he's still alive," the author of *The Last Circle* said to me. "They say he's living in Liechtenstein. Or Cambodia. Or Bali. I haven't drawn any conclusions one way or the other."

Sam, however, had no doubt. Nichols had layered escape routes into his life for years. There was a small city called My Tho in the Mekong Delta in Vietnam where Nichols knew he could find refuge. Nichols had accumulated an array of fake IDs. He had bank accounts all over the world in different names. There was no way anyone could catch him—if the law ever even realized that he hadn't passed away.

"Bob isn't dead," Sam told me. "He's very much alive and well— somewhere. Bob is the real thing, not a con man like the government says. There is too much smoke for there to be no fire. He is literally the man who does not exist. He told me that many times. He left no footprint. Bob was seriously connected to American intelligence agencies and the people who really run the world—to the Octopus. How else can it be explained that he was never charged with a crime? If you believe in the shadow government, as I do, there have to be people like Bob alive in the world. Think about Iran-Contra. Think about Iraq and the supposed weapons of mass destruction and how the public swallows all the bullshit fed to them by the government. Like the death of Osama bin Laden. Bob told me about the Corps Command and the Pakistani generals and how they all knew exactly where bin Laden was hiding. That was years before bin Laden was killed inside a compound right next to a major Pakistani military base. The truth was just like Bob described it. I sometimes think Bob was the only real person I met."

In prison, Israel has commenced legal proceedings to recover the Federal Reserve bonds. But the government refuses to give them back.

"I want the bonds," Sam said. "If they're worthless, give them back to me. If they're worth something—if they're worth, say, one hundred million—then Bayou's investors should be paid back with that money. I'm doing everything I can. I won't stop. The truth is going to come out."

Acknowledgments

I am grateful to Sam Israel. I am convinced that he is sincerely remorseful for his actions and the pain he has caused his family and friends. I know Sam also deeply regrets the losses suffered by Bayou's investors and those who trusted him. It is my hope that this book will provide some measure of closure for all concerned.

Debra Ryan was kind enough to relive extremely painful events, and I appreciate her generosity. Likewise, I thank Dan Marino for telling his side of this story. Jeff Singer and Graham Wellesley were invaluable guides, as were Carl Catauro, Kevin Walsh, and Steven Garfinkel. I thank Israel's defense attorney, Barry Bohrer, for making it possible for me to gain access to his client in the first place; his partner Barbara Trencher did a huge amount of the research I relied upon; both were unfailingly gracious in their dealings with me. Investment fraud attorney Ross Intellisano assisted me in understanding how Bayou interacted with the financial world, most especially Goldman Sachs. Anna Lenzer and Mary Cuddehe provided valuable research assistance.

At Crown, Rick Horgan proved an outstanding editor, as did his associate Julian Pavia. Their attention to story and detail made this a much better book. Dennelle Catlett ably spearheaded the publicity effort, and Julie Cepler was a stalwart on the marketing side. I'm grateful

Acknowledgments

to them and Crown's publisher, Molly Stern, for believing in this project. Jody Hotchkiss, who handles my film affairs, was with me every step of the way and remains a great collaborator. I'm also thankful to my literary agent, Susan Golomb.

On a more personal level, Charles Foran, Scott Anderson, and Merrily Weisbord are trusted confidants in matters literary and otherwise. Elyce and Andy Arons are the best pals anybody could hope for. My daughters Lucy and Anna, who avidly followed my progress, will one day be big enough to read *Octopus* and find out what all the hard work was about. To my beautiful wife, Maya, I am eternally grateful for your patience, wisdom, grace, and love.

There were countless others who cannot be named who assisted me with *Octopus*. To them I offer my sincere thanks. Some can be found among the complete list of the book's pseudonyms:

Golo Barthe	Kumar
Katherine Carnegie	Lew Malouf
John Cassidy	Barry McNeil
Tim Conlan	Derek Mirsky
James Fairweather	Phil Ratner
Nigel Finch	Phil Severt
Emily Hardwick	Prince and Princess Stromboli
Alan Jacobs	Philip Winsler-Stuart
Charles Jones	

Index

Index

Index

McNeil, Barry (pseud.): as con man, 309,
321, 322; fear of failure of, 268; Nichols
and, 265–66, 272–73, 283–85, 297;
Nichols-Sam first meeting with, 265–66;
Nichols-Sam signing ceremony with,
272–73; ODL and, 265–66, 267–76, 278,
279, 288–89, 293, 294–95, 320–21; op-
timism of, 269; Paribas/BNP deal and,
286–88, 293–94; personal effects of, 320;
personal and professional background of,
265; Rothschild House scam and, 272–73;
Société Générale Bank trade and, 267,
278, 282; Wellesley views about, 273–74,
294–95, 320–21; Yamashita's gold and,
283–85, 297
men's support group: Sam at, 111–12
metal box, Nichols's, 243–45, 247, 277, 299,
313–14, 315–16, 318–19, 340–41
Michael's Too bar, 36, 37
Mirsky, Derek (pseud.), 237–38, 239, 251,
252, 253, 261
money: Sam's views about, 32
money laundering, 253
Morgan Stanley, 4, 5, 37–38, 39
Morgenthau, Henry, 315
Mosaic (O'Halloran), 130–33, 159
Mossad: Sam as agent of, 164–65, 269
murder: and Sam's shooting of man in
Hamburg, 234–37, 237n, 246, 253

National Association of Securities Dealers,
102
National Security Agency, 148, 166, 184,
186, 187, 211
New York State Accounting Society, 77
New York Stock Exchange, 3, 5, 6–8, 17, 18
New York Times, 242, 329, 339
Nichols, Ellen, 199, 203–4, 207–8, 222,
239–40, 251, 273, 299
Nichols, Robert Booth: agreement between
Sam and, 277–78, 299, 316, 318; aliases/
code names of, 186; appearance of, 150;
as Bayou employee, 206–7; as CIA black
ops agent, 142, 143, 146, 147, 150, 166,
184, 185, 186, 187–88, 189, 207, 222,
226–27, 230–31, 246, 277, 317; CIA
thumbprint identification system and,
149, 150–51; as con man, 179, 181–83,
185–86, 225, 227, 228, 246–48, 257,
258, 277, 316–17, 322; death of, 209–10,
339–40; drinking of, 203, 208, 222, 240,
251, 283; FBI reports/views about, 185–
86, 185n, 187–88, 257, 277, 296, 330, 339;
fear of failure of, 268; freezing of accounts
of, 316; government negotiations with,

339; Hardwick failure to deliver gains
and, 175; health problems of, 206–7,
238, 317; in Hollywood, 187–88, 246;
homes of, 186, 246; *The Last Circle* and,
143–46, 150, 152, 155, 209–10; lawsuit
against Los Angeles by, 189; life story of,
184–89; Malouf-Sam deal and, 298–99;
Marino learns about, 165–66; Marino-
Sam meeting with, 166–67; metal box
of, 243–45, 247, 277, 299, 313–14, 318–19,
340–41; New York/Trump House visit
of, 206–10; Octopus connection of, 142,
147; ODL and, 261–62, 265–66, 282,
293; O'Halloran tells Sam about, 141–42;
personality and character of, 143, 158–59,
187–88, 193; PROMIS program and,
151–52, 154, 161; religion and, 207, 222;
reputation of, 226–27; Sam-FBI interview about, 256, 276–77; Sam as fugitive
and, 330; Sam as night trader in shadow
market and, 176; Sam seeks meeting
with, 147–48; Sam as successor to, 238;
Sam's belief in, 168, 174, 184, 226, 340;
Sam's celebrations with, 169–70; Sam's
first meeting with, 149–58, 318; Sam's
paranoia and, 190–91, 192, 199, 202,
203–4, 205–6, 216, 270; Sam's relationship with, 158, 165, 167, 173, 189, 202–3,
206–10, 222–23, 225–26, 227, 235, 236–37,
238–39, 247, 253, 258, 269–70, 285, 286,
293, 299, 335; Sam's views about death
of, 340; Sam's Westchester mansion idea
and, 215–16; shadow market and, 154–58,
161–72, 183–84, 217–18, 299, 316–17, 318;
shared psychosis of Sam and, 268; tales
of, 218–21; $10 million loan and, 239–46,
247, 258, 277, 285, 299, 309, 316, 318, 319;
testimony of, 317–19. *See also specific person or topic*
Nixon, Richard, 131, 157
nondepletion accounts: Bayou money in,
169, 301
Nord–21, 65

Octopus: as Casolaro's name for cabal, 145;
charities and, 264; FBI interest in Sam
and, 257; Marino and Sam sign nondisclosure agreement about shadow market
and, 166; Nichols as connected to, 142,
147; as run by American intelligence
agencies, 145; Sam's paranoia and, 328;
Sam's shooting of man in Hamburg and,
236; Sam's "suicide" and, xiv; violence by,
210. *See also* shadow market
The Octopus (Casolaro), 145–46